Demons Be Gone

A Romance

Tuna Cole

Cover concept by Tuna Cole
Cover design help from Kirsty Munn

Demons Be Gone, A Romance
Tuna Cole

Copyright: 2017
ISBN # 978-1-365-90011-2

Keywords: Japan/Nippon; Japanese history, culture, language, religion, geographic/geologic/demographic features; memoir; gonzo ethnography and linguistics; American-Japanese cross-cultural pratfalls and anomalies.

Also by the author:
Ragnarok, A Plausible Future (2009)

Voyage of the Yellow Submarine, A multi-voice chronicle of life in a commune (with contributions from Pip Cole and eleven other former communards: 2012)

Shards, a Life in Pieces (2014)

Demons Be Gone
A Romance

by
Tuna Cole

Oni wa soto   Demons be gone
fuku wa uchi   good fortune enter

The second day of the second month of the lunar calendar is known as
Setsubun, the advent of spring, signaling the family ceremony in which all
the lingering ghosts and spirits of ill intent are banished from the home.

"…everything interesting happens at the borders between domains of power."

David Eagleman, *Sum* (2009)

Prologue

It must have been summer of 1984, probably during a weekend since he was at home instead of at his summer parks job out on the coast. What was he doing? Probably putzing around the place getting caught up on one or more of the quotidian tasks postponed all week during his stint maintaining the nearby campground and the string of state waysides for twenty miles up and down the Oregon coast. Whatever he'd been attending to was interrupted when he heard—or more, felt—a vehicle start up the steep quarter-mile driveway that served as his access to the civilized world. A minute or more later, with the sound of the engine growing louder, crawling uphill in low gear, an unfamiliar car appeared at the entrance of the meadow.

His cabin is six miles up a dirt road from Highway 101, itself following closely the Pacific Ocean from the lowlands and dunes near Florence, 15 miles to the south, and continuing another ten miles beyond the Small River turnoff before encountering the next town to the north, Yachats. He had lived a solitary life for about four years at that point. He was pretty much a recluse since the dissolution of his family, and still coping with the loneliness and emotional upheaval as a result of that schism. Still, he made an effort to interact with whomever he could, when the opportunity presented itself. You don't live on the Oregon Coast for many years without knowing, directly or indirectly, something about most of your "neighbors" for miles around. Rural folks network with the other locals for resources, advice, information (aka gossip), and plain old camaraderie. If you survive several winters on the Oregon Coast, you've invariably developed idiosyncrasies, quirks that, in an odd way, seem to help you cope with 100 mile-per-hour winds, storms that bring inches of rain in a couple of days, trees blown down, roads regularly washed out, and a catch-as-catch-can economy putting survival—forget "prosperity" — in doubt on a regular basis.

1

He was not expecting guests, so it was with considerable curiosity that he went out on his front porch to see who had come calling. With some relief he recognized Owen Hubrisson, a guy he had known causally from the Florence area. Owen was an odd duck, but clearly in the sub-culture they shared, one's peculiarities—short of life threatening—accorded him more cachet than opprobrium among most of their coastie peers, a loose affiliation of loose affiliates. In any case, he'd come to respect Owen's take on things through various events they'd participated in together.

One conspicuous project they'd cooperated on with a handful of other odd-ball locals was to dismantle the aging covered bleachers at the Florence High School track and football field for the salvageable materials. It took them a good month of hard, dangerous work, but by the end of the job, they all had plenty of usable building materials: literally tons of 2" x 12" x 16' to 24' lumber planking from the benches; 8" x 8" beams that supported the overhanging roof; 2" x 10" rafters; an unbelievable amount of full 4' x 8' sheets of 5/8" plywood as substrate for the roof; and concrete pads as support for the whole structure. Hell, the whole thing must have been at least 40 yards, maybe 60 yards long! It had been a serious undertaking and they'd pulled it off without any major glitches. Collectively, they'd done themselves proud. So, it was good to see Owen and catch up on old times, friends in common, and finally, get down to what it was that had brought him all this way.

Along with catching up on the noteworthy events that had transpired since they'd last met—a two-year-or-so gap, they reckoned—Owen explained that he'd gone back to teaching English in Japan, and gave an overview of what that entailed. He painted an attractive picture, especially from a local perspective, which was an omnipresent struggle to make enough money to meet the court's demands for support of three children, as well as enough to keep life and limb together. The State Parks job paid reasonably well, but it was seasonal employment; he was employed for the peak tourist period, the summer months only. He also worked odd jobs, handyman projects and yard maintenance, mostly. Furthermore, through the good graces of another friend, he was able to find work in the fall of 1983 at a winery in the Valley, and parlayed that beyond crush (the grape harvest and initial processing toward the finished wine), to vineyard pruning during the winter. Owing to the good will experienced, he was invited back for the '84 crush. But his working prospects were dismal beyond that.

These jobs generated just enough to make ends meet; he was able to meet his child support obligations and take care of his basic needs, but nothing else—and his life was anything but profligate. So he was instantly intrigued when Owen suggested he come to Japan and try his hand a teaching English along the lines of what he had been doing. By his account, he taught some business classes, a few at community centers, and private groups of housewives. Almost exclusively, he taught conversation classes, which meant he needed very little preparation and virtually no homework, no papers to grade, and no term grades to assign. Most of his classes were open-ended; there was no built-in final date. The classes would continue until he and/or the students decided to conclude it. He made it sound like a piece of cake. What was not to like about this proposal?

Owen indicated that if our guy could afford the flight there, he could stay at Owen's apartment—until he got established, anyway—and he would be included on his teaching circuit. In this way, he could observe Owen's teaching methodology, meet his students, and begin to cultivate classes of his own. What was there to lose? Considering his dead-end, barely-making- ends-meet situation at the time, it sounded too good to be true!

By summer's end he had received his new passport and was plotting his departure. Of course he had no way of knowing how well he would adapt to this very different culture, so he bought a "one-year-open-return" ticket. It was more expensive than a fixed-return ticket, but he reasoned, he might need the flexibility of choice. One thing he had going for him was his world-traveler experience, including two weeks in Japan in December of 1966, at the end of a year-and-eight-month, round the world pilgrimage. He was not a novice at encountering exotic and profoundly different cultures, those far-away places with strange-sounding names...

He wrote to Owen that he would fly into Narita (Tokyo) in mid-December, after having participated in another six-to-seven-week crush at a Yamhill County winery, paid up child support obligations a couple months in advance, and pocketed a small nest egg for Japan. Life has a way of presenting opportunities that you could say were pivotal, having the potential

3

to be life altering. You either take the challenge and accept the risk, or face the possibility of regretting it the rest of your life.

Ready or not, he was coming!

Better get drunk and cry
than show off your learning in public
Otomo no Tabito (665-731 CE)1

Some four thousand years ago, give or take, the supreme goddess, Amaterasu Omikami, created the Japanese archipelago and proclaimed her spectacular creation the "Source of the Rising Sun." Every year the Japanese people celebrate the *day* this event took place: February 11th. By way of reconciliation of this anomaly (attribution of the day of creation with nothing but sheer speculation as to the year, decade, or even century), allow me to present a *kotowaza,* or proverb: *Nagai mono ni wa makareru,* loosely translated as, "One is apt to get tangled in long things." Now, if that statement seems more convoluted than it need be, veiled in ambiguity, as it were, you are starting to learn an important distinction between the Japanese language and culture, and the English language/American culture, a subject to be revisited from time to time. The author begs the reader's indulgence for the occasional insertion of a Japanese expression deemed to be apropos of the context, as it often captures in a few words an essential view point embedded in this "inscrutable" culture.

In *Nihon* (a softer, gentler way to say Nippon, the choice is context driven), I am a *gaikoku-jin,* commonly shortened to *gaijin,* an "outside-country person." As a six-foot, fair-complexioned, sandy haired Caucasian, with a fair amount of facial hair—and conspicuously absent epicanthic eyelids—I could hardly be otherwise. I will always be a cultural outsider (even to a few personal loved ones and close friends); I could never be an insider, which frees me on many an occasion to flaunt my gaijin-ness.

Japan is far and away the most homogeneous developed nation, and quite possibly any nation. *Nihonjin,* the Japanese, aren't all the *same,* of course, and this is absolutely not the case among urban youth, say, between 15 and 20. Those who don't get into a university by then may stretch the defiance of lifestyle and appearance expectations a few years longer, and either make it professionally in that role (actor, musician), or succumb to occupying a niche within the range of societal normalcy. Otherwise, the Japanese are more alike in appearance and behavior than the citizenry of any other nation on earth. (*I know, I know, that is a very harsh, blunt statement. I spend most of the book*

5

showing how, in different ways, the homogeneity is maintained and reinforced.) In any event, for an outside person in looks and demeanor, I stick out like the proverbial woody pecker.

I suspect I'm on relatively safe ground when I'm confabulating, er, reporting, my own experiences. The perilous waters appear when I begin to characterize aspects of Japan. Only a fatuous, self-absorbed foreigner would have the insolence to discourse on this or that aspect of Japan and the Japanese—without any real credentials. My interpretations, no matter how eloquently presented, are basically empty words unless I compare them to similar circumstances, say, in the Pacific Northwest of the US. It is inevitable that we make such comparisons between the familiar and the unfamiliar, the *other*. Some of my characterizations are bound to veer from the commonly accepted narrative, so it's unlikely that I could avoid erring. Ten years with my finger on the pulse, ear to the rail, grants me null status as to "special" knowledge of Japan, and yet here I am: Another arrogant gaijin, thinks he's got something to say, some unique insight into this venerable culture, symbolized by Nippon, the nation. You want certainty? You want *The Truth*? You'd have better luck conducting that search on another planet.

With (tenuous) knowledge aforethought, herewith, I commit my folly.

Saru mo ki kara ochiru
Even monkeys (sometimes) fall from trees.

Social relevance? Nobody's perfect; we all falter. Blundering is our fate. You could say, I'm copping a plea here before the commission of a "crime."

The reader is alerted to expect some *discontinuities* in the elaboration of the central relationship. Unlike fiction, where we might expect the principle characters to behave consistently in a tidy, plausible story line, often leading to dramatic, if not tragicomic consequences, this is a real-life account with long gaps—weeks, *months*—where nothing is known of the relationship. The reader is offered precious little by way of reinforcement, often no more than a crumb, a nibble of fleeting connection, then hastily returned to limbo. Precisely as it happened for the principles! The reader is required to endure the ambiguity as, indeed, did the protagonists. *Shikata ga nai,* it can't be helped.

Finally, just to be explicit, the author wishes to acknowledge that he, a bag of mixed blessings (like any other mortal, though conspicuously not of this culture), might qualify for consideration of placement among the "demons" to be cast out, exorcised, though he believes generally he pursued an Aristotelian happiness—or perhaps more accurately, contentment—as a result of a life mostly governed by reason: a state of *Eudemonia.*

I'll start with some easy stuff, some reference factoids, "immutable" geographical, geological and climatological considerations, and some demographics for the uninitiated, or should I say, less than fully immersed. Japan, the Eastern-most nation in Asia, is an archipelago comprising of four main islands—Northeast to Southwest, Hokkaido, Honshu (the central and biggest island), Shikoku, and Kyushu—and hundreds of smaller islands of which the Okinawa chain are the most prominent. Sum totally the land mass of Japan is slightly less than that of California, though it is stretched out twice the length, and is far more mountainous.

California is the most populous state in the US, currently sporting around 40 million people (2016 data), whereas Japan's population is 130 million. Metropolitan Tokyo is said to have the world's most highly concentrated urban population at 40 to 42 million people. California is fortunate to have abundant arable land, around 43%, and in the event of sufficient water—becoming more and more dubious as *climate change* gains momentum—the Golden State has been the nation's top producer of fruit and vegetables. Japan is primarily coastal, transitioning quickly to alpine, with comparatively little arable land, about 12 % (2).

California has several tectonic fault lines running along or near much of the Pacific Coast causing occasional earthquakes. The last major quake, in 1989, destroyed much property in the San Francisco Bay area, and caused 63 fatalities and nearly 4000 injuries. Japan is riddled with wandering, sometimes converging fault lines the plates of which regularly slip against each other, causing seismic lurches, sometimes on a colossal scale. It is a rare occurrence to go more than two weeks in the Kanto Plain (Greater Tokyo) without a noticeable temblor. The last major event to hit Japan was the March 2011,

Richter 9.0 magnitude quake off the Pacific coast of Tohoku. This was the strongest quake ever recorded in Japan (2), causing a tsunami that devastated the coast for a hundred kilometers north and south of the inland city of Fukushima (ironically, "Lucky Island"). Something like 16,000 people lost their lives, 2600 are still "missing," and tens of thousands continue to exist in "temporary relocation."

Furthermore, the worst possible outcome that could occur to a nuclear power facility did just that when four out of a possible six nuclear reactors melted down, owing to sudden lack of coolant, a direct result of the earthquake and subsequent tsunami. This exposed the globe to immense amounts of highly toxic radioactive materials, and this leakage continues to this day. Before that, a January 1995, 7.3 magnitude quake destroyed major portions of Kobe, a relatively new, post-WWII-reconstructed city, causing 6,500 fatalities, according to the venerable Wikipedia.

California has one dormant volcano (Lausen); in fact, the whole of the US has only thirty or so active volcanos—primarily in Alaska and Hawaii, and one, Mt. St. Helens, in Washington State. Japan has 108 active volcanos, including Fuji-san, 60 miles from Tokyo, and *Kowaku dani*, a bubbling, sulfurous wound in the earth a mere forty miles from the capital. One gets the sense that the Japanese are far too busy accounting for/reacting to the active, spitting, flatulating, and belching *kazan*, volcanos—literally, "fire mountains" —to have much concern for the sleeping ones.

The Wakanai Hanto (peninsula), at the Northern-most tip of Hokkaido, is on the same latitude as Portland, Oregon, while the southern part of Okinawa is just shy of the latitude of Mazatlan, Sinaloa, Mexico, itself barely north of the Tropic of Cancer. From the equator, the Pacific Ocean current runs north along the eastern seaboard of Asia all the way to the Bering Sea, where it dips south along the West Coast of Alaska, Canada, and continental US. From the equator, this northern Asian current accounts for the warm ocean along most of Japan for most of the year. And the incredibly high moisture content in the air during summertime. Conversely, the southern flow—from the frigid Bearing Sea—brings cold waters along the western seaboard of the US that moderate summer weather patterns, with essentially no humidity.

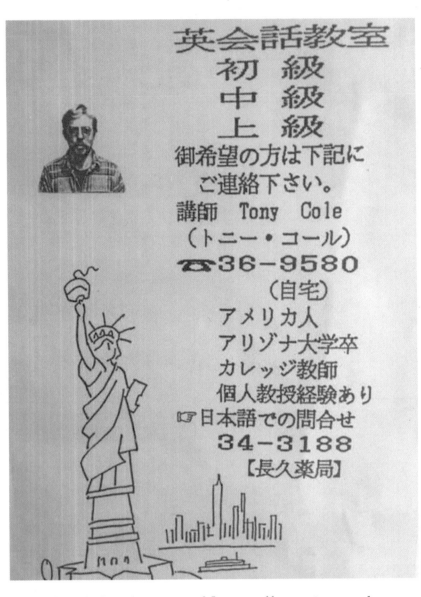

In the early days, this visage and flagrant self-promotion graced many a power pole in the Tsujido area.

from my journal

1985

<u>January 2</u>: *Akemashite, Omedetoh Gozaimasu!* Happy New Year, and Untranslatable Salutations! Year of the Cow—or is it Bull? Bovine quadruped? Domesticated ungulate? I'm three weeks into this Japan experiment, comprising a willingness to radically alter my living circumstances from merely scraping by, psychically and financially, on the Oregon coast, to the drastic changes relocation to a foreign country requires. Thus, a new beginning. The intent is to relieve the ennui resultant from my inability to establish a new focus since the dissolution of my family four years ago. Coupled with the hope of turning some coin through the time-honored device of teaching English to non-native speakers, "yearning, hungry for the opportunities English language proficiency presumes to offer." *So much depends on one's perception of events.* The groundwork has been laid in the latter regard; I've attended most of Owen's classes, and feel confident I could fulfill a comparable role. The community feelers are out, including postings on neighborhood power poles. Now, to have the patience to see who bites. Meanwhile, there is an inexhaustible amount to see and learn. Nose to the ground, eyes and ears on alert!

Here is my working hypothesis, based on the flimsiest of speculations. I am poised to be the beneficiary of post-war Japanese curiosity for things American: all things modern and assertive, pop culture, music, movies, TV, emphasis on youth and fashion, and an air of power and success. Notice I said *curiosity*, not envy. Not admiration. The Japanese are curious about this superpower that is capable of humane and progressive behavior internationally, while ostensibly permitting more personal freedom to its citizenry than all but a very few other nations. Curious, in the sense of *wary,* about this relative upstart of a country that wields so much power.

Well, I'm here to help remedy this dilemma. Through the medium of English I can provide them with a "better" *gaijin* interpretation than they are apt to receive from the impersonal media, by virtue of being in this teacher/student relationship over time, face to face, and therefore, subject to questioning. My assertions should, and will be challenged. I am a real-life "outside person," here to help my students improve their English, and provide

11

insights into the world view/core ethical orientation of Westerners, specifically this college educated, middle-aged, Caucasian male from the Pacific Northwest of the US.

January 3: Awoke this morning to snowfall. Thick, wet flakes that tended to melt too quickly. The first snow of the winter, Owen said. I got out in it right away but didn't stay out long as I was getting pretty wet. Spent the rest of the day hunkered down in my six-tatami room reading and catching up on correspondence. People don't heat the whole house, but rather the immediate area around which one tends to stay. My room is plumbed with a gas outlet and I've got a small heater on a flex hose that heats my space adequately. Owen's rooms upstairs are similarly equipped. Just beyond my sliding panel door is the quite cold kitchen, which goes for the rest of the house, for the nights are all below freezing even though the days can be warm and pleasant in the sun.

Sachiko came over for a while this afternoon, ostensibly to listen to Owen's new toy—his compact disc player—while they engaged in some licentious clutching. She's gotten less self-conscious about these trysts. Previously, I had to leave the premises for several hours in order to maintain the subterfuge of their liaisons. I expect Owen has convinced her that we gaijin can be discreet about these private indiscretions. (*Who would I divulge them to, anyway?*) She is after all a respectable matron in the community, married with two adult children. In any case I was glad not to have to make myself scarce, aimlessly wandering the streets of Tsujido for hours on end.

January 7: With the holidays behind us Owen's classes are picking up where they left off. I am to accompany, charming my way into the hearts, minds, and not least, pocketbooks of his students. On one of those early January Sunday mornings Owen took me to the Tsujido *Kominkan,* or community center, to meet Howard Levy in his role as *sensei* of TEC, the Tsujido English Class, the longest running English class in the Shonan area. Owen didn't stick around but Levy-san made me feel welcome, so for most of those twice-a-month Sunday mornings for several months I would drop in on the two-hour TEC show, keep my mouth shut until spoken to, and sit at the foot of the master, so to speak. Levy was a wizened, affable, aging New York Jew from the younger

12

end of my parents' generation. He got his PhD is Asian studies, and could read, write, and speak Chinese (Mandarin), Korean (Hangeul), and Nihongo. His current wife is Japanese; former wives were Chinese, and Korean, I believe. He's self-published at least a dozen books, half English acquisition, and the other half old Japanese poetry translations, his favorite being classical love poems. Dr. Levy has produced his own translation of *Hyakunin Isshu*, "100 Poets, One Poem Each," a classic collection of poems from the tenth to the early part of the fourteenth centuries (3).

Hyakunin Isshu is also a traditional card game where the opening line from each poem is read and the players scramble to locate the card with the remainder of the poem included. The one who remembers the most poems the quickest, wins. This card game has been a tradition with the royalty/nobility since the Kamakura Era, and popular with the common folk since the Edo Period. It grieves me to say, however, with post-war prosperity and miraculous advances in electronic self-entertainment devices, the custom has all but died out from common practice—collateral damage along the superhighway called *Progress*. But I'm unable to think of a parallel under the American cultural umbrella. Families don't often get together over games of any kind, especially designed to reward players who read the first two lines and recognize the rest of the poem composed from 800 to 1100 years ago. For us Americans, Shakespeare is a heavy lift, and this English-language giant of a playwright precedes us by "only" four hundred years.

Levy-san's PhD dissertation was a treatise on the venerable Chinese custom of foot binding, while another of his popular works is a translation of the *Tao of Sex* (4), wherein we are instructed on how to apply our "jade stalk." I could not help but learn much—about teaching, Asian history, and life in Japan—from this easy-going, thoroughly intriguing man. Before the year was out, Levy-sensei would give over this Sunday morning TEC class to me. Fortune had smiled on me; based on this class over the years many other classes came to life.

January 10: Every evening around seven o'clock the sweet potato man comes around in his ancient, faded-blue pickup with the charcoal brazier in the bed. You can hear his approach three or four streets away; he tracks crisscrossed streets in patterns that only he must know. Tonight I succumbed, stopping him when he got close. For 200 yen I got a couple of hot roasted sweet potato nuggets. His singsong dirge is amplified, but not one of the sources of noise pollution I object to. In fact it's come to be the signal of wintertime evening: *Yaki imo-o-o, yaki imo! Oishii yaki imo!* (Roasted sweet potato! Delicious roasted sweet potato!) I guess I'm a sucker for the recurring street venders. I remember as a kid hearing the tamale vendor making his rounds through our neighborhood in post-war South Tucson. And much later, occupying a sub-street level apartment in Kolonaki, a hillside neighborhood of Athens, being awakened on an early Saturday morning by the call for "old clothing, and all such unwanted things"—*Palliotis, o-palliotis, kei al'afta ta pragmata...*

January 18: Last night Isezawa-san took me to a Kabuki performance. A business connection had turned him on to some tickets so he invited us gaijin. Owen had a class conflict, so only the two of us went. The Kabuki Theater was in Asakusa, a ward of Tokyo, and the site of one of the oldest and most venerable temples. Arriving a little early we wandered around the grounds that only a few days prior (New Year's Eve, Day, and the next two days) had seen hundreds of thousands of visitors come in supplication for an auspicious year to come. There were still signs of the hordes: white strips of paper—prayers?—tied to the bare branches of nearby trees, and the large banners expansively extolling this or that announcement in completely illegible Kanji. Before heading to the theater, Ikezawa-san and I mounted the steps of the central temple, observed the tradition of tossing some 10-yen coins into a slatted box, while making a silent prayer. (I invariably pay my respects to the local deities, a kind of backlash, I suppose, from my many years of total irreverence.)

This performance consisted of two completely different "acts"—perhaps linked in ways too subtle for my ignorant gaijin brain. The first act had begun before our arrival, but we walk in on a male and a "female" (in Kabuki, all the roles are played by men) conducting a very elaborate and formal slow-motion dance, alternately and together, accompanied by two rows of musicians in the background. These latter were all the more striking by their lack of animation, bodies held rigid, faces staring straight ahead with just enough movement to pluck the appropriate string of the *shamisen*, a three-stringed, banjo-like instrument; play a percussive noise maker: three or four varieties of drums and a couple of wood block players; and intone a stilted sort of chant. The dancers said nothing. The male's face was painted up and his attire looked rather buffoonish, but his demeanor was more tragic. The woman was geisha-like, also seriously painted, hairdos piled up and elaborate, sumptuous layers of kimonos, still graceful and demure.

The second act was more to my liking, comprising an actual play—first performed over 200 years ago—with an actual story that develops with the aid of the participants. Two samurai lords, or *Daimyo*, with their entourage and servants were ensconced in front of Tsurgaoka Hachiman-gu, Kamakura's most illustrious shrine, generally congratulating themselves on a military victory when up rides another samurai lord with his complement of warriors and servants. This newcomer is regarded as a sword expert, but he keeps himself aloof from the others—though he does agree to stick around for the celebration. Who should appear next but an old woodcutter and his winsome daughter. The old geezer asks if anyone wants to buy a samurai sword, wrapped in his bundle of firewood, for 300 yen, a paltry sum on today's market, though it's fair to assume there's been some currency inflation over the last eight centuries. The two hotshots are interested but think the price is too high. They ask the expert to evaluate the prized weapon, which he does, noticing a seal near the haft indicating it's from the enemy camp, though he doesn't let on, being secretly a sympathizer. While all this is transpiring front and center, in the background is a "chorus" of six or eight men—much in the style of an ancient Greek drama—providing a running commentary in a very stylized, melodramatic Nihongo.

Probably, there was a stirring conclusion to the play(s) we saw. If such is the case, the impression eluded me before I was able to attach words to it. In my defense, let me point out I've been in country just a month now; my life is a 24/7, four-dimensional play that I'm trying to make sense of *as it is occurring*. Sometimes this play, this drama, tends toward the tragic. More often it flows in the direction of the tragicomic with a generous dollop of farce, not to mention a ration of satire/irony thrown in. I'm not at all familiar with the social protocols yet, how to maintain some dignity when I put my foot in it, while learning how not to repeat the folly.

15

<u>Sometime in March to sometime in April</u>: I got a shot at a big-bucks (to me), short-term job. One of Owen's students heard from a source that a native English speaker job was coming open and, knowing my plight of under-employment, she recommended me. The job initially was to read over the text of Nihongo translations a time or two, then record the text for pilot trainees from various Asian countries. I was interviewed and hired for the job working at the flight simulation and training facility of All Nippon Airways (ANA), near Haneda Airport, the only such facility at the time, for the entire Asian region. Several stories high, this fairly new, glamorous building took about an hour one way to get there. I needed three different train lines—the Odakyu Line to Fujisawa, Tokaido to Yokohama, and Keihin Kyuko to Haneda—not to mention the three-industrial-block trek along factory row from the nearest *eki* (station).

One quick peek at the training manual and I knew the job was going to require some serious editing, retranslating, and rewriting. This involved a technical understanding of the abstruse systems necessary to operate an airplane. And all the parts of all the systems. And how they all work together to get this aluminum and plastic tube-with-wings off the ground, of which, of course, I was wholly ignorant. This English version of the training manual would be used by aspiring pilots from the entire Asian region. They would not be expected to speak Nihongo, the language of the host nation, but regardless of their native language (Tagalog, Chinese, Hangeul, Malaysian, what have you), they would be required to understand English, the *lingua franca* of international aviation.

This English version of the Nihongo original training manual was going to be their lifeline to comprehending critical workings of this enormously complicated flying mechanism. People's lives would depend on how well the future pilot knew, for example, the correct response to mitigate a currently minor/soon-to-be major aberration in one of the operating systems. If not for my valiant efforts, this future pilot would be fated to agonize over the tortured English, where it was not even possible, in some cases, to discern, from the figure displayed and the text provided, what it's role was, related to *anything* else. Was the device pictured in front of you—accompanying explanation below—functioning as a cause, or was it designed as a reactant? Without serious editing and significant rewriting of the text, the reader was not going to have enough coherent clues to make sense of it.

I spent over a month largely on rendering the rough language into something approaching mainstream and comprehensible English, with a good deal of consultation with a Japanese flight engineer to explain or verify terminology and applications. Maybe half the time I spent recording the text in their own sound-proof recording studio. It was my first experience, and a heady one at that, working in a fancy office building teeming with workers, a thriving ant colony, each member, in concert with every other, busily performing the assigned tasks as if orchestrated.

The OLs (office ladies) wear the same winter time corporate uniforms: brown or black, low-heeled pumps; dark, solid blue-to-black stockings; a knee-length, pleated skirt, gray-to-dark blue; with a matching vest and/or jacket; over a seasonal long sleeve shirt, ranging from white to a hint of pink, pastel yellow or orange, followed up with a black ribbon tie. The men also conform to a dress protocol. They are expected to wear dark suits with white, or off-white shirts, dark ties, and dark shoes. There is some subtle leeway as to dress. Just as Edo Period merchants were prohibited from wearing overtly showy or gaudy clothing, but skirted the law by flashing a fancy sleeve hem, so too modern dressers, men *and* women, find ways to call attention to a better quality of garment, a tailored fit.

I'm sorry to report that all the women I saw performed subservient roles. There were no women in administrative or management roles. On the other hand, there were only women who occupied the roles of preparing and serving tea. They were attractive, and they were generally good at locating and fetching things. Most importantly, women served as the all-important first line of interface between the corporation, its goods and services, and everyone else. And that's where the real action takes place, at the front. Japan, emphasis on Japanese women, has "public relations," be that inter- or intra-culturally, refined to a high art. Did I mention, the office ladies I encountered were not hard to look at? That recognition probably says more about my testosterone-clouded condition than "objective reality"—should there turn out to be such a thing.

Towards the end of that month-long job the three-block, one-third-mile walk from station to job site was utterly transformed from drab, dingy, gray industrial backdrops to an explosion of dazzling off-white cherry blossoms. All those stunted, dead-looking trunks supporting a few scraggly branches along the roadway turned out to be dormant, wintering-over Sakura patiently waiting, gauging the lengthening sunlight and the advancing increments of warmth when, as if on cue, each branch of each tree produced a botanical explosion. These sticks simply burst forth, and the contrast was stunning. From nothing naturally beautiful in sight, to suddenly, a brash statement of defiance and splendor from each tree, the whole of the tree.

There is a price to be paid for this sudden exuberance of delicate beauty, however; the price is the short duration. Two weeks is the life cycle of the Sakura blossom; half a month is all you get. Beauty and life itself are fleeting; it's here today, gone tomorrow. So, enjoy the blossoms against the background of dull tones and too often gray skies. Behold this splendor nature is capable of under the harshest of conditions. Enjoy this botanical audacity for its two-week bedazzlement. Above all, enjoy them *because* they are short lived.

Fractured *Eigo*, or English:
Only who knows the taste can really appreciate it.
      Lotte Chocolate

Home, Sweet Home

As of <u>May 10,</u> I've been the proud tenant of my own private space. 4-4-19 Matsugaoka, Kugenuma, Fujisawa-shi, Kanagawa-ken, is the official designation of my digs. Generally, the Japanese don't name their streets, so I don't have a *street* address, per se. As near as I understand it, I live at 4-19, in the fourth *chome,* or district, of Matsu ga oka (Pine Hill), an area of Kugenuma (Pintail Swamp), a distinct area of Fujisawa (Wisteria Creek), one of many cities in Kanagawa Ken—Yokohama being its capital—one of seven or eight Prefectures (counties? States?) that make up the Kanto Plain, Greater Tokyo.

For ¥100,000 ($850~900) per month, my aging domicile sports several advantages that could just as easily have been otherwise. My kitchen has a bona fide gas range *with an oven!* Ovens were trending in new kitchens, but it was still commonplace to visit modern homes with all the amenities of an average American home—except on a smaller scale—relying on stovetop burners and a microwave, exclusively, for cooking meals. I could survive without an oven, but I would miss one. I like to bake once in a while: pies, quiche, nut breads, cookies, and pizza, even baked potatoes, yams/sweet potatoes, casseroles, and meatloaf… I'm making myself hungry.

Another feature for which I am seriously grateful is the sit-down, flush toilet. Again, I would have survived with the old standard of Hole in the Floor, but the *porcelain throne,* for one who was raised on them, defines comfort, relative to crouching unstably over a dark gap in the flooring, hoping I wouldn't slip off one of the foot pads. This was an older house, so expectation of a contemporary toilet, as well as an oven and stovetop combo in my kitchen, would have been inviting folly. For a couple, three months, it would be adapting to the reality at hand, but over the long haul—the ten years I was to occupy the place—both of these features significantly added to the quality of my life, and I was fortunate in this regard.

My house is located behind two houses that front this little no-name side street. The access is a meter-wide, 15-meter long, paved walkway between the two houses on the street, whereupon, you come to the front of my house, a porch sheltered by the roof overhang at the corner. This porch has an external door that is usually left unlocked when people are at home. This door leads to a thoroughly respectable *genkan,* a completely enclosed ante-chamber where outside people are bidden to take off their shoes and put on house-provided slippers—good for anywhere inside the house except the toilet room—hang up their raingear, prop up the umbrella, all before entering the house proper. This threshold divides outside dust/dirt/mud from an inside which has been scrupulously cleaned, especially the floor, since many of the daily activities take place on the floor. It is not at all uncommon for a complete stranger to enter your genkan, this intermediary space, unannounced, no door bell, before calling for the woman, or man, of the house: *Gomen kudsai!* (untranslatable, but having the meaning equivalence of, "Excuse me for intruding, but could I bother you for just a moment/have a brief word with you?")

Next to the genkan is my living room, then, stacked in a row toward the back of the house, an eight-tatami room, *hachi-jo,* that is mostly useless since it is a part of the corridor from the genkan and living room at the front of the house, to the kitchen, my default bedroom, the toilet stall and sink, and finally

19

more space at the complete back of the house, a small part of which is my *furo*/shower, as well as my washing machine.

My all-purpose, front room is a square, *ju jo*, or ten tatami room, with the outside face a bank of sliding windows, built-in book shelves above enclosed cupboards. The flooring is carpeted. One of my first acquisitions via the local *sodai gomi*, periodic large refuse disposal, was a *kotatsu*, a square coffee table with an electric heat lamp built under the surface. One puts a large quilted blanket over the frame of the coffee table and then, a hard square surface on top of the blanket over the table frame. Up to four people can sit at this table with their feet and lower legs beneath the blanket, being heated by the heat lamp, attached to the underside of the table frame. Typically, these people sit on *zabuton*, a floor cushion about two feet on a side, stuffed with cotton batting.

On the *kotatsu* table surface, it is common for family members to eat, play games, write/record transactions, drink tea while watching the sumo tournament on TV, you name it. I generally prefer to teach my students at their homes, in community centers, or even in public places, coffee shops and the like, but sometimes circumstances dictate my charming digs, or no class at all. Thus, my modest *kotatsu* has served as the tea-and-study surface with from one to four students at one session.

In the winter months, even Shonan Kaigan, the "Miami Beach" of Japan, can and does get freezing cold at night, from around two months in a mild year, to more than three months in a severe one. Older, traditional houses were unheated throughout, and insulation was unheard of until recent history. A kerosene heater could be moved site to site to give a semblance of a warm space; more modern houses (e.g., Owen's apartment) are plumbed room by room with gas fixtures so that more efficient gas, portable space heaters may provide local warmth, but such is not the case in my abode.

Then, no matter how miserable the weather outside and, as a consequence of the lack of insulation, the temperature inside, hunkered down in your *kotatsu*, feet and legs all toasty, wearing your *hanten*, a quilted housecoat for upper-body heat retention, a fool might be so bold as to say, Bring on the deluge! *Though, probably no true Nihon-jin would ever so wantonly and foolishly taunt Nature to provide more death and destruction. Especially, since She is frequently inclined, wholly without provocation, to*

20

unleash some manifestation of her fury on Nippon—like few other places on earth. The demonic trinity of volcanos, typhoons, and earthquakes are all-too-frequent reminders of Nature's might. Furthermore, Nihonjin are not exactly strangers to flooding, tsunami, or severe ice/snow storms, either. No season without its thrills!

My "bedroom" was parallel with my somewhat narrow kitchen. For an industrious Nihonjin this room would be all-purpose for most of the day with the futons, blankets, and pillows stored in the deep cabinetry built into the north wall. I generally didn't suffer for lack of space, my front or living room serving most of my waking-hour needs. Thus, my excuse for acting like a lazy gaijin, and failing to observe the Japanese custom of folding up and putting away my bedding each morning. Only to take it out each night.

Do you face difficulties falling asleep when crawling into a freezing bed? My winter-time, fool-proof method is to soak a few minutes in a *furo*, say, in the 103~4 degree F. range. I don't actually keep a thermometer, and your hand is not a particularly sensitive organ in terms of temperature, but by the immersion of your forearm, you should be able to get a pretty accurate reading. You want to lower yourself slowly, feeling a slight sense of discomfort owing to the startling contrast of air to water temperatures. Without injuring yourself, soak your bag of bones in a fairly hot bath—pretty much as hot as you can stand it—for a while, say, eight to ten minutes, if you can endure it. When you climb out of the tub and towel off, glance at yourself in the mirror. Don't you resemble *yu de dako*? Boiled-red octopus? Flushed, bright red? Your skin radiating steam as well as heat waves? Well, dive into the bedding. No matter how cold and clammy, your heat-stored, "fevered" body temperature is enough to counter the ambient temperature for a while. Long enough for you to warm up a little cavity in the futon. Sometimes it takes all of three or four minutes before you are in the realm of Morpheus.

During my "vacation," brought about by the necessity of my exiting the country in order to qualify for an automatic visa renewal for three months, Nagahisa-san, my landlady, painted the walls of my most decrepit room, replaced the worn tatami mats, and repapered the tattered *fusuma* and *shoji*, opaque, sometimes decorated vs. plain white papered sliding screens, respectively. These screens offer the ability to open up the "walls" to the outside, as well as virtually all the interior. Or conversely, completely close

21

out the exterior space, as well as divide up the interior into a series of separable cells. At times before the remodel, I had joked that my house was built during the Meiji Period (1868~1912). Seriously, in areas of the internal wall you could see the plaster was a mud/clay slip over crudely woven straw (wattle and daub). Now, my house is really quite presentable.

Step into my parlor, said the spider to the fly…

July 20, Saturday morning 7:00: Just four days after returning from a month in Oregon.

I've resumed classes as of Wednesday—not exactly with a bang, but adequately. With accounts of the wilds of Small River, complete with pictures. The contrast between Shonan exurbia and Oregon coast wilderness is about as extreme as imaginable. In a former incarnation—for nine years before coming to Japan—I lived in a cabin six miles from mail delivery and a paved road. I built this cabin myself, with a lot of help, from siding, flooring, framing, some plumbing and windows I salvaged from a 75-year-old house on the coast. My cabin had no electricity; we cooked and heated the cabin from firewood I cut from the surrounding forest. Water came from the hillside. I built a rough stone dam in a nearby creek, and uncoiled 350 feet of 5/8 inch polyvinyl-chloride flex tubing from the settling tank down the hill, having plumbed the cabin for a shower/bath and bathroom sink, as well as the kitchen sink. Light at night was via kerosene lamps and candles. After some months we got a propane cylinder, which made possible a propane cook stove, refrigerator, and hot-water heater. It was absolutely civilized! Toward the primitive side, but civilized.

My son, Loren Cedar, was a natural birth in that cabin.

For a time, I kept goats—for milk, meat, and targeted brush clearing. And companionship. Among the 15 or so of mankind's domesticated species, I'm prepared to go on record that goats, ol' *capra*, are the most rambunctious and curious, perhaps second only to dogs. But in matters of *deviousness*, goats win, hooves down. They are amazing creatures; I have spent many an hour "herding" them, assuming that's really possible, trying to understand their thinking. We also had chickens (for eggs, occasionally, meat), rabbits (meat; I didn't know how to cure the hides), and bees (honey—and stings). These and other aspects of country living are beyond the ken of most urban Japanese. So

22

I do what I can to highlight the contrast and reinforce that there are heads-up humans who don't fit the standard preconceptions of Americans, the ones who are not stamped out of some kind of mold. My feeling is, my students are paying me explicitly for language instruction, but just as importantly, though more indirectly, cultural exposure. For my conversation classes, the form of the communication is interactive spoken, and sometimes written, English, and the content is whatever my students want to talk about—no taboos. It is primarily what the students know best, their own experience and knowledge of life in Japan, as explained to an ignoramus, not a difficult role for me. This often entails comparisons of Japanese and American cultures. Interculturalization.

Via English, over the months, I get exposed to some fascinating interpretations of Japanese culture. And I hope I provide my students a valid, progressive, hopeful, agnostic picture of the US—in lieu of a more typical conservative view. Most of my students have a pretty good idea I'm not mainstream American, but it's tricky trying to pin down who or what a typical, mainstream American is, owing to the diversity of immigrants who have fundamentally made the USA what it is. I'd say, America is a rich blend of peoples from all over the world, the cultures, languages, and religions. The US is a plurality of many cultures, lifestyles, philosophies, the arts, cuisines, and religions. To that extent, for better or worse, the US is the closest thing the world has for a microcosm.

Due to the homogeneity here, the fool in me would say, it is much easier to characterize an "average" Nihonjin—until we begin to peel away the layers of culturally driven requirements for communication, and begin to discover a more unique and personal identity. Maybe. I'd say the jury is still out on that one. Because it's entirely possible we'd find, that with each sloughing of an aspect of socially-required conduct, a deeper, more fundamental, core constituent of group identity is revealed.

In the last couple of weeks in 1984, just after I arrived, I taught one or two try-out classes, and on a fluke, Kimiko, an attractive, guileless, insouciant young woman, came to one of them. I coaxed her phone number, toward a possible coffee date, and after some trepidation of reaching a startled mother or father, neither of whom spoke any English, while my Nihongo couldn't have been more basic, I called her. We went out a few times—she has her own car—and the mutual attraction developed a certain inevitable trajectory.

It is almost unbearably humid these daze. I left with the weather warm, nights still cool, and *tsuyu*, the rainy season, about to begin. Gratefully, the rains have expended themselves in my absence, but now I'm told we face six to seven weeks of unrelenting steamy-hot, sticky, sultry, muggy, torpid misery. I know what *hot* is like. I grew up in the 1940s and '50s, in pre-refrigeration Arizona where peak summer lows were, and continue to be, in the 90s F. and the highs, 116~118. While these numbers don't signal "comfort," or anything like it, people managed to accomplish physical undertakings in all but the worst of the heat. It's just that heat by itself, in Japan doesn't tell the whole story. As far as I'm concerned, it is the heat saturated with humidity that is not fit for civilized society. To go through a day dripping sweat over major portions of one's body is no way to live and, a Westerner might be apt to think, only those who've never lived in a more benign climate, that is to say, those who didn't know any better, would continue to submit to this misery. (Of course, it's a little more complicated than that…)

This might be a good place to talk about a phenomenon that is significantly enhanced by the heat and humidity. I'm referring to *Mushi*, the Phylum of Arthropoda, specifically insects, beetles, spiders, centipedes, and their ilk: Bugs. Japanese lore is rife with tales of the feats of *tombo*, dragonflies; *semi*, cicada; *hotaru*, fireflies; *kumo*, spiders; and *korogi*, crickets, the list is long. *Semi*, for example, are referenced in many haiku to signal the season. (To make allusion, without having to explicitly say it, is perhaps the essence of the Japanese aesthetic. *Bimyo na kotoba*, subtle, metaphoric allusions.) Whole festivals are devoted to dragonflies. Lafcadio Hearn cites 32 distinct types of dragonflies from around the country! (5) Furthermore, he devotes a lengthy discourse to the "singing insects," primarily the dozen or so different species of *korogi*, or crickets, collected for their mournful, high-pitched *scritch, sc-cr-ri-iitch,* the sound of Autumn. *Ah, what a guy won't do to get laid!*

24

It simply will not do to end a discussion of bugs without taking into consideration humanity's dependable, old companion, *Gokiburi*, the cockroach, the Rat of Arthropoda. Interestingly, this creature is not featured in poetry or other artistic expressions that I could find. Perhaps Nihonjin of old were more discriminating in their choice of bugs to wax rhapsodic about. Or could it be that *la cucaracha* is a recent arrival on these shores? Perchance, a gift of the Portuguese? In a fairly exhaustive search, I can find only one reference to cockroaches in Koizumi sensei (6). Around here, they might be dormant in winter—certainly less active, true the world over—but the rest of the year, they are squatters, uninvited co-occupants of "my" house, especially the kitchen.

Meanwhile, back to the reality of my cosy little domicile at 4-4-19 Matsu ga Oka: It's hot and humid, such that the place is an optimal breeding site for every arthropod denizen known to the Shonan Coast, except for scorpions; thanks for small favors. You may be sure, there have been vicissitudes attendant on these "optimal" conditions. I once had to persuade a friend to hold completely still while I carefully brushed a five-inch-long centipede out of her hair. On another occasion I was sitting at the kotatsu one evening going through lesson preparations when I caught some movement out of the corner of my eye. Glancing quickly in the direction of the flutter at the periphery of my vision, on the wall an arm's length away was a light-brown hairless spider—say, two-thirds the size of an average outspread hand—motionless, alert to my every movement.

To anthropomorphize a moment, especially if this *kumo*, spider, harbored the spirit of a recently deceased human, still in the *gaki*, or hungry-ghost realm, and not happy about it, she might have been contemplating leaping on me and quickly injecting me with her nerve toxin, which would render me paralyzed, but not dead. Then, like as not, she'd invite the neighbors over, traditional interspecies feuds suspended, for a free-for-all. On me. I'd be paying the tab, but it would be one hell of a feast! One for the books! The kind multi-generational legends would be built on—hell, I might support five or six generations myself. She was working out the logistics when I spied her.

My discovery of her presence altered her plan somewhat; she was still confident she could carry out the mission of dispatching me, but the cost

25

might be significant. Having lost the aspect of surprise meant the giant biped could wield some damage in his defense—torn limbs, dismemberment, even death—before the slow onset of her irreversible toxin. Needless to say, if she were killed or severely dismembered, she would not be able to deposit her eggs in strategic places around the carcass. Her DNA would run out. This required circumspect arachnid contemplation.

Well, possessed of a human spirit or not, I leapt up and smashed that spider into the wall with a folded *manga*, which had to have changed her outlook considerably. Propelled her on to the "next round" of Existence. She left a small protoplasmic stain on the wallpaper, which faded over the years, a little reminder to reflect on my Journey—and that of the *kumo*: Gone in the blink of a polyhedral eye.

* * * * *

One of the discoveries I made in getting to know Kimiko was that she had a good exposure to and appreciation of basic rock'n'roll, a genre of music dear to my heart. *Queen* was a particular favorite of hers. I knew of them, of course, but had not paid them much attention beyond "We are the Champions" (a truly wretched song, beyond the first two or three listenings), and "Bohemian Rhapsody" (a stunning achievement, a rock'n'roll anthem). She made me cassette tapes of her Queen favorites to banish some of the clouds of doubt and ignorance I'd been laboring under, and when she got wind of Freddy Mercury and the boys coming to town, well, you can bet we got tickets. We actually saw them twice, separated by a couple of years, once at Budokan and once at the Tokyo Big Egg. Freddy was an amazing performer, more eccentric than most, with a truly magnificent voice. It was well worth the effort to see him live. In those last few years while he was still alive.

Other musical concerts we've attended together over the years include the Stones on two different tours; George Harrison, with Clapton as guest; Heart; Def Leopard; REM; Elton John, with Mark Knopfler and Clapton; and Ry Cooder with David Lindley at a Shibuya concert hall that couldn't hold more than about a thousand audience members. And Yo Yo Ma at the Yokohama Prefectural Hall. Needless to say, attending anything like this number and variety of musicians would not have been possible in Portland,

26

and probably not in Seattle—even if I were able to afford the tab. These performances in Tokyo/Yokohama were certainly not cheap, but compared to everything else in Japan, they didn't seem conspicuously out of line with, say, dining out, or any other type of evening entertainment. At $100 each per person, per event, on average, it was the going fare, and not a terrific hit to the pocketbook.

Kuro bune, the Black Ships

Modern Japan, by most measures, began with the *Kuro bune*, the black ships of Commodore Matthew Perry and the American Pacific fleet. In 1853 Perry shelled some Japanese ports, Shimonoseki and Kagoshima, to extort compliance. None of Japan's ports were "fortified" against modern navel artillery, so in short order, the local magistrates were forced to agree to resupply American whaling ships, and one hopes the irony is not lost on the reader. Japan, as a closed society, was managing its domestic affairs, minding its own business, posing no threat whatsoever to any external national entity when the US appears out of nowhere and forces Japan to provision the American whaling fleet. *So that it might continue its plunder of Cetacea.* Nowadays *Bekoku*, the US, presumes to criticize Japan's annual whaling hunts, consisting mostly of minke whales in Antarctic seas, neither an endangered, nor a threatened species. But I stray…

For 260-plus years the Tokugawa shogunate had maintained absolute authority over the home isles (except for the northernmost island of Hokkaido, and the Satsuma clan of Kyushu who settled for an uneasy truce). That meant for the first time *ever* communities didn't have to worry about those wicked people on the other side of the mountain springing an attack on us—and those people too were spared the same anxiety. No more internecine warring. Without this overarching defensive/aggressive preparedness imposing the constant immediacy of fight or flight, the arts in all their expressions were free to flourish like never before. This included ceremonies, like *Sado*, the Way of Tea; popular drama, like *Noh, Bunraku*, half-life-sized puppets performing famous plays, and especially *Kabuki*; and *Tanka* and *Haiku* poetry events where people competed on ability to compose 31 and 17-syllable poems, respectively, impromptu to spontaneous themes.

27

Shuji, or calligraphy, became highly refined. Three distinct styles developed: *Kaisho,* or normal, standard; *Gyosho,* or cursive; and *Sosho,* the artistic, highly stylized form of writing. Annual contests—city, prefecture, and nation—were held on behalf of this highly respected skill. Nihongo uses the same basic verb, *kaku,* to paint or draw a picture, and to write letters-words-paragraphs-page ideas. So, *E-okaku* is picture drawing, and *Ji-okaku* is character or word drawing, very much an art, as is the picture-drawing form. Both disciplines are executed with a brush. *Sumi-e* is the Japanese equivalent of a watercolor, minus the color. *Sumi* is ground up charcoal, the same material, along with a brush, that is used in writing.

Then, there is everybody's favorite, *Origami,* the art, dexterity and eye-hand coordination of folding colored paper into intricate forms. *Ikebana:* I am troubled that the standard translation of "flower arrangement" doesn't do it justice: What flowers? Selected and arranged according to what criteria? In what manner of presentation? In a bamboo container, *raku* ceramic, some kind of metal, or porcelain? Placed where, in relation to other features of the environment? Is the choice of flowers and arrangement appropriate for the family *Butsudan,* Buddhist altar, or for the *genkan,* the transition entry room? These disciplines, among others, developed into a highly sophisticated and detailed *people's* art.

Recall that Japan was a closed society. Except for Dejima, a strictly controlled port in the bay of Nagasaki where the Dutch and Chinese had exclusive contract to trade and serve as a very limited conduit to the outside world, with very rare exception, nobody came and nobody left Japan during 260 years of the Tokugawa *bakafu,* the military regime.

I stress this point because of the astonishingly short interval of time it took Japan, once she understood the real-world politics she was up against, to completely transform the society from the ground up. It is likely that the *Kuro Bune,* those hated Black Ships, stunned and shocked the putative defenders of the homeland into taking serious stock of the geopolitics of the day, the Asian region in particular. In short order, it must have been brutally clear that a mere handful of Western powers had colonized vast lands in the Asian Pacific. A half-dozen European nations had absolute control or were suzerain to most of the globe, from the vast island chain of Indonesia and Malaysia (the Netherlands); to Vietnam (France); to Goa, East Timor, and Macau (Portugal);

to the Philippines (Spain, until the US whupped the Spanish in 1902 and took over: *Meet the new boss!*); to Honk Kong, Singapore, the entire Indian subcontinent, Australia and New Zealand—the "Big Daddy" of colonial powers, the United Kingdom. At its height, during the Victorian Age, a common adage was, *The sun never sets on the British Empire.*

Japan was no doubt already on someone's list, a juicy peach, ripe for despoliation—a la the *Conquistadores* in the New World? It would not be out of the question. Another of Europe's small and unassuming countries, Belgium's King Leopold II, born to European education and aristocracy, was historically late to the table of colonial rapine. This European monarch, eager to make up for lost time, would covertly promote slave labor of the "colonized" in Africa's Congo well into the 20th century in pursuit of rubber and ivory primarily, resulting in the deaths of some *10 million* Africans, not to mention the wholesale obliteration of untold unique, autonomous cultures (7).

If Japan were unable, or worse, unwilling, to master the means by which these white devils were able to conquer and control these lands—critically, their strategic military superiority—it was a sure bet they would succumb like the others had. This must not happen! These half-pint, pipsqueak European entities—the Netherlands, Portugal, Belgium, the United Kingdom—*World* Powers? What a colossal injustice! Ah, but the secret of their power was their knowledge of the latest advancements in science and its applications, technology, coupled with manufacturing ability on an increasingly massive scale—thanks to the industrial revolution—as a result of a fundamental understanding of higher realms of mathematics, physics and chemistry, mechanics and engineering, which is to say, current empirical knowledge of *all* the sciences. Nippon, by matching European and American technological prowess, might yet avert subjugation by one or more of these arrogant barbarian nations.

Thus, early in the Meiji Restoration (1868 to 1912) the decision was made to send the brightest scholars abroad; for the most part, these would be the lay-about samurai. They would travel to the US, and the politically dominant European countries—Germany, France, and the UK, mostly—to study at the most prestigious institutions. In a few short years these students began trickling back conversant with the state of the art in medicine, modern military weaponry and tactics, a legal framework on which to build a civil society, architecture, a health care system, electrification, urban planning/engineering, and public transportation/railroads, power generation, a post, telephone, and telegraph network—the list was staggering in terms of what Japan would have to accomplish in order to compete on an equal footing with the Western powers.

Evidence of this very achievement came by 1906 when Japan defeated the Russians on the Pacific seaboard, for which Teddy Roosevelt won the Nobel Peace Prize in brokering the Peace Accord. By 1910 Japan had annexed the Korean Peninsula as its first, full-fledged colony, with Manchuria, the vast, northeastern province of China, and Formosa (Taiwan) in her sights. In 35 years of maniacally driven social upheaval, Japan had arrived on the world stage, scrappy, ready to go toe to toe with the colonial powers for primacy in Asia.

By the late-1930s Japan was justifying its own bold steps at colonizing foreign lands as "Asia for Asiatics," and in 1940 the *Greater East Asia Co-Prosperity Sphere* was formally proposed (8). Within powerful Japanese groups, there was increasing recognition of the need to liberate Asian countries from foreign imperialist powers. Only Nippon was in the position to take the leadership role in confronting these abhorrent non-Asian colonialists. Of course, sacrifices would be necessary. Much of the economic productivity and raw materials of the member states—Chosen (Korea), Formosa (Taiwan), Manchukuo (Manchuria), and others—would have to be redirected to the war effort. "Protection" doesn't come cheap. *Sound familiar?*

Needless to say, without justifying anyone's colonial conquests in any way, it doesn't take much to see the hypocrisy in this setup. Thus, you might imagine my shock when I discovered that Japan had based her legal right to assert authority over lesser developed nations of its region on *a precedent established by the good ol' USA!* How curiously life unfolds! After I'd picked myself up off the floor, I learned that America, under the guise of the early-19th-century Monroe Doctrine, presumed to exclude European (and, hypothetically, any other) powers from meddling in the Western Hemisphere—that's *two whole continents*, folks, North *and* South America—under the pretext of preserving our own safety and stability. Proving, once again, that a little arrogance and territorial over-reach go a long way.

The Japanese militarists must have taken one look at this geopolitical precedent and said, *The operative concept here is, Who's the Big Dog in the neighborhood?* Sure enough, from a local and regional perspective, Nippon was uncontested. In hindsight, however, it does appear that the war lords of Nippon in the late-1930s/early-'40s lacked sufficient appreciation of the global reach of Uncle Sam. And the rest, as they say, is history.

Only the Meiji period rivalled the reconstruction period following Japan's total defeat in World War II, for the breadth, depth, and extent of the transformation. So far as I know, Japan is the only nation-state in modern times—from all recorded time?—to have undergone such a profound political, economic, social, and physical upheaval not once, but *twice* in less than a century. *And* managed to preserve the 2000-years-in-the-making *Nihon no kokoro*, the heart, the essence, the soul of Japan. Bruised, but intact.

* * * * *

One of my students, herself an English teacher, taught me a valuable expression early on: *San tan gen no "s."* This little gem means, "The *s* that refers to third (person), present (tense), singular." Or the "he, she, or it" position of a verb that requires a final "s." English has three—and only three—final-s uses to signal a change in usage: 1) Countable, plural *nouns*: books, trees, molecules, ad infinitum. 2) Possessives: the rays of the sun = the sun's rays; the park of the children = the children's park. And 3) Third person, singular, present tense rule of English syntax. I talk, we talk, you (singular) talk, you (plural) talk, and they talk. *But...* He talk<u>s</u>! She talk<u>s</u>! Even, assuming it's semantically feasible, It talk<u>s</u>! That is the only particular change in verb form distinguishing *only* third-person singular, present-tense—with a final *s*. It is a handy shortcut I can use by way of explanation to my students of this quirky aspect of English.

Tuesday evening (July 23): After my Nihon Roche class of stiff, tight-lipped *kaisha-in*, business men, here I am plopped on my bed in front of the fan having just emerged from the *furo,* traditional bath, in my birthday suit: the coolest I've been all day. Over the last few days I've come to realize why I've been out of sync. Aside from having broken the routine for the five weeks'

31

home visit with my kids, I indulged the fruits of my labors of the previous six months, and now I'm back to the arduous task of replenishing the coffers. How true it is that earning it comes harder than spending it…

Kimiko was here last night when I returned from a class about 8:30, putting the finishing touches on a dinner. She's a good cook: hot weather, Nihon *tabemono*, e.g., cold soba noodles to slurp after dipping in some wasabi broth, and some *chu-hi*s to chase it with, put the evening in a convivial mood. I wish her English—and my Nihongo—were better, though we seem to manage just fine with the basics. *Ishin denshin*, an intuited, non-verbal communication; a close implicit, empathic affinity. We seem to be intrigued with each other, in spite of—might it not be just a little "because of"?—a challenging language barrier…

Sunday Blues (<u>August 18</u>): Again, lounging in my birthday suit in front of my electric fan, coping with the physical and emotional torpor. After six days of air-conditioned hotels in exotic surroundings, elegant dining, to say nothing of the intriguing sight-seeing, by way of meaningful, if temporary, distractions to the episodic carnal feast, well, yes, a return to normalcy is decidedly a let-down.

She came last Sunday evening and it was hot, sweaty love making deep into the night. Then, we were up by 4:30 in order to make the necessary local train connections to Odawara, a castle town in the foothills of the Tanzawa Mountains on the western edge of the Kanto Plain. We needed to catch the *shinkansen*, or bullet train, bound for Hiroshima at 6:55. Every train appeared exactly as scheduled. We settled into a reserved seat/air conditioned car, breakfast in the dining car, and had time for part of a magazine because four and a half hours later we arrived in Hiroshima. Taxi to the ANA Hotel; now *this* is living! We had a great room on the 20th floor with a view of the city stretching to the bay, Miajima, and other islands. This hotel is probably the tallest building in Hiroshima and quite near Peace Park, where we headed as soon as we unpacked, borrowing an umbrella from the hotel (western Honshu was undergoing the tail end of a typhoon, and there was a light drizzle all day).

The museum really clobbered me. I'd read a fair amount of the literature on the effects of the Atomic Bomb and I was rationally prepared for evidence of the destruction, but during a half-hour documentary of mostly stills of the post-bomb landscape, bodies, and people in the process of dying, I started to come apart. I remember, at one point the documentary profiled a couple of sisters, maybe ten and twelve, with vacant and scared looks on their faces, their hair falling out in big clumps. They'd been *X* thousand meters from the epicenter of the blast, and were thus not killed outright. The narrator reported, however, these girls did succumb to radiation poisoning a short time after being filmed. By the film's end I was silently weeping and shaking, and Kimiko was in the awkward position of consoling me. Without trying, I'd made the immediate connection to my own two daughters in far-off Florida, about the same age. Ah, what incredible suffering we inflict on each other!

The next day by 1 pm we caught the *shinkansen* back to Kyoto where we made a bus connection to our *ryokan,* a traditional Japanese inn, at Arashiyama. We told the *obasan* we wanted dinner at eight, and went for a leisurely walk up the river that fronted our ryokan. This river and entire area figure richly in Kyoto lore; it was fun to muse over lovers walking this same river bank on a similar summer eve—1000 to 1200 years ago when Kyoto was the capital. On the walk back we were charmed by a line of floating candles on both sides of the river, being carried downstream. Just before a low dam upstream of the bridge, in the last of the twilight several boats were being poled into the current. These long-prowed boats had flaming baskets hanging from booms at the bow. Each fire lures schools of river fish, *aiyu*, to swim closer to see what all the fuss is about, whereby they are greeted by three to five cormorants per boat, restrained by close-fitting metal collars. After much thrashing around the birds were hauled aboard and made to disgorge their catch.

Back inside our room we were treated to an 11-course spread exquisitely arrayed. A visual and gustatory extravaganza, including this same river fish. *Obasan*, the room attendant, cleared away the dinner wreckage and made up our futons. Our bath was not the traditional *furo,* but a wooden tub allowing us to bathe together; the lady is fast overcoming her reticence to our nakedness.

Next morning we made the trek up a nearby hill to view the city—and to see the wild *saru*, or monkeys, very much acclimated to human handouts. The size of a cocker spaniel with a stub of a tail, they were very endearing—

something about their resemblance to *Homo sapiens* that fascinates (facial expressions and reciprocal grooming?). Back down on the river we rented a rowboat and rowed quite a way up river; an idyllic episode, complete with our self-conscious attempt to sing snatches of remembered Beatles songs...

Here and there people stare each and every day.
Gather 'round, all you clowns, let me hear you say,
Hey, you've got to hide your love away!

"You've Got to Hide Your Love Away," from the album/movie "Help"
John Lennon & Paul McCartney, 1965

After, it was fetch our bags, catch a bus to a famous TV/movie set, *Eiga Mura*, and our first taste of the throngs of people inundating Kyoto for Obon—the traditional summertime holiday when people return to their family homes to clean ancestral graves, present offerings to the returning family spirits, and reconnect with living relatives. Since I have limited experience of vast crowds, I am negatively impressed.

The New Miyako Hotel provides us with a spectacular second-floor view of... the sheet metal siding of a dingy warehouse. As it turns out, we're not prone to spending a lot of time gazing out of windows, anyway. After a cleanup, we are off on a tour of downtown featuring a trip up the Kyoto Tower in time for sunset. Our promenade of the central district fails to yield a promising sushi bar, so we go back to the Miyako where we find a surprisingly good one. Back upstairs we change into our *yukatas*, summertime cotton house robes. But only briefly...

Thursday we rented bicycles nearby and commence a tour of Kyoto antiquities. This city is chock a block with historical monuments, shrines (*Shinto*) and temples (*Bukyo,* Buddhist), and other assorted antiquities; arguably more per square kilometer than any other continuously occupied city on earth. As the second of four ancient capitals, and the longest lasting, there are several dozen unique sites listed on any decent map of the city, and hundreds of sites considered less noteworthy—on virtually every street—that would be hot stuff in another earthly locale. You could be blindfolded and plunked down in any neighborhood in Kyoto, spun around twice, and, tossing

34

a dead cat at random, could not help but strike some prized cultural relic—or some eager tourist scurrying to one, at the very least.

Our first stop, Sanjusangen-do, was, for me, our antiquities-hopping highlight. Over 1000 meticulously replicated (wood carved, gold leafed) Buddhas, four rows deep, fill the entire length of the 390 ft. building, but only half the width. The other side has some 28 highly individualistic sculptures of *Niorai*, the gods, demigods, demons, other assorted spirits created to exorcise the evil that might lurk in the area. One is humbled by the piety expressed here. Like pre-and early renaissance art in Europe, most of the themes for artistic expression were inspired by religious accounts. Virtually all ancient architecture is Buddhist or Shinto. After, it was a stiff bike ride up the low hills east to Kyomizu-dera, a massive temple accompanied by a five-tiered pagoda in a small copse of pine. There is a small spring, the waters of which are said to have magical properties. The day's remaining highlight was a leisurely pass through Nijojo, the imperial palace, complete with massive bulwarks and a moat, built by a 17th century Tokugawa shogun and later donated to the imperial family. Wandering around the grounds arm in arm, it was fun to fanaticize hiding out in the foliage at closing time and stealing a night together as the military and political master of the land and one of his favorite concubines in any one of his 30 or so tatamied halls—though, truth to tell, the ol' boy would certainly have traded our fairly straightforward, utilitarian, air-conditioned, electrically lit, hot and cold water provided plumbing for his dimly lit, mosquito haunted, sultry tomb, in a hot second!

That evening—Holy Priapus!—it was slow and gentle, hot and raunchy, over and under, a yin/yang of the libido, which stretched into hours. I didn't know I had it in me; it had been a long time. Next morning, we broke fast in the café downstairs and managed one final clinch before vacating the premises by 11.

We checked our bags in a locker at the train station across the street from the hotel, and caught a bus for Kinkaku-ji, the Golden Pavillion, covered in gold leaf, making it very showy and ostentatious. The grounds are exquisite, though, and in any event, swarming with people. To clear our heads we walked the 20 minutes it took to reach Ryoanji, the temple with the famous rock garden. It's basically a 10 by 15 meter +/-, finely graveled field, framed by a two meter high, plain, stuccoed wall on the sides and back. On this plot seven or so large, and perhaps another five smaller, differently shaped rocks are interestingly arrayed on a sea of combed gravel. Fronting this display is a set of tiered bleachers for perhaps as many as 120 people to sit and consider whatever it is the stone arrangement conjures. Unfortunately, this place was also swarming with people. While we sat over the course of 15 or 20 minutes, one round of uniformed middle school students, *chugaku sei,* left as another group took their place. For me, appreciation of a zen experience— or anything remotely natural and contemplative, for that matter—must necessarily take place in a quiet and peaceful setting. The dilemma of group enjoyment, group thought, and group action is nowhere so apparent as at Ryoan-ji in August. Queued in a line of hundreds of slowly moving people with the attendant grunts, murmurs, chuckle/snickers, jostles, bumps, farts, and sneezes is the absolute antithesis of a contemplation of subtlety, or balance, forget serenity. It was going through the motions for me: *A bunch of rocks in front of a wall? That's it? Ok, what's next?*

What's next was to catch a *shinkansen* back to Odawara, stop there long enough for a bite to eat before taking the local Tokaido line to Fujisawa, connect with the Odakyu line to Kugenuma Kaigan and home by 11 pm. Ms. K changed her plans in order to stay one last night. Sticky tenderness, somewhat anticlimactic. Saturday morn I made pancakes to go with yogurt and raspberry jam, juice and coffee, before putting her on the train for Machida, her family and job. Currently, this is looking like one of those ill-fated love affairs the melodramas are full of, a budding blossom full of promise, cut short before reaching full flower.

August 24: I have lately had occasion to gain insight, and perhaps new respect for alcohol and other drug abuse. More than the pursuit of kicks (*cheap thrills,* as the ol' cliché had it), it serves to blunt the steady pain of loneliness, to numb the ache of separation. Any drug worth its salt—certainly alcohol in enough quantities—is effective at curbing the despair in the knowledge that you are all alone in his world, and that frequently life seems to have no meaning. Such was my state in the days following my honeymoon-like idyll with Kimiko. I've managed to cope some of the time writing a few letters, I'm afraid, with some self-pity on display. Here's a kotowaza that doesn't help, as such, but suggests to me that others face a similar plight:

Kaho wa nete mate.
For better luck, sleep and wait.

I interpret this to mean, one is incapable of making "good luck" occur. What one can do, however, is to rest—and cultivate patience, which is what we do when we wait.

Ku gatsu, ju shichi nichi; September 17: As of this month classes have increased, though I still have several time gaps I could teach. The first week of this month I worked 25 hours (not counting preparation, or transportation to and from the class site), and earned ¥100,000. Week two was 27 ½ hours for ¥111,000, though this week will be less. I think I surprise myself with my earning capacity.

The weather has changed. In the scope of three days it has gone from summertime hot/ humid to deep-fall cool, with off-and-on drizzle. A welcome relief.

Trains

If Japan were to be praised for mastery of a particular aspect of modern technology, applied to the benefit of society, a prime candidate would be for the engineering, construction, maintenance, and constant upgrading of the greater Tokyo train network. This vast system works seamlessly, since one line frequently shares a station with several other lines. Yokohama station has eleven separate train lines converging at this one location; Tokyo has fourteen lines; Ueno, ten; Shinjuku, with 12, had something like 3.65 million commuters per day through the station, a world record as of 2013 (according to Wikipedia). Delays are so rare—outside of winter-storm or earthquake related—that suicide by train has become a factor, statistically. This railway network is so efficient and effective that millions of people live all their rich and varied lives without ever owning an automobile! A reckless and heretical concept, to most Americans.

Modern commuter-train cars typically have 54 seats, with some variations according to the line. These same cars, around rush-hour time, regularly accommodate 300 people. One of my students reported that under such conditions, she was still able to stand and read a book—standard sized (6" x 4"), held close to her face. She also said, at 350 people per car, the density requires the services of the *osuya,* the "shoving brigade," sometimes seen on train platforms, white gloves complementing natty uniforms, pushing people into the cars with all their might. No book reading under such conditions. And decidedly *not* the place for a claustrophobe! Here in Nihon, it's called *Sushi zumi.* The English idiom equivalent is "packed like sardines in a can." In Japanese, it's "stuffed like rolled sushi in a *bento*" (a small lunch container).

Someone made a tentative calculation that at 350 people per car, there would have to be eight people per square meter of available floor space. Surely that's wrong, even for Japan. *Pureed*, maybe, but even then, given the mass of the average adult, they'd all have to be six year olds, or younger, and we'd have to be talking about *cubic* meters, or liters, to contain the volume.

Profanity and Vulgarity

Or at least verbal impropriety: I don't think profanity is possible in Nihongo. Japanese "gods" are amorphous, animist, and in many cases not anthropomorphic. To be profane in Nihongo, it is necessary to have a target to blaspheme. Japanese deities are non-hierarchical and don't lend themselves to verbal or sexual abuse, unlike, say, Christianity with Jesus and God the Father very much in human form and, thus, subject to human-familiar, imaginative foibles, an easy step toward ridicule out of anger and extreme frustration. By contrast, however, both languages share a rich vocabulary of vulgarity. Synonyms for penis, vagina, and variations of the sex act are numerous, but, at least in colloquial speech, far from infinite. In fact, a very few terms wind up getting used over and over. As a sub-set of vulgarity, terms that express extreme dissatisfaction with events associated with the person being addressed may be demeaning and derogatory, and yet, be artfully addressed.

Among this group, consider: *Chiku-shou!,* delivered *con brio*, with gusto. Usually by the potential victim, calling out the perpetrator, in order to humiliate him and ward off further assault. The only time I heard it used was on a crowded evening outbound train. Since it was a young woman's voice, we might surmise that a tired and beleaguered office lady had reached her limit with some hormonally challenged troglodyte, tracing through the fabric of her skirt the outline of her cheeks with deliberate fingertips. The term has doubtless been translated to mean a person less than human; a brute, an animal. A person totally devoid of decency, or respect for the woman being fondled. The best definition I've heard, the one that really stuck with me, was *Bestial life form!* More creative than *asshole,* to be sure.

Then, there's *Aho* and *Baka*, accentuated with *Yaro: Baka-yaro!* Personally, I've never really understood which demeaning term to use for what occasion: Idiot, moron, cretin, imbecile, retard(ed), fool, stupid; if you stoop to character denigrations, no matter who wins the face-off contest, I think the argument is lost, and all the participants have surrendered an important piece of their humanity—for the duration of that episode. The participants, by this stage, are intent on emphasizing the differences, and have no stomach for reconciliation. Those few epithets are, from my limited experience, the most commonly used in Nihongo, and used not at all commonly in polite society.

In deference to someone worthy of superlative dismissiveness, becoming an object (not even a real person) of supreme insignificance, my favorite is:
> ...*doko no uma no hone tomo shirenu yatsu* (9)

"(What, that/him? That's/he's nothing but) a horse's bone from nobody knows where." Utterly beneath human dignity.

September 21: *Marriage is the graveyard of love*, a comment out of the mouth of the sage, himself, Owen. In order to evaluate the statement, we have to carefully consider the meanings of *love*. Well, in at least one sense—e.g., the rapturous, blissful, ecstatic state of heightened sensation between two lovers, *the body electric*—the condition is unsustainable by definition, with or without the false bulwark of the marriage institution. That being the case, why is it we so often desperately seek to contain the feeling? As in wed*lock*? People must not be possessed. Love is the one clear expression in relationship that cannot be taken, but only given. It is a morally flawed statement to say, *You are mine*, in the sense of possession, though in the case of parent/child relationships, it is true in the sense that, *You are of me. You came from me, which makes me responsible for you—for a while.* By contrast, it is an expression of love to say, *I am yours.* Consequently, there are no guarantees, no absolute security on one's future feelings, not through writ, community customs, or religious dogma. As we know too well, fools rush in…

Knowing all this intuitively, why is it I feel uneasy about Kimiko's ambiguity of our future? I'm used to thinking that somewhat, at least, I am the "master" of my fate; I'm asserting my will, in this instance. It's fair to say Kimiko does not feel this way, certainly not under these circumstances.

Part of my unease stems from the assumption that I am/we are "just a good time," and that a lack of commitment to anything implying a future suggests, at some point, an ending. It is manifestly true that we enjoy each other's company. And if one really has no moral justification to codify so fragile and perhaps transient a connection, what more has one the right to hope for than to *have a good time*? She gives her love to me wholly; I want nothing else than what I now have. I'll have to work on ways to banish thoughts of permanency, or perhaps exclusivity. This evening she comes, and again we will take up our intercultural experiment.

As a landed family there were expectations, cultural traditions, obligations that needed to be upheld. She was 29 years old, and by common convention, the "Christmas cake" was growing peaked. The Christmas cake is freshest, most delicious and desirable when ravished on the 25th day of December, corresponding to the chronological year of age. 29 is becoming just a little tired, stale—or some would have us believe. But there is truth to some of this attention, as it relates marriageable age to the prime baby-making years. What a difference a century makes! Up until Meiji certainly, prime marriage age for girls was sixteen, and fifteen wasn't unusual.

Unmarried women, beyond Christmas cake, face the *petit Kanreki* of 30—since full *Kanreki* is 60 years, or five times around the 12-year zodiac. Finally, the last designation of old maid-ness is "Dried Flowers," from 35 years of age, on.

September 22: Hamlet's dilemma, *To be or not to be*, is everyone's. In contemporary terms, How (or What, since they are essentially the same) to be is the question. Too often, I think, people are content to let circumstances define their identities. For me, there is a kind of built in resistance to the inertia of the Great Wheel's implacable revolving. To be pitted against that momentum seldom yields serenity and calm. The personal victories are few, modest, and short lived. Yet, for my own self-esteem, I deem it more of value to chart my own course and pursue it, however ineffectually, than to acquiesce meekly to whatever fate I am dealt. Is this an illusion? Don't I delude myself into believing *I* actually make the significant choices? *Any* choices? Isn't the presumption of mastery of one's own destiny an ego pipe dream? *Whatcha got in that pipe, bubba?*

It is true that we often fail to achieve our goals—life presents many distractions and obstacles, often unforeseeable. And the price we pay in falling short, the disappointment, frustration, and sense of inadequacy, can be very debilitating. That said, I still generally believe we underestimate the importance of the force of one's will. Carefully, continuously applied, like water dribbling on a stone, it can produce astonishing results. So much can be reduced to the question: What is it you really *want?* With quiet, patient dedication invariably more can be accomplished than originally imagined. *Exampli gratia*, witness the mountains of verbiage generated from the flimsiest of abstractions—what, or how to be. *Because, you see, What/how to be presupposes we have the choice.* And then perhaps, the even-more important question: *Why? Toward what end?* I mean, who would have thought there could be so much to say about such a transient consideration?

(For the next 20 to 24 months this relationship teetered and tripped through a series of intense periods together, followed by periods of no contact, nothing. During these dark stretches, Kimiko went through the motions of complying with her family's expectations. There was a six or seven month phase where she succumbed to family sanctioned, arranged "dates" toward the selection of a marriage partner—and was completely out of touch for that duration.)

Here's a little tongue twister you might find amusing. I stumbled across this one while trying to memorize a list of adjectives. Enormously important, adjectives, as modifiers of nouns, don't you think? *Atatakai* means "warm," as in a warm day.

Except that Japanese don't say *It's a warm,* or *cool, day.* They basically say, *Atsui desu,* or *Samui desu.* It's hot, or It's cold, as if the whole society were prepared to assert the extremes in weather, with no gradations. I've raised this observation dozens of times with Nihonjin in various contexts, such as a brisk or blustery day that doesn't sink to the level of cold—as considered by most people, I assert. Invariably, they nod politely, and acknowledge the logic of my observation, conceding its validity, all the while thinking to themselves, *This poor booby of an outsider thinks "precision" and "accuracy" of observed data, given a normal range of human perception, could possibly be more important than building a sense of rapport with your fellow interlocutor. Precise interpretation of weather conditions, except as crude statistical data, is virtually irrelevant, given that we are all free to experience and interpret the weather as we choose.*

Ahem, if you please, let us return to the development of our "Warm" treatise, progressing nicely before that rude interruption: To state the negative of warm in *Eigo,* English, we'd say, It isn't warm. *Nihongo de: Atatakakunai desu.* Now, if you were to render this into a past-tense, negative statement—It wasn't warm—in Japanese, it would be *Atatakakunakata,* an almost-palindrome. Say that three times in a row, quickly!

Now, for your follow-up, existential puzzlement: What (or who?) is "It" in the following combinations: "*It* is/was/wasn't a warm day"?

September 23: *Shumbun,* the Autumnal Equinox. Ms. Kimiko came last night. Bread just out of the oven, blackberry pie still baking. It turns out the flowers I bought for her are sold, especially this time of year, to commemorate the dead. The Spring and Autumn Equinoxes are ceremonial occasions for people to attend family cemetery plots to show respect for relatives who have passed before. She understood my error and was appreciative of the gesture, nonetheless. We had warm pie with yogurt and coffee. Followed by a tasty rendition of Vivaldi's Four Seasons, and drawn-out lust—most of "Spring," all of "Summer," and a bit of "Fall," if memory serves. Our plan was to play all day: picnic in the mountains nearby, if weather permitted. Or go see a movie, or?

Alas, we never got the chance to create the day together. She was summoned by a dawn phone call. Her grandfather, after a long struggle with throat cancer, had finally succumbed. I immediately sent him a little prayer of gratitude for hanging on through the night.

September 30: Excerpts from a letter to Hobbit and Faery Godmother

You ask about the damsel of the raven tresses. Ah, what can I tell you... The ancient adage, "Opposites attract," has a certain poignant veracity here in Japan, a study in contrasts with Yours Truly as a principle. The lady and I enjoy each other's company, which is generally speaking every week to 10 days, or not often enough. Where it goes from here is anybody's guess. I'd say, however, that we are both in deep enough to make it pretty tough to cut it loose. A factor pushing in that direction (dissolution) is family pressure—she is the elder of two daughters (no sons), younger sister having just gotten married. Her traditional/feudal family "expects" her to settle down with an acceptable hubby and begin engaging the management of the family business. Ergo, to get serious about me would mean for her to leave the family, a very difficult decision for a Nihonjin (Japanese) to make. Other factors that influence this lady with a bold streak of realism: I'm 16 years her senior (not a real biggie), I've been divorced and have three half-grown children (not too serious of itself, but getting there), and I can't make any more babies, owing to a vasectomy. This one is a serious obstacle—the maternal urge in Japanese women is formidable.

For my part, what could dampen my ardor would be an attempt to get me to conform to the total Japanese lifestyle, i.e., sedate conventionality, materialism and a serious dedication to pecuniary pursuits, to name but a few. As you might have guessed by now, I'm too much a burned out old hippie to find any lasting benefits in a blatant devotion to Mammon—it's not for nothing these people are referred to as "economic animals." Lord knows I'm corruptible, but Dionysius and his ilk have greater allure for me than wealth or power...

Religion

The 400-or-so years that made up much of the Fifth through the Ninth Centuries saw accelerated trade with China. This corresponded with the wholesale importation of Buddhism. Along with language, Japan had a well-established indigenous "religion," Shinto. However, over the course of a few centuries, Buddhism became popular among the nobility and the ruling families, and so avid adherents of Shinto learned to accommodate. Each religion commands its own realm of authority, but generally they seem to have a co-existence pact; basically they ignore each other. My guess is most Japanese, from the Heian *Jidai*, Epoch or Period (794~1185 CE) to the present day, don't see these two religions as mutually exclusive—unlike, say, the followers of Christianity who are bound by the commandment, *Thou shalt have no other God before me.* These days most people would admit they are *nominally* Buddhist *and* Shintoist, alternately as the occasion requires. Buddhism and Shintoism are cultural icons, woven into and inseparable from the culture. They are very much of what it means to be Japanese.

Shinto

Shinto is the native religion of Japan; it has been a practice based on ancestor-worship since centuries before the advent of Buddhism, the "latecomer" beginning in the mid-6th century. It is animist; gods/divine spirits/ghosts of our predecessors dwell in natural sites, such as mountains, forests and individual trees, stunning rocky configurations, streams, the moon, even breezes. Places that inspire you through a unique and striking set of features are considered sacred, and often become the site of a shrine. In broad stroke, I see it as parallel to Druidism, a pre-Christian, European religious practice, in its polytheistic nature reverence. No doubt, a great deal of Japan's aesthetic sense originates in Shinto's deep reverence for beautiful places, as well as commonplace, simple, natural phenomena that we Americans as a rule take too much for granted —*Fuji-no-hana*, Wisteria; the moon in all its phases; the passing of the seasons; sakura, *man kai*, cherry blossoms in full bloom; wind-blown leaves. And truly, who isn't humbled and speechless before a spectacular waterfall?

Lafcadio Hearn—Koizumi Yakumo, his Japanese name—had a lot to say about Shintoism (10), but any paraphrase of his ideas on the subject would have to start with the concept of *Shoryo*, ancestor worship, as origin of everything that follows in Shintoism. But then, Mr. Hearn asserts something I hadn't thought of before: Ancestor worship, in one form or another, is the basis of *all* religions. Today's dominant European and Middle Eastern religions, the Abrahamic Religions, are examples of that evolution from ancestor cults into the "Period of the Greater Gods"—Koizumi's terminology—while Shinto remained very much intact. I suspect a lot of the basic rituals and ceremonies of Shintoism got codified by the Heian Jidai (794~1185), or earlier, partly because the rituals and official dress to this day are straight out of that period, complete with an impressive range of quaint caps.

Japanese native mythology/religion never developed concepts of heaven or hell. Therefore, no reward/punishment as a consequence of life on earth. As you were in life, so you will be in death—*O-higan*, the place where all the dead dwell. We all become ghost/spirit/gods in death, and unfortunately, some of us aren't going to be so beneficial and supportive of the living, regardless of the incense, flowers, and sake offerings, because we were such shitheads in life. Friends and family members who have died all continue to exist as ghosts, and in a sense, gods without hierarchy. So, you can understand, *Ohigan* is getting fairly crowded since we never really lose any, but get more every day.

Two basic considerations to hold: First, these ghosts or spirits acquire supernatural powers in the hereafter, and second, their well-being is dependent on the care and attention they are shown, in the form of food and drink (more symbolic than substantive), flowers, incense, and frequent prayer. When the aforementioned regimen is adhered to rigorously, the deceased will be inclined to act kindly on your behalf. If not, well, who knows, right?

The inference is an important existential choice: Which is more troublesome, paying your respects to your dead relatives on a routine basis, or trying to cope with an indifferent world without the sometime aid and material support of benign spirits? Which choice is likely to be the way of humility? Which is the way of arrogance, even foolhardiness? By such means, a Nihonjin might reckon. But here's the thing: It's hard to imagine that any Nihonjin would even consider the notion in the first place. For Japanese people, this isn't really a matter of belief. It goes deeper than the implied choice of belief, especially since there is no cultural awareness of choice at this level. Specifically, these rites are performed as per how families/communities learned them, generation after generation, throughout centuries. This is what we do. You may choose not to participate in these rituals once in a while, but if you outright cease performing a short, silent prayer before the family *Kamidan*, Shinto altar, family and friends will eventually take note of it, and you will have taken a huge step toward being considered an *outsider*, an almost unbearably lonely feeling. Ostracism is one of the worst things that could happen to a Nihonjin. Again, Koizumi sensei:

Human society, in this most eastern East, has been held together from immemorial time by virtue of that cult which exacts the gratitude of the present to the past, the reverence of the living for the dead, the descendent for the ancestor. Far beyond the visible world extends the duty of the child to the parent, of the servant to the master, of the subject to the sovereign. Therefore do the dead preside in the family council, in the community assembly, in the high seats of judgement, in the governing of cities, in the ruling of the land (10).

According to Edwin O. Reischauer, long-time Japan scholar and former American Ambassador to Japan, "The underlying stream of Shinto today remains little changed since pre-historic times..." It is a "simple and naïve nature worship" (11). Shinto lays claim to pride and prestige based on its original, native status. It asserts a connection with the Emperor from ancient times. In the first half of the twentieth century Shinto was used, some would say manipulated, by the militarists and chauvinists to achieve nationalist consensus on Japanese military ambitions. This turned out to be an unfortunate alliance, as we came to learn.

Shintoism provides unique services at the traditional societal landmarks: *Shichi-go-san*, The Seven-five-three ceremony, benchmark rites of passage for girls at three and seven years old, and boys at five years old, on November 10th. Also, marriages are typically Shinto ceremonies, as are Adult Day ceremonies on January 15th. On this day twenty-year-old men are seen in their new suits—nothing special, there, while women go all out by having their hair done, and dressed up in their finest, colorful (rented) kimono, white *tabi*, socks with a cleft between the big toe and the others, in order to slip on *geta*, wooden clogs. Struttin' their stuff. Ah, but they are a sight to behold!

For Japan's indigenous sport, sumo, Japan's indigenous religion, Shinto, is represented by priest-like officials at the tournaments—straight out of the eleventh century. Only for year-end/year-beginning celebrations do Shinto events share services, glory, and profit with the Buddhists. And this is probable because neither of the two institutions is able to handle the public load separately, the desire of large masses of people to agglomerate before a mere handful of shrines and temples in the entire Tokyo area, in supplication of New Year's blessings. These decades, Kamakura's Tsurugaoka Hachiman-gu is among the most famous and popular. The hive swarms on this often very cold occasion, and hive members celebrate group solidarity by the millions.

Buddhism

There are something like six popular branches of Buddhism: Tendai shu, Jodo shu, Jodo Shin shu, Nichiren shu, Zen shu, and Shingon shu. And, according to Lafcadio Hearn, there are at least six other, esoteric branches that are obscure and not taught to the masses. These separate iterations of Buddhism would be analogous to Protestantism in Christianity, except that there was no presumption of supreme authority among these sects to rebel against, a la Protestants vs. Catholicism in the West. Also, somewhat analogous to Christianity's holy Trinity (God the Father, Jesus Christ the son, and the Holy Ghost, or Spirit), Buddhism has other sacred incarnations of the Buddha: Kwannon, the Goddess of Mercy (note the feminine gender), and Jizo-sama, Patron of travelers, babies and kids.

Among the various Buddhist sects, to most Westerners, including myself, Zen Buddhism is the most mysterious, elusive, and as such, alluring. Zen—*Cha'n* in Chinese—means meditation. Through rigorous meditation, one attempts to cease all rational machinations. When one accomplishes this task and suspends thought, one is said to have achieved Enlightenment, or *Satori*. Which isn't going to happen while trying to take the measure of an entity that, by its own account, is beyond space and time. Needless to say, this practice does not lend itself to a here-and-now, snappy, 140-characters-or-less handle for the Western mind to absorb, and thereby presume some "understanding."

For starters, I give you Koizumi Yakumo (10) at his most cosmic:
The very delusion of delusions is the idea of death as loss. There is no loss—because there is not any self that can be lost. Whatsoever was, that you

47

have been; whatsoever is, that you are; whatsoever will be, that you must become. Personality!—individuality!—the ghosts of a dream in a dream!

Makes you wonder if Koizumi *sensei* didn't, you know, take a dip of laudanum now and then. For his aches and pains... But let's entertain the notion that *personality* and *individuality*—what we've come to call *ego*—are delusional. Because if you don't subscribe to the standard-issue Abrahamic religions' concept of the eternal soul, or some variant, then you are faced with something like Koizumi's interpretation. Since we Americans are socially, culturally reinforced to show somesort of uniqueness of personality, we are programmed to project a socially acceptable, hopefully creative persona. But along the way, hubris is apt to set in; pride and a defensive role in "protecting" this unique and special persona from life's slings and arrows.

It's interesting that cross-culturally, regardless of which religion or lack thereof, we humans pretty uniformly subscribe to the "mass delusion" that collectively, and especially, individually, people grow attached to each other, especially family members, and become distraught when these close comrades die. Grief over the loss of loved ones seems to be universal. Well, soul or no soul, since there is no obvious, palpable connection between the dead and the living, at least from my personal, Western point of view, we might as well disregard the afterlife altogether, in deference to making the most of our relationships with the rest of life in the here and now.

Yaozah, dat's tellin 'em!

無 (Mu)

In Zen Buddhism *Mu* is taken to mean nothingness, emptiness, no thing, or the absence of cognition, rational thought, our hard-wired, survival-driven disposition to organize and evaluate the universe as we encounter it. In this way—*only* in this way, according to Zen—are we able to escape, no matter how fleetingly, the irritation and annoyance, even the pain and suffering, that arise from a life of assumptions and beliefs as to how we expect life to proceed. The essential paradox: How to define (in order to understand) a state of being in words, meta-linguistically, that only attempt to limit or trap that which is beyond, or other than, definition, meaning, and comprehension. *Mu!*

A Zen *koan* is a little, logically-impossible puzzle for you to ponder as a kind of aide toward the suspension of logical thinking, *Mu*. The cliché of koans is *What is the sound of one hand clapping?* A nudge on the bumpy road to Enlightenment. Here's a koan-like story from *101 Zen Stories,* transcribed by Nyogen Senzaki and Paul Epps:

In modern times a great deal of nonsense is talked about masters and disciples, and about the inheritance of a master's teaching by favorite pupils, entitling them to pass the truth on to their adherents. Of course Zen should be imparted in this way, from heart to heart, and in the past it was really accomplished. Silence and humility reigned rather than profession and assertion. The one who received such a teaching kept the matter hidden even after twenty years. Not until another discovered through his own need that a real master was at hand was it learned that the teaching had been imparted, and even then, the occasion arose quite naturally and the teaching made its way in its own right. Under no circumstance did the teacher ever claim "I am the successor of So-and-so." Such a claim would prove quite the contrary.

The Zen master Mu-nan had only one successor. His name was Shoju. After Shoju had completed his study of Zen, Mu-nan called him into his room. "I am getting old," he said, "and as far as I know, Shoju, you are the only one who will carry on this teaching. Here is a book. It has been passed down from master to master for seven generations. I also have added many points according to my understanding. The book is very valuable, and I am giving it to you to represent your successorship."

"If the book is such an important thing, you had better keep it." Shoju replied. "I received your Zen without writing and am satisfied with it as it is."

"I know that," said Mu-nan. "Even so... you may keep it as a symbol of having received the teaching. Here."

The two happened to be talking before a brazier. The instant Shoju felt the book in his hands he thrust it into the flaming coals. He had no lust for possessions.

Mu-nan, who had never been angry before, yelled: "What are you doing!"

Shoju shouted back, "What are you saying!"(12)

This story must be deeply unsettling to Westerners—and not a few Nihonjin, as well. The overwhelming majority of North Americans would say they couldn't live without their possessions and attachments; it is part of our cultural makeup to take pride in our things. North Americans would also say, life might very well be unbearable without our relationships, our attachments to others. Throughout our lives the toys changed as our interests and desires evolved, but never the underlying notion of possession. Many people, including me, believe our love and need for our friends and loved ones, even our *things* (ok, not me so much concerning physical possessions), are the source of our happiness, and, yes, some unhappiness as well, but wouldn't dream of willingly surrendering them. Yet according to Zen, a condition of the ascetic life is the necessity to rid oneself of one's earthly possessions. The goal is to live a life without *any* possessions, or attachments. Does anyone, short of death, really succeed at putting *all* attachments and possessions behind him?

The answer seems to be Yes, if only for some, and in brief episodes. In deep meditation, perhaps an hour or so.

Permit me to segue to this firecracker of a koan:

> *Has a dog Buddha-nature?*
> *This is the most serious question of all.*
> *If you say yes, or no,*
> *You lose your own Buddha-nature.* (12)

Appropriately enough—in spite of issues pertaining to manifesting the Buddha—one's spontaneous response is apt to be, *A dog? Certainly not! Any creature that can be kept amused by endlessly fetching a tossed stick could not possibly possess a Buddha-nature.*

> However, if one
>   were only to consider
> the sublime grace,
>   the quiet dignity,
> the earned acceptance
>   of *cats*...

For corroboration, I offer one of Japan's "Big Guns" of the literary world, Soseki Natsume. Did this illustrious author write three volumes (in English translation) on personifying a *dog's* psyche? No, he did not!

Buddhism in Japan has many things to recommend it. As a primary example, in many another culture it is assumed a Buddhist priest—or high-ranking religious figure of any stripe—would remain celibate, denied the life of a family, denied connubial bliss, required to focus on spirituality alone. But not in Japan, at least in the case of some sects, like *Jodo Shin Shu*. Here, it is understood that priests are real people who are not necessarily less qualified to interpret the Sutras simply because they also devote attention to being a husband and a father; no impurity here. Thoroughly admirable, I say! Besides, the Shinto priests had already set the precedent. But here's my beef: As near as I can tell, every Buddhist sect in Japan treats Death as an unlimited-withdrawal cash machine. It is the natural conclusion to all life, *the* essential, ultimate counterpoint to everyone's birth, absolutely no exceptions. So, who declares a monopoly on the traditionally authorized management of the passage from the living to post-living existence? Well, the Buddhists! And you are going to pay through the nose to hire their exclusive services. The higher the prestige of the dearly deceased, the bigger the payoff to the Buddhists, the "exclusive" gatekeepers to a serene eternal repose.

Why am I so harsh on the self-same people I've more-or-less consistently praised up to now? For starters, tradition dictates that you need a Buddhist official/priest, *Obo-san,* to officiate from five to eight ceremonies *for each person who dies! Which is everybody!* To be sure, the ceremonies nearest the person's death are the most elaborate and expensive: The wake, the funeral, the 49-day ceremony, the first, and the second anniversaries. After that, it gets stretched out, the seventh anniversary, then the thirteenth, the twenty-first(?), and the 35th. Who keeps up with these events? (Well, the Roman Catholics, for one. Isn't this what the Catholics were up to, at least until the Reformation? Hands out for pre-payment for preferential treatment in the Hereafter. To be sure, for the Catholics it wasn't high-cost, exclusive names for the hereafter, but some other ecclesiastic hurdle—resolvable for a price. Abuse of power of any strip transcends cultures.)

51

Another way the Buddhists cash in on Death is claiming authority in issuing a specific, propitious name to be identified with the deceased throughout eternity, called a *Kaimyo,* one's posthumous name. Never mind that all your friends, companions, family knew you all your life as someone else; henceforth you are to have this completely different name. For a big, fat fee. The more auspicious the name, the higher the price, but we're talking eternity, here; no price is too much to ensure a Great Beyond without care... Your average Westerner is in varying degree conversant with Christianity and its evolution since the life of Christ, but might not appreciate the importance of possessing a proper death name, *at cost*—to be discussed by appointment, during business hours.

We knew him as Willie all his life, but what'll he be now, Cognerskoweitz Turnip, or Mortissimus Abner? Well, it's a good deal more complicated than that. The appropriateness of the name to the deceased depends on a number of factors, some of which are satisfied in selection of the name with the optimal number of strokes in writing it. For a price. I think the name is represented in at least two kanji, with, let's say, 47 strokes of the brush to execute the task. It's possible for those two kanji to require 28 in the first and 19 strokes in the second figure, but what happens if another kanji, or two, get tossed into the mix. Because it appears the appropriate-number-of-strokes requirement precedes the number-of-kanji requirement, or more importantly, the semantic values of these kanji. As to the appropriate meaning and pronunciation to apply to these two or more special kanji that make up one's own *kaimyo*, among the dozen or more possible, along with any other questions pertaining to this death/name process, please apply to your local temple. Oh, and don't neglect to bring money.

Ota-san, a valued student, experienced a recent tragedy; her father died. He was a well-respected and loved man from a strictly middle-class family—nothing in the way of lavish accoutrements; house, car, lifestyle choices, all indicative of a modest propriety. The *In*, or *Kaimyo* ceremony where the death name is selected, cost this man's family a cool ¥2,000,000, out of a total funeral cost of ¥6,000,000. *Ouch! You bring our beloved family member back to life and we'll talk about six million fornicating yen!*

The Morikawa family has probably been members of the local *Jodo Shin shu* temple as long as they've had roots there, something in the neighborhood of 400 years. This temple has accumulated a great deal of knowledge about this and every other prominent family as a result of officiating in family rituals, but let's say a visiting monk wound up performing the second anniversary's rites, *san-kaiiki.* (Then why, you ask, is it *san-kaiiki* instead of *ni-kaiiki*, if it's the second annual memorial service, and not the third? It turns out, this tradition came from China where people were one year dead when they die, just as they are one year old at birth—as if they didn't have the zero yet and couldn't calculate below one, no such thing as portions of one).

This hypothetical visiting priest would be able to read the room for community clout based on the number of *zabuton,* seat cushions, set up in rows in front of the large family *Butsudan,* Buddhist altar, a large photo of the deceased draped in black, front and center, flanked by candles and incense smoking. The Obo-san would also note the array of large fruit-and-ersatz-flower displays. These frames are tripods built to hold maybe 30 lbs. of assorted fruit. I saw a lot of tropical fruit in the display I sat directly in front of during a winter *ii-kaiiki*, first year memorial ceremony: melons and citrus fruit, papayas. Then, an arching rainbow frame at the back of the fruit basket, to support synthetic flowers and a banner to indicate the doner's name, the whole display some four feet wide by five feet high. Small-scale funerary events might have three to five of these garish fruit and flower demonstrations, the outpouring of grief at the loss of this particular person, made manifest. Twelve or more of these displays would signal the loss of a high-profile member of the community, a great tragedy with broad consequences. *Ka-ching!*

The Catholic Onslaught

In the mid-16th century Francis Xavier, a Jesuit missionary, sailed to Asia seeking converts to the "true faith"—not to mention trading agreements to fund his expanding missionary work. Through a canny balance of guile and bluster, he was enormously successful at finding new souls to rescue from their degenerate and depraved indigenous lifestyles, by starting new missions in Angola and Mozambique (Africa), Goa (India), East Timor (Indonesia), and Macau (China). In each case, he had been preceded by Portuguese traders, who had made tentative trade inroads with *Zipango*, particularly the Nagasaki area, introducing firearms in 1543. Over the years these Ambassadors of the

Lord got to be slick at proselytizing. They had realized early on, if they could convert regional clan lords (*daimyo*), the vassal occupants of their respective fiefdoms would perforce follow along. Something like eleven daimyo got a leg up on their obdurate and obsolete neighbors, thanks to the Jesuits who were not above providing guns, lots of guns—and the wherewithal to make them domestically—in exchange for the surrender of their immortal souls.

By 1588 some 300,000 Tanegashima *arquebuses*, a smooth bore, muzzle loading, short, heavy, precursor to the rifle, were estimated to have been manufactured in Japan—thanks to the Portuguese. It is a curious footnote to history that for a period toward the end of the 16th century, Japan had more *teppo*, firearms, in absolute numbers, *and* as a per-capita ratio, than any other country in the world (13). Whereas, a far more relevant comparison might inquire about the number of homicides by firearms in the city of Chicago *last month*, compared to the entire country of Japan in all of *last year*—since we were skirting the subject vicinity of an armed citizenry, and ease of access to firearms, not to mention, considerations of what constitutes a civil society functioning with a minimum of lethal violence. And isn't it interesting how quickly a country can change on so fundamental a policy? Over years, clans learned the advantages of firearms in skirmishes with their enemies, which led to competition among rivals for possession of such weapons. Arquebuses figured more and more in violent encounters for decades, and then, by Tokugawa fiat, no more guns were allowed for the general populous.

Frankie Savior came to Japan in 1549 and, despite being told by traders in and out of Macau that *Zipango* would be a fertile ground for Christianity, he was not as successful as he had hoped. The Japanese Francis Xavier encountered were impressed that he had come to Japan after "completing" his missionary work in India. At first, they believed he preached a version of Buddhism, since by this date they had already encountered and assimilated five or six Buddhist sects, while maintaining their own native Shinto practices. As a result, the locals were not easily converted, presumably having experienced sufficient spiritual guidance from established Buddhism and Shintoism. Furthermore, many were said to be troubled by some of the Christian tenets. To wit, "How could a God who created everything—including evil—be all good?" *How, indeed!* The concept of Hell was also difficult to accept, given that nobody wanted to believe his or her ancestors could possibly reside there. I mean, it's not like they'd renounced Christianity; they'd simply not had the choice, a less-than-sufficient reason, by any sensible measure, to be damned throughout eternity.

Those previous ports of call that became thriving Christian outposts surely presented communication challenges initially, but they paled by Japanese standards. Ol' Frank the "Savior" was haunted by language barriers in Japan he'd not known in previous locations. From this frustrating experience, after two years, he gave up trying to curry favor with this or that *daimyo*, succeeding for a while, only to fall out of favor partly due to his own curious demands, and partly by the shifting power alliances of the day. This period, roughly, the century culminating in Ieyasu's victory at Sekigahara in September 1600, was known as *Sengoku Jidai*, the Warring Years, when power struggles among sparring clans were especially volatile.

One of Frankie's primary frustrations was his failure to obtain outright permission to build a coastal fortress and port to protect Portuguese ships, and I, for one, am eternally grateful. Every Nihonjin should be overwhelmed with gratitude that the authorities of the day denied the weasely Portuguese a foot hold anywhere in Japan. This is the third instance, in my opinion, where fate, the roll of the dice, or dare I say, *devine intervention*, brought about a fortuitous outcome: "protection" of the homeland. The earlier two instances of god-like intercession refer to the attempted Mongol invasions of 1274 and 1281, during the Kamakura *bakafu*, military administration, both of which were thwarted by *kamikaze*, or devine winds, severe tempests that came up quickly, causing the invading—but not particularly seaworthy—ships to founder. In the case of the second attack, something like 140,000 Mongol, Chinese and Korean warriors were said to have perished at sea. That was one hell of a lucky break! Had that size a force succeeded in making the crossing, they would surely have overpowered any homeland defenses, and established a foothold in Kyushu.

Clearly in this instance, the volatile, unpredictable times, the shifting alliances—as much as the shrewd appraisal of the feudal lords—made it too difficult for Francis Xavier to feel he could build foundations; the vagaries made it too much of a long shot. He had to throw in the towel and beat a retreat back to Macau. These people spoke a language too abstract and vague and equivocating for this man of the cloth ever to feel confident in serious

55

negotiations. It was simply *the Devil's language*. Still, it's sobering to speculate how different Zipango might look today if the Portuguese had become the colonial overlords. *Shudder!*

After solidifying power, the Tokugawa *bakafu* finally banned Christianity in 1614, and by mid-century, demanded the expulsion of all European missionaries, and execution of all converts, many of whom went underground to avoid detection. The number of active Christians at the high point of those days was estimated (by Wikipedia) to be 200,000 people, mostly in the Nagasaki area.

In modern times, there are estimated to be around a half million Christians in Japan, or less than ½ of 1% of the whole population, whereas in South Korea, Japan's nearest neighbor, the Christian population is said to be about 30%. I wonder what the Christian population of South Korea was at the end of World War II. I mean, America, a putative Christian nation, delivered Korea from her Japanese overlords of 35 years, and then prevented the North Korean Communists and their Chinese backers from over-running the peninsula. It shouldn't be surprising to discover a receptivity on the part of South Koreans to the religious foundations presumably underlying the culture and geopolitics of this "savior" nation.

Manga

Until the proliferation of truly miniature sound reproduction and communication devices over the last couple of decades, believe it or not, people used to devote their attention to *reading* in one form or another. Newspapers of all persuasion had maintained a robust readership, as we might expect. In the mid-1980s total newspaper output was 67.5 million per day, or more than one for every two people in the country (9). Maybe the following is true everywhere there are cities, with crowded transportation networks and a literate populous: On the train, Nihonjin fold their newspaper first lengthwise, like an accordion, before folding the length in half, making a convenient newspaper "sandwich" to digest with minimum intrusion on fellow-passenger space.

Beyond newspapers, people read books, often small, with exterior dimensions conveniently sized to fit handily in a suitcoat pocket or a purse. Then of course there are the magazines of every taste, from the religious and new-age spiritual, to women's lifestyle and fashion, to politics/economics, to sports, catering to every conceivable fan base. That newspaper statistic caught your eye, right? Well, try this: 3 billion 500 million copies of 3,600 different magazines are published every year. But surely the largest form of magazine sales, no, the largest sales of any print form in Japan, is Manga! Some weekly and monthly publications have "circulations of over four million" (9). Virtually all the genres of magazines, even the most august and straight-laced nowadays devote a small section, eight to twenty pages, to a cartoon rendition of real-life issues thematically related to readership concerns. Or fantasies, more like it.

Over the months and years, I had ample opportunity to scrutinize a range of manga, mostly abandoned on the train, when the passenger departs. This is invariably intentional rather than a *wasure mono*, a forgotten item. Businessmen regularly pick up at the station platform kiosk, the latest copy of popular events and manga, cartoon mini-stories that run 12 to 16 pages each, one after another, in a 250-page magazine. There is often a four to six page spread on the latest celebrity, often in provocative poses. And there's usually a short feature of soft-core pornography, say, a seventeen year old dressed to look fourteen, in various stages of disrobing her middle school uniform, while way too many men complement their Lolita fantasy, savoring each snapshot. The full exposure of breasts is not considered pornographic in Japan, but display of pubic hair is strictly prohibited. Armpit hair on a young woman has occasioned national controversy.

One of these mostly-manga magazines is capable of holding your slightly boozy, benumbed attention the hour or so it will take the train to whisk you to your home station. You've milked it for its entertainment value; there was never a presumption of anything serious or profound to arise from this pulp material, nothing of lasting value. You sure don't need to bring it home. It's just kinky enough that the wife won't appreciate it—though she would never show it—and the kids get enough of the ragged edge of the social contract, thanks to their curious and risk-taking peers, and their elder relatives. *Besides scholarship, what were you up to during those teen years?*

So, you leave it on the train, for scavengers like me to "recycle."

Ni gatsu hutsuka: the second day of the second month

In the US, <u>February 2nd</u> is somewhat noteworthy. It is known as Groundhog Day. Perhaps 2/3rds of the continental US is sufficiently north in latitude to experience severe winter weather: months of freezing temperatures, snow, and ice. Groundhog Day is a faux ceremony sponsored by residents of Punxsutawney, Pennsylvania. It is designed to lighten up the millions of New Englanders' and Mid-Westerners' winter doldrums. According to "legend," on this day a befuddled and sleepy groundhog (think, a twenty-five-pound rat with a short tail) is roused from its hibernation den and paraded before a clot of journalists with nothing more pressing on their schedules. If Phil, the name of this rodent, is able to see its own shadow—if the sun happens to be shining at that time—he will be startled by his shadow into scuttling back into his den, to remain six more weeks until the end of winter. If, on the other hand, he cannot see his shadow, due to clouds of any sort obscuring direct sun light, he will take that as an indication of the immediate onset of spring. *Break out the shorts and sun glasses!*

In Japan, this day takes on a different mantle. *Setsubun* is literally season passing, or renewing. There used to be a celebration with the advent of each season, but this is the only one remaining. This particular custom has been around since Japan started appropriating ideas from China—early Nara Period (710 to 794), or before, at least 1300 years ago, a relatively peaceful time. It has to do with the advent of spring on the lunar (or Chinese) calendar, which, one assumes, was a time for spiritual, as well as material cleansing, purification, and renewal.

However, on the current calendar, the second day of February could hardly be said to herald spring in the Kanto Plain; the first significant snow of "winter" fell last night. There was quite a bit of it left on the roads this morning to make the motorbike trip to my Chigasaki class more than a little perilous. Interestingly, the lunar calendar was a pretty good predictor of spring. The Meiji Reformation decided to go 100% Western in terms of distances, weights, and standard measures, and as a result, things got a little confused, including calendar designations. The Western Gregorian calendar starts the year with January first, going back to 1582. The event we acknowledge in Japan today is five-to-six weeks before the lunar calendar's second month, second day, the same system the Chinese use today.

This celebration of the "arrival of spring" often takes place around nightfall, hopefully with all the family assembled—though often as not, the husband is still off with his colleagues in that "gray" area between legitimate work and quasi-obligatory collegial socializing time. Anyway, the idea was for some senior family member to don a demonic costume—in the old days, it was doubtless elaborate. These years, it has come to be a simple cardboard mask, while the rest of the family chase him around the house and finally out the front door, shouting at the top of their lungs, *Oni wa soto! Fuku wa uchi!* Literally, "As for demons (or evil spirits), outside; as for good luck, or good fortune, house (meaning *inside*)!" Or in passable English, Evil spirits, get out. Good fortune, come in! These ever-vigilant family members throw roasted soybeans at this apparition throughout the process. It's great fun, especially for the younger family members, who sometimes switch off playing the part of the *Oni.*

No adult professes to believe this custom, but stages the event for the delight of the children—as has happened for countless generations. Traditionally, care was taken to throw beans out of windows and/or doors representing the four directions. After this frivolity has transpired each family member with teeth (between the ages of two and 70 plus?) is bidden to eat the exact number of beans as his/her age—to assure health and longevity. It appears, however, few people take this aspect seriously. Children often exceed their allotted number by untold amounts, while adults often resort to a shortcut version: A 38-year-old would be expected to consume eleven beans, since 38 is three and eight, which equals eleven. No doubt there is more to the myth that I am (yet) privy to.

Housewives in my conversation classes have confided that they view the full expression of this pageant with mixed blessings, as it implies a complete housecleaning, what with beans under foot everywhere. Consequently, some housewives have resorted to the symbolic gesture of assembling the kids at the entrance of the house, and with *genkan* (entry way) doors open, exhorting everybody to throw soybeans out the open doors, shouting in unison for the household purging of malevolent spirits—and in focusing only on this one room, the main access to the house, taking an awful chance on the rest of the house. It is doubtless laudable to rid the genkan of evil spirits, but rather amiss to leave those unspeakable horrors lurking, say, up in the back bedroom… when the lights are out… and you *thought* you just heard something…

It's easy to sympathize with the harried family manager in not wanting to take on any more menial labor than necessary, sweeping up the beans from every room—behind every *tansu*, dresser, under every *zabuton*, cushion, desk and chair. Perhaps the symbolic exorcism is adequate after all.

Having a passably decent aim, I went through my pre-WWII house devoting one well-thrown bean to a room. While my humble dwelling could not be said to be "clean" in the conventional sense of the word, I feel reassured that it is purified of those rascally evil spirits.

Beyond this simple ritual, some of my students report that you are supposed to hang uncooked sardine heads in a cluster of holly leaves (which have several needle tips to each leaf) outside the front door or by the main gate. To serve warning to the devils what's in store for them should they be rash enough to enter this particular house. One surmises that even desperate demons are apt to shy away from a welcome of smelly fish heads and thorny vegetation. I was careful to inquire of my students the duration of this latter observance. One or two days, was the unanimous reply. Just as well, I say, lest the reeking mess ward off the good spirits along with the bad—to say nothing of benign, flesh-and-blood callers.

Modern day adults—think, urban, multistory condo occupants—tend to dismiss the custom as a foolish superstition, while the kids and the grandparents' generation still have fun with it. Superstition it may well be, but what constitutes *foolishness*? Is it any more foolish than a session at the local *pachinko* parlor? Or an average evening in front of the TV set? For me, it isn't a question of belief or disbelief—we have the ability to suspend belief (to paraphrase an old philosopher)—and treat the custom as a charming and harmless link with the deepest roots of Nihon. All the same, however, this kind of connection to the past is gradually dying out, and a part of me regrets the incremental diminution of another ancient and delightful custom.

Thanks to a recommendation by Yoshida Tomoko-san, for the better part of a year, I taught the three children of the priest of Tokeiji, a lovely 13th century temple in Kita (North) Kamakura. One of the most memorable events occurred there on the afternoon of February 2ⁿᵈ while I was teaching the middle child in the family room. From somewhere in the bowels of the temple came this deep, thundering basso-profundo voice: *O-o-oni wa soto!... Fu-u-uku wa uchi!* Almost sung, as if by a Kabuki chorus professional. The resident priest was exorcising the temple residence of demons to the delight of his youngest, a six-year-old son. I was quite charmed by this overall teaching opportunity, and quite a bit awed by the temple and its grounds, though it was somewhat time consuming getting there, and back. Ultimately, however, I was unable to keep the children's attention on the lessons, despite my best efforts, and so had to give up just shy of a year the only class I ever taught at a Buddhist temple.

Beans seem to be imbued with mystical qualities. *Mame* means bean(s). If the proper quantity of these soaked, dried, and roasted beans are consumed they are said to preserve one's health. It's a compliment to be called *mame*, and I have been so complimented, on the occasion around Christmas/end-of-year celebrations when I sometimes made banana bread mini-loaves for each of the *shufu*, housewives, in the class. This is above and beyond what was expected, or necessary. Apparently, water-soaked beans in the roasting process can pop and jump around the pan, giving the impression of being lively, and energetic. Rambunctious, feisty, full of piss and vinegar.

So, how did I celebrate *Setsubun*, you ask? By spilling the beans with the little lady. Yes, the relationship continues. And yes, it still threatens to dissolve, but she is reluctant to cut the cord and I take joy in its continuation, be that another day or another month. Don't all beginnings imply endings?

February 12 (Showa 61): Yesterday was a national holiday, Foundation Day, or *Tencho setsu*. In a country with a culture going back in excess of 2,000 years I've been baffled as to how anyone could fix February 11 as the date the nation was "founded." So I asked several of my students, suspecting that the answer was related to post-WW II implementation of democracy, etc, but they all assured me the concept goes back long before the Meiji Era—and Commodore Perry's "black ship" intrusion. Pressed as to why this particular date, they all appeared puzzled. Since very few Nihonjin in my experience are that fuzzy-minded about their historical dates, I conclude that the date is entirely arbitrary. Wouldn't it have to be? After all, the Western, Gregorian calendar has been in effect in Japan only since Meiji times.

On the other hand, who am I to argue against a holiday!

February 17: Last weekend I went skiing for the first time. I'd gotten acquainted with Fujiko and her husband, Minoru, at Sally's bar, "The Gaijin Bochi" (Foreigner's Graveyard) a while back, and they suggested I accompany them and friends on a ski outing. How could I refuse? With a couple weeks' lead time I was able to reschedule or cancel classes—one of the advantages of teaching privately. We met at Fujisawa Station at 6 pm Friday in time to buy a few supplies/snacks before catching the Tokaido to Tokyo, then Ueno Station where we were met by brother-in-law and two other guys in this tiny Subaru van. From Ueno it was a two hour drive to Minakami, a small ski area in Gunma Ken, in the Japan Alps. With the mad Tobari-san at the wheel, intent on navigating the highway at top speed, the rest of us sipped sake and listened to the new Dire Straits cassette I'd brought back from the states, "Brothers in Arms:"

> ...for it's written in the starlight, and every line in your palms:
> We are fools to make war on our brothers in arms...

I learned that nine members owned this mountain cabin, of which five were along this weekend (Nariya showed up later that night with Nishi). After unloading the van we all huddled around this little stove in the center of the main room, drinking til the wee hours. Next morning, 7 am (ugh! About four hours of sleep), we were up wrestling with equipment, and gulping down miso shiru, rice and salad, before driving to a ski rental shop (skis, boots and stocks for two days: ¥5000), and on to the slopes. Saturday Shibata-san and Yoshinaga-san unselfishly took turns offering me tips and encouragement in this beginner's basin about half way up an intermediate slope. I learned how to stand up, fall down (to the novice, this may seem strange; after all, what newcomer to the ski slopes needs help falling down? In short, no one! Ah, but like most things, there are good ways, and decidedly bad ways, to fall down. Feet together, skis pointed in the same direction, falling to one side or the other is far superior to falling forward (skis splayed to opposite sides, a recipe

63

.

for compound fractures), and maintain somesort of balance and turning ability, none of which come intuitively, at least not to me. But then, not so many people wait until their mid-forties to take up skiing… Needless to say, I had no trouble falling down, but all morning I needed help getting up. Embarrassing. Finally I could master that task, and I didn't feel so badly about falling thereafter. From that beginner's basin, I skied down the long, steep (for me) slope, a couple of times before lunch and another couple of times before leaving that day.

The only way I knew to stop—to avoid colliding with someone, usually—was to fall down intentionally. On my first descent this occurred probably a half dozen times. I'd get going so fast that all my concentration was focused on keeping some semblance of balance—control was minimal. But by the last time I only had to dump it twice to get down and that on a much more congested slope. I could actually manage some crude, rudimentary turns, and I didn't feel as if I were hurtling down the mountain 40 mph paralyzed with fear. Without a hint of grace, to be sure, but oh! what an exhilarating experience of exercising a portion of control of this momentum over this physical equation of mass on a slick slope. Amount of friction? Degree of slope? Multiplied by gravity, the constant. It could be likened to the awareness of increased power and control that we experienced when we took our first confident steps, though at +/- one year old, that experience would have been pre-verbal and hence, pre-long-term memory.

I want to ski some more. Maybe in March before the snows melt. Talk about yer natch'l high! Except the next day, every muscle in my body screamed, *What did you do to me?!?*

March 15: It's the Ides of March, but I'd just as soon it were the Ides of April. Spring is a reluctant visitor to this part of Japan. She makes a coy, hesitant appearance, just enough for everyone at the banquet to take notice, then she bolts for the door. The folks around here say, "three days warm, four days cold." Currently, we're in the midst of *Haru ichi ban,* which translates to the first storm of spring. Let me tell you, it takes a bit of finesse to distinguish between storms of the latter part of winter from the one presently under consideration. A scant three weeks ago we caught better than 30 cm. of snow in one 24-hour period whereas this one seems to be characterized by a three-day (thus far) howling gale, and the slushy snow seems to be giving way to rain. Winter was definitely cold but at least it was mostly dry. This freezing fecal deposit makes a 20-minute crosstown motorbike ride like "swimming" to work. Any impression you may be getting that the weather here is less than ideal is wholly intentional. *Complain, complain! Got nothin' better to do, you can always complain about the weather.*

<u>March 16</u>, Sunday Today is laid back: No pedagogical commitments. After breakfast, I took my dirty clothes to the coin-op Laundromat in Hon Kugenuma, then actually vacuumed the house—once every couple of months, whether it needs it or not, *dessho* (right? Isn't that so?). This afternoon it was polish off a letter to friends back in Oregon crouched over the *kotatsu* while watching the spring sumo tournament in Osaka: Quivering mountains of scantily clad flesh slamming into each other. The big question on everyone's lips these weeks is who will be promoted to Yokozuna (Grand Master) from the herd of able and surprisingly agile bulls (though one, Asashio, definitely resembles a Berkshire hog) occupying the Ozeki ranks. Will it be Onokuni? Hokutenyu perhaps? Or the giant Kitao? Wakashimazu seems to have lost the killer instinct. The little scrapper of a bulldog, Hoshi, is leading the tournament, so far. Kirishima is in his prime, and looks to be in fine health, but doesn't seem to have that extra little toughness, that push when you really need it. Maybe it's because of his sumo name. Kirishima means "Foggy Island," (or "Shrouded Isle," if you really wanted to get into it), more the stuff of mystery, romance, and poetry than the psychic focus and sheer, concentrated, full-body power launched at the precise moment, in order to knock down (in about ten different ways), or force the opponent out of the ring—in at least six different techniques.

Then there's the 233 kg., or 513 lb. Samoan, Konishiki, the most obese creature to hit sumodom, who looks like nothing so much as a bipedal hippopotamus. The media report Konishiki is conducting a discreet search for a wife. *What do you think, ladies? Assuming this behemoth could coax you out of your frillies, how would you like to be served? Do we have any takers for the "missionary position"? It's important to think of these things...*

65

<u>March 25</u> (from a letter of encouragement to my brother, on the occasion of his coming to Japan for the purpose of touring China together during "Golden Week")

Dear Phip, I got reservations from Narita to Hong Kong April 24th, returning May 8th. Since that is well within your time of arrival and departure to/from Japan, I'm going to assume this is alright and I'll pay for the tickets in the next few days. Let me know when you are due to arrive, on what airline and flight number, and I'll <u>try</u> to meet you, but the chances are I'll be committed for class work, busy language entrepreneur that I am, so here are detailed instructions.

Don't worry. I know you can do this because I did it without help from Owen when I first got here. I recommend you bring just one modest-sized suitcase with mostly warm-weather clothes—it could be a little cool yet in Japan, especially in the evenings, but I've got extra sweaters, jackets, long underwear, snow boots, everything you are apt to need. Also, you'd better not come loaded down with a bunch of illicit drugs, as the immigration authorities tend to lose their sense of humor where that's concerned, though Japanese bureaucrats are a sorry lot generally, and could probably benefit from a therapeutic, surprise jolt of LSD.

No fire arms or heavy-duty explosives either, right? Much of the rest of the world, it turns out, is not as "enlightened" as us Merkans regarding gun totin', or our god-given right to blow shit up. But on to the matter at hand. Assuming you clear customs under your current alias, you should be entirely anonymous here. Anonymous, like an albino in south Chicago, like a strapping Scandinavian chica in East Los Angeles. So, once you clear Immigration/ Customs, go to the information booth in the main airport lobby and ask for the limousine bus service to Tokyo Station. I want to emphasize there are at least four ways to get to Fujisawa, but these means are by far the easiest. OK, so cash in $50, or better, $100 into yen—those currency exchange booths are all the same—and pay the cute ladies at the bus counter for your ticket to Tokyo; they will tell where and when to catch the right bus— quite nearby.

About an hour and a half after boarding, you'll arrive in one of Tokyo's "centers," you are across a massive street from the station. Never mind that the colossus of the Tokyo station is vaster than your home township of

66

Florence, Oregon. Never mind that it is one of the three or four largest train stations in Japan, and hence, the world. Never mind that hapless tourists have been found wandering around the endless neon-lit catacombs bleating like wounded sheep after days of searching for an exit. Any exit! You just let those unnatural fears slide off your back like cold sweat over gooseflesh. Perhaps this would be an appropriate time to recite one of those Buddhist mantras designed to aid you in such dark and foreboding instances. Then, with serene equanimity you just shuffle into the jaws of the beast, the maw, as it were.

Before you come to the ticket takers, you'll see on the right a wall of ticket dispensing machines. Some of these devices have a slot for inserting a 1000 yen (¥) bill. This you are to do, and push the ¥850 button when it lights up. Out comes your ticket and change (will these miracles never cease?). Pass through the turnstile of ticket punchers and proceed to track 7, bound for Shimbashi (and possibly another station or two more), Shinagawa, Kawasaki, Yokohama, Totsuka, Ofuna, and yes, folks, about an hour and a half after you start, Fujisawa! This is the Tokaido Line originating at Tokyo station, and— THIS IS IMPORTANT—you have a chance at a seat if you hot-foot it into the car when the doors open. This would be a good idea since your chances of getting a seat before Yokohama 45 minutes out are nil, and arguably worse thereafter. Seriously, if you are at the back of a clot of people waiting to board the train and you are unable to find a seat initially, I recommend you get back off and stand at or near the front of a line to board the next train some ten minutes later. Waiting another ten minutes to secure a seat on a train that will get very crowded quickly, and stay that way for most or all of the way to Fujisawa, is surely one of the best pieces of advice I have for you in your exciting transition from country rube, to international traveler, jetting in to one side of greater Tokyo, and fearlessly threading the labyrinth of surface transportation to my Kugenuma, Fujisawa-shi, Kanagawa-ken sanctuary on the opposite side of the world's number one megalopolis. As the crow flies, the distance between Narita Airport and my little cottage in the Kugenuma district of Fujisawa might be no more than 60 miles; I seriously doubt if it's more than 75 miles; however, in terms of humans and their imprint on the land, it is the densest place on earth.

At Fujisawa station get off and follow the herd upstairs, and give the nice man your ticket. The signs in kanji aren't going to help you choose the

South exit over the North one, so stay on that second level until you're sure you are on the south side: You'll be able to see Seibu, Costa, and Odakyu Department Stores (signage in Roman letters!) on the side you want. Then, go downstairs and get in line to catch a taxi. Show the driver my address and he will be able to deliver you to my doorstep for a ¥500 to ¥1000 consideration. If I am not at home, the place will be unlocked.

No doubt, this all seems complicated, but better too many details than not enough. Navigating your way through 40 million people (instead of, what, 5,000?), by itself, does require a different set of "skills," on top of being thrust into a very different language and culture.

But follow these instructions and, short of a natural calamity, I can't see how you could fuck up. If you have any doubts along the way, just ask someone. Speak slowly, minimizing the panic of a crazed gaijin in your voice, and they will understand. They won't volunteer to help because they are scared shitless of making an English language gaffe in front of total strangers—their peers, not you—but once approached they feel duty-bound to help. And everyone over the age of 12 has had extensive (if impractical) English in school. So, good luck and see you soon!

<u>March 26</u>: This letter is a little hot air I felt compelled to vent at "the Daily Yomiuri," one of five or six English rags published in Japan—the cheapest, but unfortunately a trifle right wing:

The Daily Yomiuri
English language newspaper
To the Editor:
The citizens of Zushi have restored my faith in democracy in Japan. By a clear majority on two occasions this month they have rejected a proposal to build housing for American military personnel in their community. But alas, that is not the end of it. Earlier in the month the Daily Yomiuri editorial (March 5) raised the specter of "national security"—that hackneyed pretext for abuse of the political process. Then came the parade of hardliners: Liberal Democratic Party (LDP) Deputy Secretary-General Uno urges the government to proceed regardless of the recent plebiscite. Mr. Sasa of the Defense Facilities Administration Agency assures us there will be no change

in the plans. And Mr. Kato of the Defense Agency is likewise determined to pursue the agenda. All cite the sacrosanct US-Japan Security Treaty, as if somehow the entire treaty were dependent on these houses being built at this location. It's hard to imagine how a few hundred housing units have anything to do with the security of Japan.

Does might make right? Do the ends of a dubiously imperiled nation justify the means of running rough-shod over a sensitive nature preserve, not to mention the wishes of the good people of Zushi? Is the democratic process just a charade, after all?

Sincerely....

(The letter got published in the Monday, March 31, edition of the paper.)

It's impossible to reason	*Naku ko to*
with authority figures	*jito ni wa*
or crying children	*katenu* (14)

<u>April 2</u>, Wed: Easter Sunday I taught TEC (Tsujido English Club). We must have read all of three pages from Kesey's *Cuckoo's Nest* before surrendering the rest of the class time to discussion. Often my adult students want to explore edgy, risqué themes. It's almost as if there were a competition among the students to see who could embarrass the teacher. Or each other. This is a class of 12 to 14 middle-aged, married (most of them) students willing, eager to go places mentally, in imagination, that they never would in reality. I think, to a person, they were fascinated by nuanced sexual concepts from this barbarian culture I represent. At one point, a distinction was requested between kinky and deviant, or perhaps, perverted. The best example I could think of: Some people might say the use of a feather for sexual purposes is kinky. On the other hand, sexual conduct involving the whole goose (Leda and a metamorphosed Zeus notwithstanding) is deviant behavior.

After TEC, I wound up hosting Mr. and Mrs. Kurabe at my house for 1 ½ hours while it piss-drizzled all afternoon. Monday Sachiko-san came for her 90 minute lesson in Espanol, of all things. Bizarre as that sounds, I know Spanish well enough to teach the fundamentals. My student could afford the lessons, and since her only experience of a second language so far is English, I was in a position to get her started with pronunciation, politeness phrases, basic verb structure, a few Q and A drills, you get the idea.

Long about that time the vague cold symptoms that flirted and flitted about me the last several days lowered the boom. It was like I was pole axed. Not in recent memory has an infection hit me so hard, so fast. Sneezing fits every 20 minutes or so, a throbbing head, and the situation where if snot were blood I'd have bled to death in short order. We are talking *true* misery. Unfortunately, Kimiko was scheduled to come. As planned, I was able to put together a quiche, which we ate along with some pretty bad Sagami Hara wine she'd brought. The quiche was underdone—the egg not quite congealed—so back in the oven with it while I rode off to a one-hour class with teenage girls in Tsujido. Kimiko wasn't exactly up to par either having just come from the dentist's drill, so she left after a somewhat pained/clumsy sense of togetherness. The stark reality was I was damn weak and feverish, not fit company.

Ah, but Tuesday, April 1st, with a good night's rest, I felt reborn! I expected more of the same, hopefully some diminution of the body wrenching symptoms, but lo and behold, them nasty little pathogens had abandoned me for more fertile pastures: Good riddance! Either I'm too ugly to support a sustained colony of cold viruses, or ramping up the vitamin C helped. In either case, I'm grateful. Too often we take our health for granted, until we've lost it…

I met Noriko-san near Yokohama Station for our 1½ hour chat (her sister-in-law was off on a mission of mercy to visit a dying family member). Then I went to Ishikawacho for a slog through government bureaucracy to renew my tourist visa. After that, I beat it back to Tsujido for "lunch" (+/- 2:20) with Tanaka-san at his restaurant and an hour of idle prattle, followed by a two hour stint with the guys at Nippon Roche, a pharmaceutical plant near Ofuna. The final 90 minutes (from 8 to 9:30) with Mr. and Mrs. Iwata over dinner back in Tsujido. Now there's a day for you.

Phip and I spent Golden Week traveling in China. From Hong Kong, once I got my visa—an extra day of bureaucratic complication, bribe recommended—we trained to Guangzhou (Canton) for a couple of days, where we black-market exchanged some of the funny money all foreigners are compelled to buy, and are supposed to spend, while in the PRC, the People's Republic of China. But on the street between the travelers' hostel and the five-star White Dove Hotel we negotiated the standard daily rate, something like a 2/3 advantage, FECs (Foreign Exchange Currency) to Renminbis, the people's money: 100 FECs got you 165~170 Renminbis. Of course, one never really knows how big a risk one takes in these circumstances; there's usually a pretty good reason for a government policy/restriction regarding foreign visitors— which we were flagrantly violating. Perhaps this is the day when the government decides to make a public example of the corruption, fostered by foreign visitors… But no, this is a win/win scam for everyone. Major hotels, first-class restaurants, and "Friendship Stores" accept nothing but FECs (or your dollars, Yen, or Euros, at a crippling rate), which cycles that hard currency right back into the government's coffers. The rest of us travelers get a break on the People's Money. Let's say the price of a good or a service is 100 yuan. You can pay for that good/service in FEC yuan (and instantly make a life-long friend of the good or service provider), or you can pay in Renminbis, the People's Money, and stretch your original investment by more than 50%.

China has resisted pegging its real currency, the Renminbi, to the global economy, so it is worth nothing outside the country. The only way for the average Chinese, say, a businessman intent on buying goods from abroad, or traveling out of the country, is with hard currency. FECs are hard currency since they are convertible to dollars, yen, etc. In order for the average Chinese person to accumulate FECs, he must pay a premium: 1 2/3 Renminbis for every FEC. My guess is the government permits a modest black market, which rewards enterprising Chinese money changers and crafty, travel-savvy on-the-roaders, in order to rake off a pretty big chunk of the currency spent by all the first-class, as well as the package-tour travelers, where the real money is, anyway. (In fact, China abandoned this Foreign Exchange Currency farce and agreed to work with the economies of the world within a few years of this trip.)

From Guangzhou, we took the river bus up the Pearl River, *Li Jaing*, to Wuzhou, and then Yang Shuo, a kind of Chinese artist community surviving on tourists who have come for the spectacular scenery, specifically the surrounding limestone crags in various evocative shapes jutting from the valley floor. So far as I know, unique in all the world.

This little town—and its inhabitants' willingness to flaunt standard Chinese convention, as long as the tourists are amused enough to pay for the edgy T-shirts and "Mao hats"—was ultimately more interesting than the unique landscape. I acquired a "Hard *Seat* Café, Yang Shuo" T-shirt with the same red ball in the center, black lettering, of the "Hard *Rock* Café" international franchise, and I believe my brother bought a "Mickey Mao's Café" shirt where, front and center, is everybody's favorite rodent sporting a Mao cap, red star emblazoned at the crest. There was no evidence of the Disney Corporation having licensed this curious juxtaposition of one of mid-20th century's prominent revolutionaries of communist ideology, with a true icon of "free-market" capitalism—speaking of Mr. Disney's initial creation, here.

The culinary highpoint for me was the "American Breakfast." I succumbed to two gelatinous eggs, sunny-side up. Two slices of very white bread, crisped, no butter. A hot cup of instant coffee. Some fried potatoes. And a couple of narrow links of some peculiar sausage. Not very fatty, and not heavily spiced in any way I could tell. After two bites, I had pretty much ruled out the standard mammalian possibilities: pork, beef, lamb/mutton, goat, rabbit, horse, venison, elk, reindeer, bison, kangaroo, oh, and whale. As for fowl, neither chicken, goose, nor duck. Concerning reptiles, I could with some confidence eliminate alligator and snake. All of these, I felt reasonably sure, were *not* the source of the sausage. Immediately raising questions of "meat" I had never knowingly eaten… Nothing to do but sop up my runny eggs with my fully desiccated toast, knock back a gulp of some "quality" powdered, instant, Swiss-manufactured coffee—and contemplate my exotic sausage. *Likely dog, and/or cat, but I couldn't help but recall a story in the "Daily Yomiuri" concerning a popular Chinese niku-man (meat wrapped in a steamed bun) food cart, and the discovery of some funny business concerning the family connection to a mortuary…*

After a few days exploring the countryside by rental bicycle and on foot, we bused to Guilin, a city of a million people in amongst more limestone crags, before returning to Guangzhou, and Hong Kong for a final couple of days before flying back to Japan. Over the years, my brother and I have put in some serious travel time together and it was good to deepen that connection, that history, with this trip.

For people who care about such things, this two-week trip involved every means of travel on the surface of the earth—except one. We flew in and out of Hong Kong, trained from Hong Kong to Guangzhou, traveled by riverboat to Yangshuo, biked and walked that area, bused to Guilin, taxied to the airport, flew back to Guangzhou, boated to Hong Kong, rode the funicular cable car, ferryboats between Hong Kong and the mainland at Kowloon, before flying back to Japan. What is that? Seven or eight means of locomotion. All, except the most common—not counting walking—throughout most of history: A beast of burden. A domesticated animal trained to pull or carry *Homo sapiens*, the dominant species.

Golden Week is one of three official, consecutive-day holidays in a year—along with three days off around New Year's, and the August break of Obon. It is a series of holidays occurring close together from April 29, The Showa Emperor's birthday; May 1, International Laborers' holiday; May 3, Constitution Day; and winding up with May 5, *Kodomo no hi*, or Children's Day, the day when the family proudly displays the heirlooms, samurai weapons and armor, if you are the first born of that lineage, and other relics from generations previous. Boys, especially the eldest, get fussed over; they will inherit the family assets (if such exist) and family obligations, i.e., periodic cleaning and attending Buddhist/Shinto rites at the family grave plot, and representing the family in all community matters. Girls marry outside the family, so they are presumed to be only "temporary" birth family members. The family flies variously colored carp banners, *Koi nobori*, for each boy in the family, the biggest banner for the eldest boy, and so on.

The service industry has to work these days, to accommodate the big-spending vacationers, but a chunk of the working class, along with most salary men take this period off: According to a local paper, sixty million people are expected to travel domestically this Golden Week.

Circumnavigation

You are a sleek caravel
dancing gracefully across
the shimmering surface
I am a coarse and unrepentant brigand
shadowing just over the horizon
tracking your coordinates
from my leaky galleon
waiting impatiently to plunder
your Treasure

Nihon and the Libido

I found Japan a liberating place to be in terms of sexuality. Being such an arcane and ritualized culture, I had frankly imagined a more convoluted attitude toward the sex act than I encountered. As a result, as regards a modest range of possibilities within the realm of heterosexuality, I was surprised, relieved, and grateful. For one thing, the Japanese don't seem to bring a lot of moral baggage to the act—from my modest, unrepresentative sample, of course. Western Civilization (i.e., Europe, but us Americans in particular), has been burdened by a heavy-handed Christian overlay of how, when, and in what manner of intent it was acceptable to engage in sex, and woe betide those who have sexual inclinations beyond or outside the rather narrow religiously sanctioned range—in this life or the Hereafter. I grew up in a post-WW II moderate household, but even now, those of us who have rationalized our departure from those archaic and obsolete religious interpretations of "acceptable" sex, still cope with those puritan proscriptions as a potent theme, or undercurrent, in the dominant narrative. They are interwoven in the fundamental fabric of our cultural identity, especially in the United States, which to this day, projects a strong fundamentalist-Christian interpretation as to propriety in all things public. To this day it remains background "noise," an unfortunate, usually subconscious, sometimes conscious impediment. But not in Japan.

In Japan, by contrast, acceptance of sexual intimacy depends on consent between approximate adults, the participants. No moralizing, period. It's been suggested that the attitude towards sex in Japan is as one of the basic hungers, like needing to eat and drink regularly, needing to sleep. In this vein, consider the notion of the "love hotel." This is a service provided by the hour to those couples driven by lust to seek respite and privacy—at substantial cost, given the time constraint. These garish, brightly lit buildings with thinly veiled names, e.g. Eros, Venus, and Diana (scantily clad Greco-Roman goddess of the hunt) are found along highways and major interchanges around most urban areas, and the sheer numbers of them give indication of their "popularity."

I don't deny that there have been times in younger days when I felt a metabolic *need* for carnal fulfillment; it was very much a hormonal hunger to me, and I'm not alone in this, am I? Thus, it was a pleasure to discover in this society a straightforward, guileless openness to sexuality. In those rare times when mutual attraction and opportunity got expressed in tandem.

That said, however, there is an old adage that says, for so many reasons, it's a bad idea for the *sensei* to be in a sexual relationship with a student. I don't think it's necessarily bad to *flirt* with one's students, a kind of play-acting, as long as everyone knows the limits. I flirted now and then, light-heartedly, in those days, and I still do, though I'm definitely older and wiser now. But, yes, I did violate that no-sex proscription with students three or four times during my tenure in Japan. To tell the truth, I would have extended that folly with at least two other students, in my first couple of years in Japan, if there had been a remote chance.

In two of the cases the class student-teacher relationship was negatively impacted—unfortunately, as anticipated. A couple involved in consensual sex suggests a high degree of mutual intimacy, which cannot carry over to a class where you are the sensei and your sometime lover is part of a class of housewives, or any other mix. As soon as she tries to signal a code for your special intimacy, other class members will begin to pick up on it, and whatever comfortable bond you'd created with this group as a whole evaporates before your eyes. You'll be lucky if you can salvage the class in the wake of this peccadillo.

In the third case, following the initial phase of sexual intimacy, we grew to be close friends. She understood the nuts and bolts of English syntax better than anyone I knew, native speaker or not, and more than once used me as a foil, in "my own" class, to illustrate my relative ignorance on this or that point of English explication and usage. Contrary to common belief, I can take some good-natured ribbing, especially when I have it coming. And no doubt, I was due in those instances.

With a tip of the hat to Henry Miller, who gave English-language writers legitimacy to write sexually explicit narratives (*magna exampli gratia*, his once-banned *Tropic of Cancer*), the following are a couple of fortuitous opportunities for wanton licentiousness that spring to mind. Solely for purposes of illustrating sexual attitudes, of course. A sort of free-lance Dr. Kinsey, if you will. *Hey, this is authentic, "case-study" caliber documentation here, absent any prurient intent. Get your mind out of the bed sheets!*

I realize this explication reads like I'm emphasizing the physical act without much reference to the emotional content. To be sure, they are not mutually exclusive, and a desirable sexual relationship, short term or long, would certainly be enhanced by a positive emotional component, a demonstrated capacity for tenderness and caring—in addition to pleasure given/pleasure received.

For maybe six months, I took the Odakyu Express weekly from Fujisawa to Shinjuku, then a connection to Kanda, the center of publishing, printing, and promotion of book products in Tokyo. It was a long, time-consuming trip to and from the work site, but I'd been hired to record some instructional materials in the company's mini-recording studio. Mostly, they were lists of vocabulary words and phrases for pronunciation drill, and little narratives, first at native speed, then at slowed speed for purposes of dictation. I was cloistered away in utter silence, and I would bash out lesson after lesson in my immaculate American West-Coast-Vernacular English. *Wakari yasui*: I'm easy to understand. Non-native speakers understand me easily—relative to most of the mono-lingual Americans they are apt to encounter. I have cultivated this ability, and it has served me well.

It was on one of those journeys into the heart of the throbbing Urban Beast that I noticed a young woman sitting near the center of the car. After a couple of stops—some people departing, others crowding aboard—I was able to maneuver near her. I could see she was looking through a photo album of the young woman, herself (*Exhibit A: "The Bait"*), in some foreign travels, in that many of the background scenes included unique geologic features not found in Japan. When a seat next to her became available, I pounced on it. Thereupon, we engaged in light conversation about her travels to Cappadocia, Turkey—from the album—in pretty halting Nihongo, for my part, and reasonably good English, for hers. We got off at Shinjuku, end of the line, and I explained that I had some work to do, but could meet her later, if she were inclined to have a late lunch/early dinner with me. Say, around 3:00 at the Kabuki-cho exit? Sure enough, after some hours of grueling, punctilious enunciation and scrupulous diction through the studied modulation of my dulcet voice, there she was, Yumiko (not her real name; I don't actually remember her name), an offering, Venus on the half-shell. Compensation for my sufferings.

We had a fine meal at a seafood establishment a couple blocks into the entertainment district of Kabuki-cho, the largest adult playground in Tokyo. (*Got kinky fantasies? You can make 'em happen in Kabuki-cho!*) We sat at the bar, sipping beers, and watching the culinary wizard behind the bar prepare our seafood "boats"—20 inch, boat-facsimile food trays. In the bed of the boat the chef laid a blanket of grated *dikon* and some lacey, red seaweed, on which to display an array of sea life: oysters, clams, sea snails, shrimp, squid, some prime cuts of jellyfish, octopus, and other *sashimi*ed fish. Center stage, or *mid-ships*, as the old salts would say, this dervish with the flailing knives presents with a flourish, the fish you had personally selected from the aquarium on the counter not four minutes before. A fish so fresh, it is still twitching in its death throes, while you pluck off pieces of its flesh with your *hashi* (chopsticks), to dip in *wasabi* (green, Japanese horseradish, ground) and *shoyu* (soy sauce), and pop those quivering morsels in your mouth. Ahh! *Gochiso sama deshita!* In this case, Thank you deeply for that tasty, *uh*, description.

Unfortunately, we had conflicting schedules for that evening, but a few days later she came for a visit by train. I met her at the Kugenuma Kaigan *eki* and we walked the six or seven minute trek to my modest Matsu-ga-Oka lair. I fed her some food, snacks probably, and I most likely plied her with alcohol, in moderate, responsible amounts, to be sure. Soon enough, without an undo amount of frivolous banter, we commenced getting to know each other a lot

77

better. Yumiko came to visit me a couple more times; she lived with her parents in a fairly small condo, so it was logistically out of the question to arrange our trysts at her place.

Not to be too blunt about it, she thoroughly enjoyed fucking. If I had to guess, I'd say she had whetted her intercultural curiosity on some foreign cock during her travels abroad—by which I mean not the uniqueness of the cock per se, but the uniqueness of the intercultural experience—along with the sex. (Witjout question, those Turks would certainly have been up to the task of providing adequate stimulation...) And here I was, presenting yet another opportunity to explore some outside-culture matching of body parts. It never ceases to amaze how well the parts fit. Gaijin sex and perhaps the novelty of my hovel held her interest the two or three times she came for my tonic ministrations, my erogenous therapy. I don't know, maybe she was counting coup on gaijin. Or conducting research. Who am I to second-guess? One should always aspire to accommodate fellow researchers.

The last time she came, toward the middle of the summer, I remember it was *almost* too hot for lewd and lascivious behavior. I mean, 90-plus degrees F. and 90% humidity, together, place a burden on *any* human activity, vertical or horizontal, young or old. It was a tradeoff between *How raging are those hormones; how fervent and intense the aching?* versus *What a struggle it is to perform anything physical, under these conditions!* It was an in-the-moment call, to be sure. On that occasion the beast won, the Satyr who, when conscious, is almost always in rut.

Yumiko and I, it's fair to say, had cultivated each other mutually. However, my one clear, serendipitous experience of sheer voluptuous lust happened in the winter, because I remember it being quite cold. I had already gone to bed and had just drifted off when I was awakened by someone banging on my front door, with a taxi waiting. In the *genkan* light, I could see it was a moderately intoxicated young woman, fashionably dressed, mid-twenties—though the age of Nihonjin, in general, is very hard to gauge.

A Kitsune for sure, I said to myself. *A fox, come to beguile me. Come to lead me astray by my already potentiating Prince of the Nether Regions.* I had no recollection of having met her before, but she was distraught and in search of shelter for the night. What was I to do? Yuri (see disclaimer, above, as to identities) paid off the taxi while I made her some hot tea—like any self-respecting Japanese host would do—and she explained that she had run away from her boyfriend, a bad seed, that one. He had been getting a trifle too rough with her.

Whoopee!, I thought. *I'm harboring the moll of some local Chimpira, a low-level turf gangsta, a ya-chan wannabe. If this were to be interpreted as a "showdown" for the young blossom's charms, it could turn out really badly...*

She had seen me once or twice at Sally's bar, the *Gaijin Bochi* (the Foreigners' Cemetery). She must have asked around. I was one of five or six local English teacher regulars; I was easy to find. Long story short, I provided sanctuary for the unfortunate girl, I think, three nights. I would leave the house to teach pretty much all day, while Yuri came and went as she pleased, met friends, and began to sort out her relationships. By the time I got home, she'd be there, playing at domesticity, something to eat, a glass of beer at hand.

Had enough to eat? Something else to drink? Well, then, how about a hot furo; and we fuck each other's brains out? I would have been amenable to a longer stay (at my own peril), but my brother was due to show up for an extended visit the following day. And I really didn't want him bewitched by Yuri-chan, the *kitsune*, to have the temptation dangle in front of him—while I was out most of the day flogging English. She and I both understood that we were but a brief respite for each other. I would miss her, but there is a good deal to be said for "short and sweet." She had other people to fall back on, so I wasn't worried. I was happy to have provided a brief waystation for the young woman, a port in the storm, a firm appendage on which to ride out the tempest. She did not leave any the worse for wear.

Could this have happened on the Oregon Coast, *a la* my former incarnation? Why not, right? Lots of real and figurative "storms" there... In short, not a scintilla of a smidgeon of a chance. Not. A. Chance. In a Shonan Kaigan (beach) lounge I was one of a handful of semi-exotic bull-frogs in a fairly big pond teeming with nubile frog*ettes*. Alas, in rural Oregon the conditions were reversed: Bull-anything were a glut on the market, while the comeliest, doe-eyed damsels had gotten smart and headed for the city, *any* city, where not only jobs were possible, but the likelihood of finding a stable, emotionally bonding relationship was more favorable, as well.

In life, you can manage your own identities somewhat, as a function of the communities and groups you choose to associate with. In my miserable,

79

iinaka (rural, provincial) existence, I had gone more than a year without a single concupiscent liaison; that's too many times at bat with nary a hit. A walk to first once in a great while, but never advanced past second base. Which only made the deprivation more acute. I mean, even deer and elk get laid at least once a year, *dessho*? Isn't that so? Thus, I take it, nobody begrudges me some discreet lascivious interplay when the opportunity presented itself. We could consider this a little balm in my recovery from my "Excruciating Celibacy" Period.

As a wrap up to this discussion on sexual attitudes, we should consider the related issue of gender *in*equality in Japan. To be sure, women have made great strides; before the Meiji Restoration (1868), women were legally little more than chattel. Property, like livestock. Even more progress has been made since the MacArthur Constitution at the close of WW II. Still, by most measures, there continues to be a bigger gap in Japan than in the US—and American women will not hesitate to assure you that the gap is not closing nearly fast enough at home. Old habits die hard, I guess.

There is a kind of consolation, however. Statistically, in both Japan and America, women live significantly longer than men, a phenomenon I facetiously refer to as *women's revenge*. It seems, a disposition that emphasizes kinder, gentler, more inclusive, more forgiving behavior is worth eight to ten more years, on average.

A relevant *kotowaza* (proverb) to ponder—and challenge—is:

> *Dan son jo hi*
> Man leads, woman follows.

Just because Confucius believed women should be subservient to men 2500 years ago, should not compel us today, to follow that tradition if it perpetuates social inequality. Some "traditions" cry out for a moral reexamination, in light of more equitable social standards. It is a tragedy in any society, not only for the historically under-privileged half of the population, but also for that society in entirety, which is depriving itself of valuable resources otherwise available to it. We are speaking of resources across the spectrum of human ability. No one to date has been able to demonstrate that these skills, this mental capacity, reside exclusively within one gender, while the other gender is devoid of said skills/capacity.

One practical outcome of this trend toward equalization of opportunity, *and* reward, is that men will sacrifice a degree of authority that they have traditionally possessed in order to achieve complete parity with women—which, we presume, accounts for men's reluctance. Meanwhile, the women themselves have nothing to lose in pushing the limits in all directions, including associating with European or American men. You could say that I have been the fortunate and grateful recipient of sexual attention owing, in part, to the perpetuation of gender disparity in Japan.

Doubtless the following would have been considered subversive activity in some circles, but I recall coaching young women who were considering marriage among a number of suitors, some of them arranged, some self-cultivated. Though these women were being considered for the role of wife, I counselled that they should certainly reciprocate in the interview process. I advised preparing a small list of questions for their prospective marriage partners, which should include, among their own particular concerns:

1) *What are your thoughts regarding sharing child-rearing responsibilities? Feeding a baby? Changing his/her diapers?* Any resistance, any demur should relegate the aspirant to the back burner.

2) *Can you cook? If so, what are you able to cook?* A response of "Cup Noodle" as an example of culinary prowess, should be grounds for immediate disqualification. (I firmly believe that my home-made quiche sealed the deal with Kimiko.)

3) *Do you appreciate humor? What or who makes you laugh?*

4) *Are you a fan of the arts? What in particular moves you? Puts you in touch with specific feelings?*

This is of course a wholly subjective evaluation. Each woman would have to weigh the answers against other factors towards a final judgement. Marriage is a serious decision, to be sure. It is my belief that there are some women out there a little more content in their marriages having left fewer variables to chance than might otherwise have been the case, thanks to my modest effort at women's empowerment.

Or these *josei-tachi*, young women, were only humoring me: They could have succumbed to the traditional marriage process, mostly having selected for earning potential and *staying power*, i.e., not apt to flop over and die in 10 years from stress and high blood pressure —*karoshii*—an alarming trend among businessmen in their 50s, even 40s. Music, a sense of humor, the arts: In this scenario, these are ephemera, the result of a roll of the dice.

Still, I've heard an aphorism from time to time, shared among men somewhat covertly, which proclaims,

For superior design, comfort, and mechanics of automobiles, seek German manufacturing;

for the subtle nuances of haute cuisine, savor French cooking;

for personal housing possibilities, check out American plans;

but when it comes to wives, Japanese women make the best.

I will catch a lot of flak for including women on this objectified product list, despite not having authored the statement, but merely report it. Though it may be an offensive comparison, it reveals the extent of respect *Nihon no josei*, marriageable Japanese women, have among Japanese men. If the author were pressed to weigh in on this latter assertion, he'd have to say, *uhmmm...* He's trying to keep an open mind, while continuing to evaluate the data. He is mindful of the prerogatives of science, and remains prudent in avoiding hasty conclusions.

* * * * *

July 30: Somewhere along this timeline Tommy Ogawa and I climbed Fuji-san, highest mountain in Japan. I remember it was mid-week with classes to face mid-morning of the following day. He picked me up at Fujisawa station around 8 pm and we headed for the mountain, stopping along the way for a high-calorie meal and hot coffee. The official climbing season is often no more than six weeks, never more than two months; the rest of the year is unpredictable, and "unseasonable" for the average climber. A warm, late-summer shower from sea level to, say, 400 meters elevation might be a welcome respite from the unrelieved heat. At 2000, not to speak of 3000 meters, that shower could become a freezing blizzard, survivable by experienced, climbers with hi-tech equipment and training. Which is not you.

Even with streamlined access to over half of the trip—toll highways—it took over two hours to drive to Gotemba, at the base of Fuji-san, then on to *gogome*, or the Fifth Station, about half way to the top in elevation, and the end of vehicular access. I don't remember what I had brought along in my backpack. Probably a sweater and a windbreaker, a thermos of hot tea, or coffee, and maybe a flashlight. I had on the only boots I owned, pretty good ankle protection but not much else. Some loose-fitting Levis and a thick-weave cotton shirt. Some kind of cap completed my mountain climbing gear. Fuji-san is a cinder cone, which makes it feel, for every step you make in ascending the mountain, you are sliding back half the distance. So much extra exertion for so compromised a result can be fairly frustrating. On the other hand, Fuji-san is considered a "walk up," it does not require special climbing techniques or gear—during the authorized season.

Fuji-san sports several well-defined trails like jagged scars up and down her flaring skirt. She's always been considered a sacred mountain. For over a thousand years she's been climbed by pilgrims, exclusively men, until well into the Meiji Restoration when women were finally permitted. The moon was full or near it, and around midnight, we headed out on a well-trod path zig zagging up the slope of the mountain. There is a rest house at each "station," where you can purchase a cup of tea and a packaged snack, even a futon by the hour, in the event you want a nap, or a nod for the rest of the night. If they are evenly situated these rest stops would occur every 1400 ft. or so of elevation. Ideally, night hikers would like to reach the summit (or 10th station) by sunrise, but in our case the sunrise caught us beyond the 9th station, just before 6 am. There was a pause and everyone faced the resurrected sun with upraised, out-stretched arms, shouting "Banzai! Banzai! Banzai!" Below us, facing east between the summit of Fuji and the sunrise, all was still plunged in darkness. It would take hours for the sun to light up the entire Kanto plain.

Twenty minutes later we were on the ridge of the caldera, basking in the sunlight (temperatures are *crisp* at 3776 meters!) above a continuous sea of gray clouds, toasting each other with a cup of tea. We didn't really dawdle, maybe a half hour to rest our legs, before heading back down the hill. What took six hours coming up took about two going down. With gravity on your side, and daylight visibility as to where to step next, descent was quick. And dangerous. Slip and fall during the slow, ponderous ascent and you can catch yourself without any damage usually. On the way down there is the temptation to step off straight down hill, five-to-eight-foot steps at a time (gravity is *sooo-oo* helpful!), but after about the first quarter hour the different set of muscles necessary to descend, especially in your thighs and calves, have turned to jello, while the knees and ankles are perilously close to being pushed a little too much at this or that odd angle and/or wrenched in ways these vulnerable flex joints are not accustomed to being used. The ascent was just one long slog: Endurance! Perseverance! Not much else is involved. I consider myself lucky, however, not to have injured myself descending Fuji-san.

For such a revered place, there sure was a lot of cast off garbage beside the trails, made conspicuous in the morning light. It amounted to a desecration of local aesthetics, and a little hard to understand the mindset of people who would pitch waste material—containers and packaging for drinks and eats, mostly—out into the open. It's that old duality of private property vs. the commons, and the responsibility entailed. That which you would never permit in your own treasured garden, becomes acceptable here, in the public domain, where anything goes…because nobody cares? From a travelogue by John Patric, an American traveling around East Asia in 1938, referring to Fuji-san:

Within the crater, sandwiched below and above the snow, rubbish lay in gigantic windrows. Along the crest the wind had pushed it into every crevice, dropped it in hollows, drifted it high against lee walls. And down the lee side of the mountain itself, mammoth rubbish glaciers moved slowly, slowly—daily reinforced by fresh accretions… But here was their own Fuji, the grandest, most sacred landmark of all Japan, and it turns out to be a colossal mound of garbage and human excrement. (15)

I hadn't read Patric's book by then, but the caldera didn't seem that blighted, but we didn't really stick around and look closely, either. The refuse along the trails and blown down the slopes, was pretty bad, though.

I can't recall if I made it to that morning's class; I probably didn't. Normally my classes started at 10 am, which would have made it all but impossible to be on time. I do remember attending an afternoon and an evening class, and presenting the feat as a conversational topic: *What do you suppose I did last night?*

August 20, Mangetsu (full moon). I've been back a week from my month-long summer escape to Oregon, and just tonight I feel like I'm getting back to the routine. Fully half my classes are canceled 'til September, this being considered still summer here.

84

She had said it before without the strength to follow through. This time, tearfully, it was clear she meant it. On returning, I called to ask her to meet me—in a restaurant, anyplace would do—to give her some modest *omiagi*, souvenirs, and show her pictures of my trip. Fearing her resolve would crumble by sitting in the same car with me—a kiss leads to a caress, as it had in the past—she asked me to mail her the present. So be it.

She has not told her parents she's been seeing a gaijin, and now it's a problem. She is 29 years old—late for getting married in Japan. She's reluctantly agreed to submit to *omiai,* or arranged marriage, knowing what the family wants, and really needs, is a *mukoh yoshi,* a son-in-law adopted into the family. This *mukoh-yoshi* would be expected to become a loyal son to the family, and the principle manager of the financial affairs. And make babies. A boy or two this time, if you don't mind.

This man, would be a second son or younger, most likely, since a first-born son is duty-bound to carry on his biological family name. A *mukoh yoshi* would legally give up his family name and accept Kimiko's family name as his own. This man would not be just an in-law, but legally adopted as a full family member. So, in order to give the *omiai* process a fair run, she's bringing us to an end.

When you come from a traditional family primogeniture of no less than 18 generations from the same base of property, certain social protocols will prevail. She is the elder of two daughters—no sons—younger sister having married recently and moved to Niigata, on the Japan Sea. It is on Kimiko to carry on the family "traditions," meaning principally, observing Shinto and Buddhist rites regarding ancestors, but also, as the head of the next generation, representing the extended family to the community at large. That is the way of *nihonjin.* Most of which I understand, in a general sense.

For a while, a short period, I hope, it will be hard to find orientation. Much of my non-working focus, both real and fanciful over the last year-plus has been wrapped up in the lady. And regardless of the compelling logic and the foredoomed quality of the relationship from the outset, it still smacks some of rejection. Yet, from a different perspective, I gave it all I could—as did she, I suppose. To some degree, I'm proud to have distracted the lady from her predestined fate as long as I did. As Mishima has said, "That which we call love is an eternal, unending sorrow" (36).

Eighteen generations of a documented family history on the same plot of land with more-or-less the same livelihood and role in the community is probably hard to fathom for most Americans. For one thing there was no US of A eighteen generations ago, and Native Americans/ First Citizens didn't keep vital statistics, or actuarial records. For another thing, most of us are more recent immigrants. Most (though by now just barely a majority) of our ancestors came directly from Europe in one of the immigrant waves, like the Irish fleeing the potato blight and consequent famine, six or seven generations ago. Even that is more than most Americans can trace back, and perhaps as a result, the family tree has little or no importance to your average *Bekoku-jin* (literally, "Rice country people," Americans). It is of no importance to me. Got some hot-shot muckity-muck in your family tree? It's just another excuse to get a fat head and take yourself way too seriously. My father got into genealogy, though. He tracked down records past his grandparents, and had basic data relating to his great-grandparents: Births, deaths, marriage certificates, birth of children. So, that's five generations to me. He must have been disappointed that I didn't express any enthusiasm. Perhaps it's a defect of somesort; I simply have no interest in investing time or energy in exhuming quaint anecdotes about my ancestry.

I realize I am not a self-made being, but I'd rather not call overt attention to some presumed beneficent identity connection, some mystical aid (a la *Shinto*?), passed down from this or that ancestor. Great-great-uncle Winnifred Theophilous Rutabaga, who earned the thanks of a grateful France for valor in the Great War, now a resident of *O-higan*, the Other Side, wishes for you to apply yourself and become a pillar of your community, so that you may publicly spout empty platitudes like these. *Blah, blah...*

I say, hold me accountable for *my* actions. Family histories, family reputations, beyond three generations, have effectively nothing to do with me, and I confess, I'm curious to what extent Americans feel something like I do on this issue. For some, however, it's either the genealogical pursuit, or forego an identity based on short-term, plebian roots, and succumb to extra terrestrial origins/"star war" fantasies.

Non sequitur

What interest there is in genealogy in the US may come from the desire to discover an identity with an ethnicity or country that predates America. Through the geopolitical luck of the draw, we Americans live in a country whose culture is not at all old, august, or replete with ancient customs, compared with many other cultures, especially Europe, with its Greco-Roman and Norse antecedents, and East Asia—conspicuously, India, China and Japan. This seeking out the Mother countries could represent a hunger for an "authentic," deep culture to claim as ancestry. Do you suppose that desire for explicit connectedness is hard-wired in the human psyche? One of my problems with this notion is that line that you draw in your retrogression of ancestors. The choice you make to *stop* pursuing the antecedents is arbitrary, because there are predecessors, those who came before, all the way back to the Rift Valley in Africa some 80,000 years ago. So, to say you come from Irish stock—or even Japanese roots—only reveals part of the story, right? Since your stock came from some "cultural" entity before it became Irish; there was something that preceded the entity that was to become Nihon.

The point of this wandering narrative is this: We are all related. We know this genetically, via DNA analysis, and we know this intuitively. To say, "We identify primarily with Norse culture because our grandparents both immigrated from the old country," empowers ethnocentrism, a distraction of historic proportions that we can no longer afford to indulge. We must now learn to share Earth's resources with each other (undifferentiated by nation-state units), and—this is the hard part—achieve homeostasis with the rest of the biosphere. It doesn't get any more blunt than this: We must learn to cooperate with each other, and drastically reduce our birth rate. Or else what remains of the biosphere will find ways to drastically increase our death rate.

In one view, because we Americans don't (for the most part) have centuries-old traditions to fall back on, we are freer to exercise our individual, idiosyncratic identities, relatively unencumbered by the chains of history. Argue, if you will, that Americans, compared to Europe and East Asia, lack the richness and depth of traditions that come with centuries; that our cultural identities are shallower, less cohesive, as a result of that paucity of history in the walls and on the streets of our communities. My instinct is to celebrate that lack of deep attachment to a multi-generational family at the same hearth, to consider it a blessing that I am not beholden to arcane protocols. But truly, what choice do I have? Neither intrinsically good nor bad: whether you were born into deep family history, or no history at all, they are simply the cards we are dealt, nothing more.

All that said, it's an amazing thing for Kimiko to be a member of a family with its roots a matter of record through several centuries. At turns, this deep connection to locality has advantages through an incredible sense of belonging—as well as demonstrating the curse it is. One thing is clear: I now realize that she would never really be able to escape her family, even if she tried.

Tenki wa hare, or fine weather: NHK (national, as opposed to commercial, TV) weather reporters indicate a region's dry, sunny weather by a t-shirt with a bull's eye in the center—suitable weather to hang out freshly washed clothes. Very few people have the luxury of a clothes dryer to go along with the washer. Is it possible this society considers it morally indefensible to use fossil fuels in this manner? Possible, yes, but it is space and habit, as well as some cost considerations, to go along with a budding environmental sensitivity, that motivate the eminently *practical* Japanese housewife.

Here's a couple of poetic shards from the days prior to a parting:

> Eyes opaque pools
> daring me to plunge
> forsaking mere oxygen
> to search the depths
> for mysteries that lie within

Mouth meager source
of such mighty utterances
diminutive cavern
beckoning kisses
recalling the moist
and quivering *other*

September 1 (Excerpts from a letter to my Oregon Coast Range cabin caretaker)

By now, hopefully, you've recovered from my frenzied pass through your otherwise peaceful domain. Hard to imagine a few short weeks ago I was paddling my feet in the cool, clear waters of Small River and sharing a smoke with valued friends. Harder still that I could forsake all that for congestion, pollution and a social structure so arcane that in a year and a half I've barely scratched the surface of comprehending it. All in the name of "filthy lucre!" And to make matters worse, it is hotter than fresh hunde scheisse here—and about as sticky. Perhaps I paint too bleak a picture; no doubt there are several benefits possible living in Japan. Just don't ask me to enumerate them right at the moment. The weather would not even remotely be considered one of them, though the Shonan area where I live is often touted as among the few most desirable places to live in all of Japan.

The dubious profession of English instruction has resumed at a slowed pace since my return—owing to school summer break—allowing me plenty of time to mope around and conjure up lengthy, introspective analyses of lost loves and otherwise pointless considerations of my lack of self-worth...but not enough time to escape the normal routine and explore new territory. All of this should change as of next week when my schedule gears up to full throttle. You see, my rather extravagant vacation calls for some applied greed for a change.

Permit me to conclude with a recent True Life Adventure: Last Thursday my Yokohama bankers' class let out unusually early due to yet another meeting the poor unfortunates were compelled to attend. Thinking I would arrive home earlier than usual, I negotiated the first of three train connections—Sakuragicho to Yokohama station. You realize that the central station of Yokohama is vast and disorienting with all the necessary transfers having to be made underground, a decided disadvantage when one is trying to locate familiar landmarks, one meandering passageway looking much like any other, all information signs rendered identical by meaningless chicken scratches. No matter! Having threaded these selfsame catacombs countless times previously, this intrepid voyager exited one train and negotiated the appropriate transfer to the next platform. Just another rat (albeit a Caucasian rat) in a sea of dark haired rats unconsciously running the maze, in time to see a "limited express" train pull up disgorging and taking on the surge of Yokohama fares. True, I didn't immediately recognize the train's destination, but it was a Tokakido Line headed in the right direction—outward bound— and I reasoned the limited express qualifier might mean we'd avoid Totsuka, the next station along the line. My fleeting pause for concern was amplified when I soon discovered the train compartments were designed to convert to sleepers. I concluded it would at least stop in Odawara (about 35 minutes past Fujisawa) as even the Shinkansen (bullet train) stops there. Alas, this was not the case. Totsuka, indeed! Two and a half hours later I was finally able to disembark at Shizuoka, to begin the lengthy and expensive trip back. I got home after midnight, a trifling four-hour misjudgment.

Stay tuned for more exciting adventures, blunders, and all manner of faux pas. Thrills abound!

Getsuyobi (Monday) <u>September 15</u>: The full moon is coming up in a few days and I was reminded, in one of my housewives' classes, of *Otsuki-mi*, Honorable moon viewing, the tradition of the full-moon viewing ceremony, especially in the fall. I've never seen a society so wrapped up in natural phenomena like moon viewing events, varying according to the season. There is a charming tale that illustrates it; I'm afraid I'm acquainted with only the bare bones of it, but, being foolhardy, I'll hold forth anyway:

Long, long ago (mukashi, mukashi), there once was an old man who lived by himself near an enchanted bamboo grove. On the occasion of the Harvest Moon (Jugoya), this man whose name is not recorded, was taking a stroll through the grove, doubtless lost in thoughts of younger, happier days, when he chanced upon an unfamiliar clearing. There, bathed in the moon's

90

soft light, lay an infant swaddled in common garments. Scarcely able to believe his eyes, the old man gathered up the waif and hurried back to his humble cottage where, warmed, fed, and comforted with soothing words, she promptly fell asleep. (Many details are left for the reader to ponder, not least of which is how this solitary old man was able to nurse this baby; perhaps he kept a nanny goat. Such matters are not included in the tale.) In the ensuing days, after cautious inquiries were made of the few people in the surrounding area, it became clear that no mishap had befallen any wayfarers; no children were missing.

The old man could hardly contain his joy, for he realized this tiny babe, whom he named Kaguya-hime (Woodcutter Princess) was the answer to his prayers, an end to his abject loneliness. Joyfully the years passed and gradually the child grew into a woman of rare beauty. So lovely was Kaguya-hime that soon her reknown spread far and wide, and though she was but seventeen years of age, it was not long before suitors began to appear at her door. To each she had but one response, a polite but emphatic No! It was rumored that even the Daimyo, the regional Lord, himself, was rebuffed... Not long after, however, during Jugoya, the maiden went walking in that same mysterious bamboo grove, never to be seen again. Curious as to her whereabouts, neighbors would ask the disconsolate old man. Wistfully, he replied, You must ask the moon.

This account turns out to be riddled with inaccuracies, a fact I was to discover by showing it to some of my students. Ok, so Koizumi Yakumo, I'm not. Still, given the sketchy details I had to start with, it's a plausible extension of imagination, *dessho*, don't you think?

Mokuyobi (Thursday), <u>September 18</u>, Jugoya. After several days of persistent rain this day began full of sun and cheer, with my mood elevated correspondingly. Alas, by noon the sky was socked in (again!), and as of 2 pm or so, a constant drizzle had set in. No moon viewing tonight. The day consisted of three classes: from 10 to noon, six housewives, this time in Ishida's house. (Most of my classes are organized on an every-other-week basis, often rotating from house to house, with the host of the day preparing a sumptuous lunch for everyone. Is this the life, or what?) In this class, I can barely contain my lust for Chieko-san. The glands start secreting, the hormones begin oozing by merely glancing in her direction, though there are two or three others who are striking. A veritable bevy of beauties! Must keep my craven lusts in check...

At 1 o'clock I meet with my next group in a spartan classroom on the third floor in an immediately post-war make-do-with-austerity office building on the Ginza of Chigasaki. Unfortunately, there's quite a range of abilities in this class from Wakamikoto-san (a good command of English with an upbeat, fearless personality), to Sato-san (a newcomer, and a fairly good speaker), to Hayashi-san (the matriarch who does alright, albeit slowly and with hesitation), to sorry Ota-san, who still can't seem to string six words of English together, after a year with me as teacher—who knows how long with the Kiwi before me—without resorting to Nihongo. She's pleasant enough, always there early, cleaning the surfaces and preparing the room. Usually brings snacks and *o-cha* (tea), but oh, what a struggle! Any teacher will tell you that one of the hardest aspects of teaching to a group is having within the group rank beginners as well as fairly competent speakers.

This disparity in individual abilities is only made worse by the deteriorating conditions of the room, which are formidable unto themselves. There is no heat in the winter, when on a cold day the temperature can hover around freezing. No cooler in the summer, so of course we open the windows and the door for some hoped-for ventilation. The building is literally next to the Tokaido Line tracks with trains of all description clattering by every five minutes or so... It's not just the roar of the trains, but the entire post-WWII cheapo office building shudders. Then, there's somesort of businessman's seminar held next door with a phone just outside their door ringing several times an hour—some vital message for one or another of the men, said message acknowledged at the top of one's voice, amplified in resounding echoes throughout the stark halls (pre-pagers, to say nothing of smart phones). To make matters worse, there is some construction work going on at the building site adjacent to ours; a giant pile-driving mechanism adding to the havoc. To top it off, we've lately been deprived of a blackboard, arguably the only feature that remotely redeemed the setup.

This was about as grim as it got for me. I show up because they pay me, but you've got to marvel at the sacrifices large numbers of Nihonjin will submit to in order to "improve" themselves. Improving one's English is one

92

example of that desire (*To one and all, I humbly thank you*). Though another reason is the opportunity to socialize in a more relaxed atmosphere than one's other social activities. There must be a dozen or more popular subjects for study or practice: *Ikebana*, flower arrangement; *Sado*, the Way of Tea; *Shuji*, calligraphy; Haiku or Tanka composition; ceramics; cooking classes for both *Yo shoku*, Western style, and *Wa shoku*, Japanese style cuisine; social dancing; the *koto*, an eleven-stringed horizontal harp; the *shamisen*, a three-stringed banjo, both instruments capable of haunting beauty; *bonsai*, and landscaping gardens through the seasons; then you got your sports realm of physical self-improvement, to rattle off a few. But even the social dancing club, or a tennis group, clearly imported from Europe and America, would still be organized along Japanese protocol, whereas a free-wheeling English conversation class, fronted by a native English speaker, can operate with the relative interpersonal freedom that English allows, though, or course, developing competence in English is a formidable task of itself.

This drive to formally improve one's skills or discipline, I'd say, is not so common in America, where individual or collective indulgences are more the norm—fans who follow their chosen sport vicariously, to Alien Wars berserkos. Self, or more accurately, *team* improvement fades pretty quickly after college years in the US. We like *the idea* of a lifetime-learning environment, but there is little follow through, on the macro scale. I suspect a low percentage of Americans, mid-40s and older, voluntarily participate on a regular basis in activities generally thought to be beneficial to community or self. Whereas in Japan, based on the entire culture emphasizing the group over the self, we could expect the results to be opposite. I regularly taught classes Friday and Saturday evenings until 9 pm, and Sunday all day from 10 am. Nothing says ambition, commitment, and discipline—to say nothing of the craven pursuit of filthy lucre—like the regular sacrifice of one's weekend.

At 3 pm I mount my trusty Honda 50 cc motor scooter, race home, exchange notebooks, excavate my mailbox of the bills and useless flyers promoting this or that sale, of course in incomprehensible kanji, gibberish; then off to Kugenuma Kaigan station where, for 90 yen, I catch the next Odakyu train to Fujisawa, transfer to the Tokaido Line (380 yen) bound for Yokohama, and one last transfer to Kannai station, for a saunter along

Isezakicho, a vehicle-less shopping street, often perusing Yurindo Bookstore, wolf down a plate of greasy yakisoba while (today) taking in five or six matches of the current *sumo basho* (traditional Japanese wrestling match of bipedal walruses slamming into each other), before heading to my last class with the yuppie businessmen at the local Bank of Tokyo, Yokohama branch. All in a Thursday's workday.

Kaiyobi, Ju Gatsu, Yohka (Tuesday, October 8): Despite "finalities," we are back together again!

Richter Magnitude 6

We hadn't met in lifetimes of months
waiting outside *Sagami-Ono Eki*
the lamp posts heave and rattle
footing is precarious as if intoxicated
Earth trembles
                in anticipation

...this being a literal account of our rendezvous last Friday evening. The papers the next day claimed it to be the largest quake (in the Kanto Plain) in 56 years. No fatalities, but several injuries mostly due to hard, heavy objects lurching from high shelves onto soft, unsuspecting bodies.

Ju gatsu, ju-san nichi, October 13: Modern Japan is what one sees and hears most of, but it's the older customs just under the veneer of the "modern miracle," the deeper waters that intrigue me. No surprise here: Post-war Japan's reconstruction—accelerated in preparation for hosting the 1964 Tokyo Olympics—has been a phenomenal achievement, given the starting point of near total devastation by the end of WWII. But it is largely a recapitulation of the latest architectural and engineering standards of urban centers of Western Europe and the US. Office buildings, department stores, restaurants, train stations, hotels, streets and traffic congestion, fashionably dressed people busy with their own agendas—it could be London, Paris, New York, or San

94

Francisco, if you were to squint your eyes somewhat and discount the homogeneity of the fair skinned, black haired masses. But back to my attempt to illustrate cultural curiosities—as interpreted by a neophyte *gaijin*—allow me to contrast a couple of highlights from last week.

The first was a garden barbeque party I was fortunate to be invited to. Among the ten or twelve adults was a ship's engineer home between voyages plying the Pacific with cargoes of Nikon cameras, the latest of Sony's electronic wizardry, and Toyotas; a woman who alternates between teaching *ikebana* (traditional flower arrangement) and gourmet French pastry classes; a theater, movie and TV luminary and wife (the Iwatas, though his stage name is Taguchi Kei—he often performs the role of a sinister samurai warrior); and my original patrons/guarantors, Dr. Yoshida and wife, Tomoko. The food was varied, abundant and delicious: grilled spare ribs, steak, salmon, squid, etc., with a full complement of vegetables, beer and wine, fruit and an assortment of the aforementioned pastries. The conversation, needless to say, was mostly in Nihongo, of which I am able to catch maybe three words in ten, but occasionally, when the topic was pertinent, they would render it in English. The sort of thing you might encounter in any middleclass backyard in America—except for language code switching. And maybe the barbequed squid. I feel immense gratitude to my hosts for being included in such social events. I did enjoy myself, though it seemed a trifle opulent for my comfort zone.

The other event was a *shamisen* mini-concert-cum-lesson. The shamisen is a three- stringed instrument used in classical drama (kabuki, at least), but has so few practitioners that it is on the verge of dying out altogether. It seems the country is swept up in a tide of "Westernization" and while learning any musical expression is to the good (there are doubtless more avid piano students per capita here than in the US, or Europe)—and while Japan definitely needs to become more international, it grieves me to discover essential cultural expressions passing away. Probably half the houses in the Shonan area sport pianos, if not violins and recorders, to boot. And virtually every neighborhood has its local piano *sensei* (teacher/master). But shamisen sensei are a different matter. Apparently, there are *kotto* schools where one can go to learn the intricacies of this six foot long, twelve-stringed instrument, but only licensed masters are permitted to teach shamisen lessons, and since there are so few, the price for such lessons are astronomical (even for Japan!). To say nothing of the cost of the shamisen, which could run anywhere from $800 to many thousands of dollars.

Admiring Tomoko's shamisen, I expressed an interest in hearing her play. She demurred, saying she hadn't practiced in ten years, but said she would arrange to take me to her sensei's house. Thus, in lieu of Wednesday's *Eigo* (English) lesson, we went to this marvelous old woman's house not far from Kugenuma Kaigan station. Dressed in traditional kimono, this septuagenarian bade us sit on her tatami floor, served us *ocha*, and commenced playing and singing this spare, plaintive music. Not melodic in the western octave-based sense, her versions of the traditional songs of the seasons were captivating, if not outright hypnotic. I was enthralled. Until the Meiji Reformation, Japan had no ability to score music. Tone, meter, everything had to be memorized and passed down from generation to generation. This gentle crone showed me a book well over 100 years old with the words to several hundred songs written out, but without any musical notation. After more *cha* and commentary of technique, she had me fret a few notes before I had to dash off to my next class. I hope to line up another occasion with this charming *Obah-chan,* elderly woman/grandmother, in hopes of recording some of her other-worldly singing and playing.

Why should a shamisen cost from one to an excess of three million yen?!? As usual when confronted with a cultural enigma, I asked my students. Their explanations (sorted from several accounts from various conversation classes ranging across Kanagawa ken) ran something like this: They are individually hand crafted (indeed, they are finely made), and cat skin is used to cover the hollow body. Half in jest, I pointed out that cats don't cost so much. The cats I've acquired over the years came to me at _no_ initial cost, in point of fact. Well, I was earnestly rebuked; only large virgin females (i.e. cats that have never borne a litter) may be used. I understand that protruding nipples might detract from the smooth appearance of the head of the instrument—hence the virginal requirement—but why a female cat? It is traditional, having to do with the superior tone only females can impart! *Okashii ne* (strange, isn't it)?

Hardly a week goes by that I don't find myself in the midst of an experience unexpected and quite different from what I would apt to have in

Oregon. In this way I am enriched beyond money. Doubly enriched; a win-win situation. I have this opportunity to absorb culture, to drink it in like spilt coffee to a sponge. I am grateful to have the means to earn my living expenses, child support, a modest amount for entertainment, and some little to save for my decrepitude. But in addition, I am grateful to behold this daily chance to acquire pieces of the puzzle that make up late-20th century Japan. And this too is win-win: Not only do I learn beguiling features of this very complicated culture, but in doing so, I automatically learn more explicitly, and in more detail, about the nation-state, and especially, the West Coast US, urban, WASP culture, I was born and raised in.

Kaiyobi (Tuesday), October 21: Today it was up for a quickie breakfast, scrambled eggs and toast, and out of the house by 8:45 to catch the train connections to Yokohama (Ishikawacho) for a 1 ½ hour class with Wang Jin, a Chinese young woman and her yakuza boyfriend. After being in Japan for only one year, she speaks Nihongo very well and now wants to learn English, towards going to Canada or the US in the upcoming year. She is highly motivated and a joy to tutor. Her *pima atama* (literally "bell-pepper head," or as we are apt to say, air head) boyfriend, on the other hand, can't even read *romaji,* the Roman alphabet. I suspect he only hangs around to keep a sharp eye on his lady. They pick me up and return me to the station in a late model, shiny black Mercedes Benz. Just another case of an attractive girl plying her notable attributes to her best advantage.

My second class of the day is with a group of charming and well-spoken housewives in Chigasaki, two stops outward bound from Fujisawa on the Tokaido Line. The class is two hours of current affairs, and whatever else is on their mind. They all submitted their mini-essays I'd assigned as homework last class on Prime Minister Nakasone's foot-in-mouth gaffe demeaning America's minorities.

Class number three was with the Nippon Roche (the Japanese affiliate of the Swiss pharmaceutical company) salary men. The class seems to be languishing after a year and a half. The class was down to five members tonight, four last class, down from nine or ten at the peak some months ago. I try to keep it snappy, interesting, current, but the novelty's worn thin. It's hard to dazzle students month in and month out, made the more difficult when they've been on the job since 8:30 in the morning, and would like nothing better to do than go home to relax with their wives and families, or lacking that, hit an *isakaya* (convivial drinking-cum-snack-food place). Who could blame them?

My final stint of the day—I can't really call it an English "class"—was with the Iwatas. It amounts to lively discussions, mostly irreverent in nature, before and during a scrumptious meal prepared by Kazu-san in their apartment over their pharmacy in Tsujido. They are by far the most provocative, atypical Nihonjin I have as "students," and a real pleasure to spend time with. On one such evening, Mr. Iwata gave me a glimpse of his world view, which I found a trifle bleak at the time. To be fair, he displayed a healthy sense of humor about human foibles, and was somewhat hopeful in regards to his family and close friends. But for prospects of a humanity devoted to its continued arrogance and aggrandizement, he had a *kotowaza* to share: *Nichi-mo sachi-mo ikanai,* loosely translated as, "No matter how hard you try, it can't be accomplished. There is no solution; you can't get there from here. The obstacle is too great. No hope. Insert another coin and ask another question." Or other nihilist utterances to that effect. If the reader is at least forty years of age, no doubt s/he could spin off another comment or three equivalent to this bleak outlook. I remember at the time, being wholly unwilling to abandon hope for a better future. Interestingly, in the nearly 30 years since, though, I have come to put behind me what I thought were the false hopes, the hackneyed naiveté, and unjustified optimism, that seemed to characterize my orientation of those days. I have come to embrace Iwata-san's bleak reality, not because I find any comfort in this dire projection; quite the contrary. I find such an outlook abhorrent. However, in my mind, it is better to face the hideous truth than some cheesy fiction, the plausibility of which is increasingly difficult to imagine...

Thus, concluded my final class of the day, 90 minutes of thoroughly engaging discussion, a meal, and to top it off, they pay me! For a grand-slam total of *san man yen,* or just under $250 for the day, at current exchange rates. If I sound like I'm gloating, it's because I still can't quite believe I'm earning so much... Needless to say, living expenses are also quite dear. For example, trains today cost 1190 yen, or $7.65 at the current exchange. I also refueled the

Talking Racehorse at the local burger franchise for less than five dollars American. So it goes.

Autumn Haiku

In a flash today
Korogi-san kept time with
Prokofiev: Awe!

(*Korogi* is Japanese for cricket. *San* is an honorific, as in *Mr.* or *Sir* Cricket.)

Mokuyobi (Thursday), <u>October 23</u>: The first gold coins to be minted in the US in over 50 years, and by yesterday were completely sold out, prompting US Treasury authorities to initiate round-the-clock production to try to meet the demand. Interestingly enough, last Thursday, a week ago today, Japan released by way of lottery (numbers 1 through 10) the right to buy by chance the first minting of Japan's gold coin in commemoration of 60 years of the Showa era. The current Emperor, Hirohito, has reigned longer than any other in Japanese history. Tickets for silver coins were released at the same time on a first come, first served basis to banks and post offices all over Japan until their allotments ran out. Lines formed hours in advance at some locations and some institutions exhausted their lottery tickets in short order—two hours or less from time of opening. Only two ticket holders in ten will have a chance to buy the much coveted gold coins (the silver coins as well) from a lottery to be held October 30th. Get this: While the face value of the US coin is $50, its equivalent in Japan is ¥100,000, or at current exchange rates, $645! It is estimated that even though more than 2.2 metric <u>tons</u> of gold were used (there is said to be not more than 45% of face value in gold per coin), the total output has not satisfied more than 1/10 of the demand, and that is with 10 million coins being minted, gold and silver each! That should give some indication of just how wealthy this country is…

Two Birds with One Stone

I propose that Japan issue a new ¥100,000 banknote. In a society rich in liquid assets without a tradition of payments by checking; with the world's highest cost of living, it has become tedious and cumbersome, and more conspicuous to pack around huge wads of ¥10,000 notes, heretofore the nation's largest denomination. To pay the rent fairly stuffs an envelope. It requires two hands to secure the volume required to purchase, say, a car, and it takes a strong man to pack your 200-plus million yen out to the nearest bamboo thicket for "safe keeping."

The problem, however, of whom to commemorate on the new bill immediately presents itself; fortunately there is an obvious choice: Yasuhiro Nakasone. He has served the people in the nation's highest office, that of Prime Minister (though there remains lingering questions as to the nature of his service, and its chief beneficiaries). And clearly he is god-like in the way he interprets his duty to the public good. Nor need he account for his dealings, so august and majestic is his eminence. My first inclination was to suggest that he holds himself above the law, but there appears to be an absence of laws to contravene. That being the case, suffice it to say that he is deserving of immortality for his (god-like) imaginative interpretation of his service to the commonweal.

Kakui Tanaka could be an alternate candidate for selection of his visage on the nation's highest monetary denomination, but in my opinion, his contributions to society pale by comparison.

October 30: I've recently rediscovered my *O-furo*, the Japanese "honorable bath." While I was in Oregon last summer my landlady installed a shower attachment on my tub heating assembly, and so on my return, I was delighted to use the shower throughout the hot weather. But alas, the weather has changed—and rather abruptly, I might add—so a few days ago I fiddled around with the controls and figured out how to heat the water in the tub. Properly speaking an *O-furo* is a container; run-of-the-mill models these days are produced from molded plastic, but in the not too distant past, were beautifully wrought from cedar, or other elegant wood, like the naturally scented cryptomeria. It usually stands above the floor, and is something like 30 inches wide, 36 inches long, and 30 inches deep, so that it is just possible to sit in it, hot water up to your neck, in an approximation of the fetal position. In the old days one would stand beside the tub and ladle water from the tub for washing and rinsing purposes. Nowadays, there is a flexible tube attached to a shower head to thoroughly wash yourself. Only after this procedure is complete with a rinse does one enter the tub for a scalding soak. In cold weather, such as is already upon us—of course, relative to the weather that preceded this phase—a thorough-going parboil is tonic for the mind and body. Regardless of how cold the room may be, after several minutes' soak, give yourself a quick towel off while your body throws off steam like you're on fire. Dive into the futon covers and sleep comes rapidly.

<u>*Doyobi*</u> (Saturday), November 1: Excerpts from a letter to a friend:

Things are rolling along for me at a typically frantic clip; everything on the verge of out of control/situation normal. Language acquisition is progressing painfully slowly. I've managed to learn a bit of vocabulary, but as we all know, mere words do not communication make. One must string them together in some coherent fashion. Regrettably, that ability yet eludes me. I did, however, manage to commit to my enfeebled brain all 92 kana, both Hiragana and Katakana. In addition to learning complicated syntax while ever building vocabulary, the killer task is beginning absorption of the dreaded Kanji (the Chinese pictographic symbols). One would think I'd be well on my way toward picking up conversational Nihongo, hearing it every day as I do. Needless to say, however, I'm employed to be the "authority" (Ha!) on English, certainly not to practice their language on their dime. I still enjoy teaching for the most part. It is very much a challenge and I feel that hardly a day goes by that I'm not learning from my students, though I suppose it's best not to bandy that notion about, lest they think I'm overpaid. Which is doubtless true.

There are the classes, to be sure, where I just grit my teeth and slog through the simple sentence patterns and pronunciation drills. But more often than not, the students are bright eyed and eager (housewives mostly, bless their hearts!), and Form melds harmoniously with Content in a dazzling display before the awe-struck assemblage (or something just shy of that). In any event, after nearly two years here, I feel I've barely scratched the surface of comprehending this culture. Doubtless, that's attributable to me being such a slow learner, but I think I'll stick around for the foreseeable future and see what I can glean. In my so-called free time I am currently wading through Koizumi Yakumo's works (Lafcadio Hearn) for insights into traditional myths and legends, and an occasional glimpse into Japanese society that is still remarkably intact and valid 80-plus years after his death.

For a "professional English teacher," I am not (yet) particularly strong in the basic rules of grammar, not to mention being a poor speller, which is without a doubt a case of "Earn while you learn." My virtues, such as they are, run to speaking clearly (I stand accused of being <u>wakari yasui</u>, or easy to understand). Also, I am reasonably polite, pay a modicum of attention to hygiene and neatness, and I show up on time. I'm open-minded, meaning I'm not shocked or judgmental about customs very different from my upbringing. I consider myself a bit of a right-brain empath—with a minimum of cues, I'm able to "understand"/identify with an interlocutor's narrative perhaps easier than most. For these few paltry graces, and precious little else, people here foist money on me in a manner that far exceeds my worth in any heretofore tried, licit profession back in sweet home, Oregon—but what say we keep that little observation to ourselves, shall we? I suspect I am learning lots, but paradoxically I can't yet seem to quantify it. The little glimpses I catch of this culture are, like the language, slowly acquired, random pieces of a giant jigsaw puzzle. Here and there a curious oddment meshes with another—more by chance than by design, I think. But this get-good-at-what you-do-while-you-do-it program these good people sponsor, places no premium on haste. So now the primary obstacle is this government, which is waxing increasingly anxious about my propensity to remain a tourist. I told the immigration functionaries recently at visa renewal time that I'm doing social research—true enough in my own slipshod fashion—towards magazine articles and/or a book.

These immigration bureaucrats know that Japan is virtually without exception (well, two exceptions: tofu, and health care), considerably more expensive than mainstream America, so I may have reached the end of my rope as a "tourist." I may have to submit to the yoke of some language institute cram school (juku) in exchange for a work visa, instead of the unfettered pastures of teaching private lessons. This would be solely for the purpose of legitimacy.

The juku system is a privately owned, parallel, supplemental educational program. Like pachinko parlors, there's at least one juku within a block of the central station of every small-and-larger city in the country, which speaks to their popularity, not to mention their perceived utility. Or it speaks of the venality of capitalism. A whole industry has developed preying on the fears of parents who could possibly fall short in their duties as parents, if they fail to provide this extra opportunity to learn the essential factoids towards passing the entrance exams of prestigious universities around the country.

As a sponsored employee, juku management usually requires 20 hours per week teaching time, in exchange for the work visa. Call it four hours of class instruction (ok, 50 minutes of teacher-fronted lesson, and ten minutes an hour to nosh on a snack, buy a coffee, release some of that barely filtered coffee you gulped last break, and consult with students or fellow instructors). Five days a week. For 2000/2500 yen per hour. This is called "Sweatshop," among those of us who find enough work through a combination of corporate, community center, and private patrons. I taught a couple of juku classes; the opportunity was there and I was curious. The stultifying regimentation was anathema to the essence of teaching, in my perspective. A teacher needs to be able to flex the general curriculum to suit the collective needs of the class, and his own pedagogic style. Building rapport is essential to an ongoing, functional class. True, there is little or no homework to contend with; no preparation necessary. Everything is set up: just follow the book; teach from the script. There is no incentive for innovation. We strive for uniformity. As the country goes, so go its institutions. This is education as a Business (with a capital B).

English instruction is of course my "business," as well. However, in my case, I either intrigue, entertain, and/or provoke, all the while educating adequately, or I fail. There are no intermediaries to manage my business—and take half the profit. I am accountable for my own failures, and rewarded for my successes—quite handsomely, I must admit. I have cultivated a tidy, personal, anarchic arrangement, and I am exceedingly grateful.

<u>Date</u>: Mid-November 1986

<u>The place</u>: Yokohama Immigration Office

<u>Personae</u>: A) Self; B) Familiar-looking gentleman; C) A cast of dozens, having no individual speaking parts, filling in the background, serving as context for the bleak, austere, bureaucratic tableaux with desultory mumbling and shuffling; and D) the *Ubermachen*.

<u>Our Story</u>: Self has been standing in line a half hour for one of the three windows available for visa application renewal, and is next to be waited on, in his line. He has passed the time alternately observing the other hapless creatures at the mercy of the immigration authorities—mostly southeast Asians, Filipinas and their Japanese "sponsors"—sometimes more accurately described as pimps—and worrying about the continued effectiveness of his ruse (free-lance journalist) as justification for tourist visa renewal. Self's line and the one immediately to his left have male clerks serving the public. Both of these lines have several people waiting, as many as ten to twelve each. The third window, the one to Self's right, the one "manned" by the *Ubermachen*, has three people acting together: A businessman lookalike, early middle-aged, bearing a striking resemblance to a prominent US politician, flanked by a Japanese woman, probably a *nisei* or *sansei* American (second or third generation), judging from her English, and a nondescript gaijin in casual clothes. These three people had stood there wrangling, negotiating, and ultimately pleading the whole time.

I refer to this female authority as *Ubermachen* because I don't know the word for it in Nihongo, though I suspect there is such a word, if rarely needed. We're not talking about a *heart*breaker, here. This one's a *ball*breaker, a woman of authority who conspicuously uses that position of power to make life a living hell for a man. Any man. I mean, the guy could be a real shithead, in which case, one might be inclined to see some cosmic justice here. But he could be a saint, bearing absolutely no ill will toward any woman. Most of us oscillate somewhere in between, I suppose—the point is, it doesn't matter to the Emasculator. It's *One size fits all* when meting out her wrath. Perhaps she was abused or taken advantage of by some mean, mistreater of a man. She really is unprecedented in Japan for her uniform hostility toward the "public" she is ostensibly there to serve. To be sure, we represent a somewhat complicated and controversial segment of the public, but still…

104

One might get lured into her clutches once, but no fool, bearing a permanently scarred psyche from that first confrontation, would willingly submit to a second helping of humiliation, ridicule, abuse, or worse, revocation of residency status. *QED*, it is revealed why so many of us willingly, *gratefully* stand in long, slow lines, when presented with this shorter, faster alternative.

You see, visitors entering the country with tourist status have three months to "tour," and then rather routinely are granted a renewal. That's *a*, signaling *one*, emphasis on the singular nature of this renewal. So you've been here six months now; what are you *really* doing here? The common assumption is, if you're a college-educated, Caucasian male, you're an English teacher of some stripe, and in practice, immigration officials are not altogether opposed to the idea, an example of *realpolitik*. However, they want you on a short leash, say, three months. Don't mess up and they will overlook your horseshit story. For a while. They know that everybody in Japan learns English in school from middle school through college, but the vast majority are terrified to speak English, especially to a gaijin, because...they might...*make a mistake!* That may be a bit of an oversimplification, but not by much. For decades, certainly since the post-war Occupation, the Japanese have assiduously learned the Roman alphabet, grammar, spelling, punctuation, everything pertaining to English...except how to speak it. *Katakana eigo*, English spoken through the limited possibilities of Katakana, is woefully inadequate in the long run. Thus, immigration authorities see some justification (*wink, wink!*) for native speakers to teach English.

Having stalled long enough, building suspense, we return to our thrilling story: The exasperated trio have bravely withstood the savaging, and they had seen it through to somesort of profane conclusion. As the "businessman" reels past me, glassy-eyed from the encounter, Self excused self and asked if anyone had pointed out the man's resemblance to Jerry Brown. He replied, "I'm Jerry Brown." We passed a minute or two shooting the breeze, mostly in observance of the vicissitudes endured braving the Troll of Window Three. Being the shameless suck up that I am, I told him I would have voted for him (governor, Senator) but I was an Oregon, not a California, resident. (The only chance I had to vote for him was during his primary presidential bid in 1980, but instead I voted for Barry Commoner of the Citizen's Party, a point I didn't feel necessary to raise at the time.)

The scene fades as Brown—just another humble petitioner at the immigration office— and cohorts disappear into the elevator. Self's visa is approved for another, "final" three months. Sounds of teeth gnashing and a throaty growl emanate from the third window as the ogre impatiently awaits her next unsuspecting supplicant.

Finis

As the fates would have it, around this time, without my making any overt pleas, my immigration plight became known to enough people with clout in the Shonan area, specifically Yamasaki Masako-san, elder sister to Dr. Yoshida, my Fujisawa patron, that a solution was found. I was given an interview and hired as the native-speaker instructor for the Chigasaki Method English Language Institute in Chigasaki. These folks became my legal sponsor. For this institute, I taught three two-hour classes, twice a month, eight to twelve students per class, and once or twice a month I taught my fellow (non-native speaker) instructors. And at a branch of the institute an hour and a half away by three trains, I taught another class twice a month, two-hour classes. That's what? Maybe 20 hours a *month* at *go sen yen*, 5000 yen, per hour. This was an amazing arrangement for me. A comfortable work schedule at top rate. For that amount of work, this institute was willing to sponsor me—formally take me under its wing as a legitimate, tax-paying employee. Additionally, I made tapes of English vocabulary and little stories for pronunciation and dictation drill, for another nudge toward my financial well-being. By this time, I had this portable cassette tape recorder on loan, complete with a microphone, which I used to make tapes to send to my parents occasionally. The Kanda office would send me the blank tapes with the script, and a stamped, return envelope. I had three of four days to make the recordings and stick it back in the mail. *Easy-peasy.*

So I became legitimate—no longer some furtive gaijin gaming the system—lurking in the shadows (*important phrase to remember; always useful for instilling menacing, fearful imagery*), squeezing money out of unsuspecting Nihonjin, while *posing* as an English Sensei. See him there:

Pssss-st! Hey, you! You wanna get on the fast track to happiness and success? Of course you do! Learn English the easy way! The first lesson is free!

God bless nepotism. It turns out Yamasaki-san has two brothers, Pediatric Physician Yoshida and family, my Fujisawa patrons, and another Yoshida of the diplomatic corps, part of the Foreign Ministry. This Yoshida had once served as Japanese Consul General in Atlanta, Georgia, as well as several ambassadorships around the world, thus he was a public servant of some clout. *If* he had been given the full accounting of this hapless gaijin's plight, from *Oneisan*, older sister, one call from his office would have greased the wheels toward a successful transfer of status from Tourist to a Work Visa. I hasten to make clear, I do not *know* this is what happened; I'm merely offering my prevailing hypothesis. It was possible that the arcs and vectors all lined up. I feel I earned their trust in me. I don't think I ever abused my role at "Chigasaki Method."

Hallelujah, it meant I didn't have to submit to any more charades at the Immigration Office, three months after (re, re)entering the country, being required to leave the country after another three months. Only to start the increasingly tenuous cycle all over again.

Regardless of the manner in which my residency status was remedied, on Yamasaki Masako's recommendation, the Fujisawa Yoshidas took me in. I taught the twins, Keiichi and Satoru, from eight to eighteen years old, when they became college students. If I may be so bold as to opine, I was like a peculiar, generally likable, old uncle who came to hang out most Thursday evenings. We learned a lot from each other, and I am eternally grateful.

November 20: The windows and door of my meager dwelling periodically rattle, quite violently at times, yet outside there is not so much as a whisper of a fugitive breeze. The nearby traffic, while audible, is rarely sufficient to shake my house, and we've had no recent earthquakes. Mt. Mihama, the volcano on Oshima, has awakened from its 12-year slumber. On a clear day Oshima is visible from the coast, about a 15-minute walk from my house. Several of my students have reported seeing the ash rising from the mountain, and in the evening, a red glow from the the oozing magma. Those violent shakes are from explosions or concussions that are right on the edge of being audible. Some 10,000 people have been evacuated from the island. What a country! One idly wonders if all this seismic/volcanic activity presages the next big quake, say, along the lines of the Kanto *dai-shinsai*, the great Kanto earthquake, of 1923. Several faults converge near here, and a massive tectonic shift has been predicted for some time. (*Invariably, by the usual doom-speculator suspects with too much time on their hands.*)

Dr. Yoshida took his twins and me to the bluff between Enoshima and Kamakura, called Shischiri-ga-hama, maybe a quarter mile inland from the coast and 150 feet above Sagami Bay, where we could see Oshima by the naked eye (well, I need prescription lenses, serious amplification, to see anything beyond two meters. The English expression means, *something seen without the aid of significant magnification, like a telescope, or binoculars—* for my Japanese idiom chasers). From our vantage point we could see the cone-like volcano shoot out puffs of smoke and ash, and have the "sound," more like a sub-sonic concussion, reach us two or three seconds later. This is literally being part of an event some twenty miles away—as verified by your witness of the eruption—through the ground you are standing on.

This country presents various and never-ending opportunities to witness, from a sense of humility, the several ways Nature demonstrates her colossal powers.

* * * * *

Kaeru no uta ga
Kikoete kuru yo
Gua! gua! gua! gua!
Gero-gero, gero-gero, gua, gua, gua!

The song of the frogs
You are about to hear (*literally, something like,* "Hearing comes")
Gua! etc...
Gero, etc...

This is one of those delightful children's playground songs that lends itself to being sung as a round. As few as four people, up to 40, I suppose, could be divided into basically two—but sometimes, three, or four groups. The first group sings the first half the song, through ...*kuru yo*, and the second group begins the song as the first group begins the *Gua, gua* part. If not everyone is terminally shy, if people actually give this a try, by the third time through it, you'll feel like you're getting the hang of it. Of course, any song that breaks into two musically complementary pieces works as well: "Row, Row, Row Your Boat" is a good example. However, there is something to be said for people practicing the song in spite of its being in an unfamiliar language.

When I was a kid, maybe five years old, my mother taught me a French round, and a lack of familiarity with the language was not at all an impediment toward learning it:

Frere Jacques, Frere Jacques, dormez-vous, dormez-vous?
Sonnez les matines, sonnez les matines: Ding, ding, dong. Ding, ding,
dong.

"Are you sleeping, are you sleeping, brother Jack, brother Jack?
Morning bells are ringing, morning bells are ringing: Ding, ding, dong. Ding, ding, dong."

Through repetition of the simple melodic structure, you "learn" without thinking about it. This round exercise needs no further justification than the pleasure generated in the doing, and the *Kaeru* song works as well as any.

1987

<u>January 15</u>: *Seijin no hi,* or Adult Day. Anyone who became twenty within the last year celebrates becoming formally an adult on this national holiday. These newly minted adults are out with their families sporting their most fashionable finery, *struttin' their stuff.* For the men, it's a new, generally dark suit and a plain, matching tie on a white shirt. Ah, but in the case of the young women, most families spring for the costs associated with wearing a formal silk kimono for maidens.

Recently, families are more likely to rent the kimono, and all the accoutrements—the *obi,* a very long sash to be wrapped around the woman's mid-section, *tabi,* white, button up, toed socks, and *geta,* wooden, sandal-like footwear. Frankly, the chances for a modern woman to wear a kimono in her lifetime are limited—and modern women are hugely grateful for that fact, when considering access and facilitation of commonplace bodily functions, to speak circumspectly. The choice of kimono is entirely dependent on the stage of life of the wearer, and the nature of the event. Is she married, or still single? Is it an evening at the Kabuki theater, or obligatory attendance of a wake or funeral? Silk is quite delicate and requires a lot of care, so nowadays most prefer renting for the dozen-or-so lifetime events that require one, thereby avoiding the dry cleaning, special care, and valuable storage space.

Adult Day is a good opportunity to spend some time loitering around a fairly big train station, say, Yokohama, and admire—or outright ogle, more like it—the opulently arrayed public presentation of "mature," ambulatory flower blossoms. My inclination is to take a bunch of pictures with my little Olympus camera, but invariably I am caught in the act and I get scowled at. They remain *bi-jin,* feminine beauties, even in the midst of a look of reproach.

Suiyobi (Wednesday), <u>February 25</u>. Thoughts on the death of a fellow gaijin and *Eigo* peddler: John Hains died 2/23/87 probably of exposure, or a heart attack; he was found in his car, likely too drunk to drive, so he just fell asleep. He was 45 years old, one month younger than me. I have decidedly conflicting feelings about the man, and I'm more than a little curious why, at the end of his life, I have this urge to come to a "final" evaluation, and render some kind of subconscious eulogy. No doubt this was enhanced by conversations with Sally and Stacy last night, and tonight with Sally and Mike. John was kin, in many ways, a fellow traveler. Through many chance meetings at Sally's "Gaijin Bochi" ("Foreigners' Graveyard") Bar, I'd gotten to know him fairly well: raised in Kansas by foster parents, joined the Navy at 17, volunteered for Vietnam. Coming from the 180-degree polar opposite on the Vietnam issue, we had ample opportunity to explore each other's perspective, and in a strange way, it drew us closer. He'd written a manuscript about his Vietnam experience, a thinly disguised autobiography. He'd nearly been killed, and had to scrape up pieces of comrades; without question, a thoroughly traumatizing experience. As far as I'm concerned, he was lucky to survive *that* time, let alone to 1987.

I come from the view that one who volunteers for Vietnam... well, it's not hard to imagine curiosity and a willingness to tempt Death in pursuit of honor through the age-old occupation of soldiering being the motivation; adventure and presumed wisdom gleaned from purposeful exposure to life-and-death situations... as a rationale for "snuffing gooks." But the sympathy I can muster for such folks stems from the realization that they weren't exposed to the same information and influences that I was, and were hence, blind to the utter immorality in allowing themselves to be put in such a situation, when the outcome of the civil war of the tiny Southeast Asian country posed no threat to the US. Few issues in my life have seemed to me to be revealed in such stark contrasts—black or white; no gradations of any color—as America's involvement in Vietnam.

But to return to John (as opposed to polemics), he was a conspicuously unhappy man. The primary means of beating back his misery was through booze and the pursuit of sex. He always drank a lot, but he was pretty good at holding his liquor until these last four or five months when he frequently got so blitzed that he got very caustic, belligerent, and offensive. After a few of these sessions when it was clear the booze was doing the talking, I could pretty much shrug off his barbs—and I'd seen Sally on more than one occasion cut him off from further alcohol purchases—but it was hard being in his presence when he was trying to put the make on some sweet young thing.

I once overheard him ask a terrified young lady, "Do you mind if I feel your leg?" She had a functional command of English, and was trying to improve it by attending Stacey's "Boston Academy." But this *in-the-field*

112

practice of basic spoken English hadn't at all prepared her for this kind of situation. Stacey and Mitch were sitting opposite the table from John and this timorous waif, about to be mauled by this leering drunk, when I walked up. I couldn't believe what I was hearing at first, but quickly intervened, advising her to tell him an emphatic *No!* I'll bet that line actually worked for him some of the time—out of naiveté, and an unwillingness to refuse intentions that run the gamut from completely abhorrent, to mildly curious, to vaguely interested.

If there was to be any thigh palpation going on, it should be me performing the research, floated my little thought bubbles. *Under more discreet circumstances, if you please. This is no way to conduct a proper seduction.* But that was John Hains in those waning months: Losing civility, not to speak of dignity.

San gatsu, mika, March 3: *Hina Matsuri,* or the Doll Festival. Families who have a daughter invariably celebrate this day by displaying a set of dolls dressed in silk finery in the style of the Heian Period (794 to 1185). Even families that live in tiny, cramped apartments usually make the effort with a correspondingly smaller display. Some are centuries old, displayed on a set of tiers, three being minimal, and seven tiers being elaborate. Rich families with large houses set aside a whole room, perhaps a 4 ½ tatami space, for a conspicuous array. On the bottom step are arranged Heian Period equipment in miniature, a chest of drawers, *tansu,* cooking materials, baskets of goods, a palanquin, tools and weapons. The second step features servants and lesser family members, and the top tier features a Heian-Period Emperor in his 9th century goofy hat, and his wife in 10 or 12 layers of silk kimono. One of my students told me, if the house wife does not set up the Hina display, no matter how modest, the dolls will weep in their wrapping and the tears will stain the clothing.

This cultural event focuses on girls, not that it matters, in terms of the dolls. These are "dolls" only in the sense of being miniature replicas of people, animals, and equipment. They are strictly not to be played with. They are expensive and far too fragile for normal rough-house play.

I feel a little sorry for the young girls: *The annual celebration in honor of you girls approaches! Here is this marvelous miniature display of dolls and trappings from days of long, long ago! Look to your heart's content, but you*

113

may not touch.... Most families set up their Hina displays a week or more before March 3 to give the family, especially the girls, a chance to gaze upon the dolls and ponder this 1000-to-1200 year tradition—and try to make sense of it all. Then, it all comes down, repackaged, and put away for another year, usually in the few days following March 3.

Nichiyobi, San gatsu, san ju nichi (Sunday, March 30). Sakura season is upon us again, the brief time when otherwise dull tree trunks and branches are transformed into radiant clouds of delicate pink blossoms. It happens in the space of a few days, rarely longer than two weeks for a specific tree. In the urban-dense area of the Kanto Plain—something approaching 40 million people within a fifty mile radius of Tokyo Bay—there are very few tree-lined streets, though small, "postage stamp" parks with their handful of trees do occur in the outlying smaller cities, like Fujisawa. And of course no self-respecting temple (Buddhist) or shrine (Shinto) would be situated without being surrounded by exquisitely maintained grounds. The final source of vegetation is the fortunate property owner who possesses a garden area. Especially in winter, when the few deciduous trees have no visible growth, the cityscape is asphalt and concrete and steel: dark, dreary colors on a human-wrought backdrop.

All the more reason to celebrate this harbinger of spring, this botanically sudden explosion of blossoms. The effect is quite striking. The Japanese Weather service alerts the entire nation regarding the advance of sakura blossoms from Kyushu through Shikoku and Southwest Honshu, our vicinity of the Kanto Plain, and finally, Tohoku/Northern Honshu and Hokkaido. Since winters vary year to year in their severity and duration, the onset of sakura bloom cannot be predicted with much accuracy more than, say, a week or so out. The approach is updated on the evening weather report, even to the finesse of predicting *man kai*, or peak bloom, after which, in a week-to-ten-days' time, the petals will be shedding in snowy banks beneath the trees.

My students have taught me that there are four distinct, popular types of sakura: The most popular and widespread, at least in the Kanto area, is

1) *Somei Yoshino*, the traditional, five-petaled, very delicately pink blossoms produced in wild profusion. No leaf growth at the time of blossoms.

114

2) *Yaei Zakura*, said to be heartier than *Somei Yoshino*, has darker pink petals with eight petals per blossom, giving the impression of a thicker flower. Also, leaves begin to appear during the blossoming period.

3) *Shidari Zakura*, a not particularly tall variety of sakura, distinctive for the tendency for its branches to droop, as they extend away from the trunk, like Weeping Willows. And

4) *Yama Sakura* tend to bloom a little later, as you might expect, since these trees are found in higher elevations. Pure white blossoms are accompanied by budding leaves.

Most people mark the occasion with a group event, often company sponsored, when they can sit on ground cloths with friends, and eat and drink too much. And sing. Everybody knows a half dozen or so old, traditional songs—the Japanese equivalent to "I've Been Working on the Railroad," "Red River Valley," or "You Are My Sunshine." With enough alcohol, virtually any group can and will engage in singing contests, such as *Who can sing the loudest? Whose attempts are the most outrageously off key?* It's one of those deals where, if you are a participant, this is one of the best get-togethers you've ever experienced! If, on the other hand, you are sitting 25 feet away with a less intoxicated group, well, it's just not as fun.

In the evenings, and holidays in particular, the parks are jammed with revelers, often company groups. It is a sight to behold; the relevant *kotowaza* for the occasion is *Hana yori dango,* which loosely means, Good food (and by implication, drink; the two are rarely taken separately in party mode) is preferable to flower blossoms, or blossom gazing. But of course, people use the Sakura bloom as a pretext to have an outdoor party, and thereby have both. We should update the proverb to say, *Hana to dango,* "Flowers <u>and</u> food." I've done the group flower-viewing party thing a few times, and have always enjoyed myself. I like social events like that; I generally manage better at them than the formal events. But if I had my druthers, I'd pick a weekday evening, and a viewing site off the beaten track, not in the midst the hordes, but in relative privacy—such as out-of-the-way crannies on the grounds of Tsurugaoka Hachiman Gu, with a comely young lady to aid me in musing on the eternal verities, not the least of which is the transitory nature of beauty, perhaps venturing a kiss in the natural interplay of things…

Kimiko and I have enjoyed more than one spring sakura bloom in Kamakura, Hachiman Gu in particular. That long, raised stone walkway up the center of Waka Miya Oji Street, known as *dan katsura*, is flanked on both sides with sakura strung with electrically lit paper lanterns. It's quite difficult to avoid being drawn into the setting. Then, if there's a moon out, well, it's surrender to the moment.

Between our two lives
there is also the life of
the cherry blossom

Inochi futatsu no
naka ni ikitaru
sakura kana
Matsuo Basho (16)

Tachi gui: Stand-up Dining, or Quickie Noodles

In the "Simple Comforts" Department, I'd like to recommend the station platform *tachi gui* experience. These are the standing-only group pods where, for around a couple hundred yen, you can get a big bowl of piping hot noodles in broth—and whatever else you want added, *kuruma ebi*, a four inch long shrimp, battered and tempura-fried, or some of the tempura cracklings, *kasu*, the little broken off pieces that give a different texture and flavor. But the important choice is between *udon* or *soba* noodles. Udon is made from wheat with a high gluten content, similar to semolina wheat that European-style noodles are made from. Soba noodles are made from buckwheat flour; the taste of these noodles is quite distinct from wheat-flour noodles. It's pretty hard to imagine you've come this far without having eaten standard semolina noodles; I mean, think of all the different Italian-food inspired pastas you've consumed. However, if you haven't yet tried soba noodles in their natural state, pilgrim, it's time you broadened your horizons.

Imagine, it's freezing-ass cold out there, and you've got a few minutes to kill until your train comes. You shoulder into a warm and cheery *tachi gui*, plug some yen into the machine near the door, push the button that'll spit out the ticket telling the *sobaya-san* manager, what you want. No matter what you order, it's the same size bowl and the same basic *dashi* broth, a mixture of

116

dried sea weed with a hint of *katsuobushi*, or dried, shaved bonito tuna. You choose which noodles, and which additions. The average businessman will have a steaming bowl of noodles in front of him, *wari bashi*, throw-away wood chopsticks, at the ready, within a minute of setting foot on the premises. This same commuter wolfs, along with the noodles, a considerable intake of air in an attempt to partially cool them. He hoovers the lot in an additional three minutes flat, with no apparent injury to the esophagus or throat from the second degree burns incurred.

Need I mention that when this harried sojourner commences sucking air and scalding hot noodles—surrounded by eight or nine other frenetic consumers—it is quite the symphony? An aural treat, as if created by a large organism (think, Jabba the Hutt's homely, larval half-brother) with many portals, all sibilant, gasping for air as if through a viscid layer. Somebody really should record one of these slurpathons for posterity.

Surreptitiously, I get scrutinized now and then in these circumstances. This is, of course, because I am unavoidably gaijin. But a part of the curiosity is the fact that I don't make a sound in consuming my noodles. Oh, the shame of it! I've tried, for the sake of assimilating into the culture and all, but I can't seem to manage it. Chalk it up to childhood upbringing, the stern parental admonition against the audible intake of air during the consumption of any liquid has left me blocked from a liberated, fully-aspirated intake of noodles and broth. The ignominy! As a result, it frequently takes me ten or twelves minutes to consume a scalding hot bowl and move on—that's three separate *kaisha-in*, businessmen, in sequence, occupying the space next to me at the stand-up counter. It appears that I over-stay my allotted time; however, thankfully, nobody is hard-nosed about it. Perhaps the entertainment value I provide, in some small way, compensates for my extended stay.

Sodai gomi

This was a system of refuse collection which focused on large-scale household throw-away items taking place once a month at designated street corners throughout the greater neighborhood—alas, this is couched in the past tense, since this popular practice was disbanded by 1993 or '94, to the dismay of a loyal cadre of avid recyclers. The Japanese term for utilizing as much as you can, to avoid throwing away anything with potential value, meaning, or use, is *Motai nai*, "Don't be wasteful," which did not seem to apply when it came to *sodai gomi* day. Small dwellings, combined with upwardly mobile consumers, equaled throwaway goods with "life"—utility, function, even beauty, sometimes—left in them. Items frequently cast off included furniture, appliances, from toaster ovens to refrigerators, kitchenware, futons, "art," antiques, you name it; anything that couldn't go out with the kitchen scraps. I basically furnished my Kugenuma house by perusing the monthly neighborhood stashes the evening before the pickup. By dusk the scavenging would begin. People would stop by on bicycle, sometimes by pickup truck, and most folks had thought to bring a flashlight. After a couple of "shopping" excursions, you got to recognize the regulars. There was a special camaraderie associated with our collective harvest of this well-to-do neighborhood's cast offs, despite it being considered a socially disreputable practice.

Kimiko was scandalized; there's a kind of built-in assumption that we were behaving like the desperately poor, rooting around in the filth and waste of others. It took her a while before she could begin to see that there might be a different interpretation, an alter-narrative. We were recycling that which was use*less* to one family, but use*ful* to another. I don't think she ever entirely came around, but chalked it up to just another eccentricity, part of the "package," the complicated totality that, for better *and* worse, is her gaijin *koibito*, lover, her *hunka hunka burnin' love*. Ah, but my kids loved the treasure hunt as much as I did.

Most of the regulars had a particular item in mind, and might snag this or that oddment beyond their focus, if it were enticing enough. Due to my haunting the local one-day-per-month dump site over the first few months, I was able to provide my initially barren digs with a prized *kotatsu*, sofa, a couple of wooden chairs, a dining table, two chests of drawers, framed paintings and photographs for the walls, lamps, a classy bookcase, a fully functional refrigerator in want of a good scrubbing, and an unbelievable assortment of plates, bowls, pots, and pans. A treasured score was a stoneware sake jug, stylized kanji of the sake brewer baked into the glaze, easily 75 to a hundred years old. To tell the truth, I had the occasional twinge of guilt, a scavenger at heart though I am, watching the bulk of it going to waste.

It's sobering to see how thoroughly Japan has become such a consumer-based society. I guess it's unreasonable to think the Japanese could long produce quality consumer goods for the world before succumbing to the temptation to own more and better quality merchandise, themselves, having been seduced by the status that comes with owning fine possessions. Otherwise, frankly, you would be left to ponder, *What is all this money for? This money that I've worked so hard to earn, what does it buy?* This form of power is a very strong narcotic. Few who are suddenly exposed to the opportunity to thoroughly explore self-indulgence—e.g., make a killing on Wall Street, or win the lottery—are able to resist the acquisitive attraction. That would certainly include the majority of Americans, *et moi*, me too, stuck in Me-First Gear. Isn't it the only, or certainly primary, "game in town"? The one we've all been groomed to pursue? In practice, God and Country represent the moral and political framework, and the social legitimation to indulge the power of your accumulated wealth. *Amen!*

As a wrap up of *sodai gomi* and related issues, I've recently heard of the term applied as a "euphemism" to aging, retired husbands. We become large, bulky, in the way, unsightly, long out of fashion, essentially useless: the common fate of geriatric husbands?!

May 27: A letter to my parents:

I've held off writing, thinking good news in the form of a work visa was imminent. After all, at least two months have elapsed since I submitted the application. However, my naïve optimism has suffered some setbacks of late. It begins to look like I won't be able to come until after my kids' visit (July 10 through August 18). It turns out the immigration department has asked for supporting documentation from my prospective sponsor—a relatively small English institute in nearby Chigasaki—as recently as last Friday. In exasperation, I had a friend call the agency for a status report. The response was, they would begin to evaluate my application when all the necessary paperwork was before them, and that the material requested last Friday had not yet been received. Thus, with this last revelation, I suppose I should cultivate some saint-like patience (decidedly not my strong suit). Another little matter requiring my patience: I sent Gina a demand draft for 3,200 dollars American to cover the cost of flight tickets for the kids, and she promptly lost the check. The initiating bank here has begun the procedure to recover the money (stop payment, etc.), which could take six months. Which means, if my kids are going to come this summer, I have to pony up the money _again_.

On to a brighter subject: She's the same young lady I've been seeing, on and off, since shortly after I arrived. Despite formidable obstacles, I guess you could say I've been persistent, so in the last few months we've been talking about making the big commitment. I've told you a little of her background; She is expected to carry on the family traditions, business and duties, being the first born of the first born (no brothers), 18 generations of the same family at the same location. Her relatives are appalled at the notion of having a barbarian in the family. The shock waves in the extended family (grandmother, parents, six uncles, two aunts, 23 cousins...) are reverberating yet.

Next month, for the first time I've been summoned to their lair for their first hand inspection of this sly beast who has ensnared their precious butterfly, spider-like in its web. These family elders need to see if they can fathom the spell I've cast on their fair maiden, to see if they can somehow break the trance, and ward off the evil curse. It should be an interesting meeting—if I'm not garroted on the spot. The big commitment means marriage, if her family approves, or living together as if married, if they don't. The assumption is they will come around eventually. There is a fairly widespread prejudice against foreigners among the older generation, especially as potential sons in law. I suppose it is rooted in ancient xenophobic myths; they are probably universal. Remember that her parents' generation would have lived through the Second World War, when the official narrative was Americans were greedy, bloodthirsty barbarians.

Her name is Kimiko Morikawa and she is charming, spirited, cheerful, guileless, and fully capable of providing a lifetime of challenge and mystery. As for "brave, clean, and reverent," she is indeed brave to take on the wrath of the older generation by living with a gaijin, to say nothing of the courage she exhibits in coping with my unique set of quirks and idiosyncrasies. Cleanliness is doubtless more intrinsically associated with the Japanese than with any other culture, certainly relative to America/Americans. For better or worse, the little lady's standards of cleanliness far outshine my own. Furthermore, I am delighted to say, she is quite irreverent!

It's likely she will come with me to visit you in the fall...

120

Tsukiji, Tokyo's Central Fish Market

Yoshi-san, the proprietor of "Fujiyoshi," a top-rank tempura shop in Fujisawa, had been my one-on-one student for more than a year when we got to talking about Tsukiji, Tokyo's central fish market. In spite of working as the primary chef for lunch and dinner, seven days a week, this poor guy trains to Tsukiji first thing six days a week in order to personally select the biggest, freshest scallops, and other shell fish; squid, *kujira*/ whale, and perhaps eight or ten different types of fish, to be trucked to his shop by 11 that morning. I guess I expressed enough interest in Yoshi-san's descriptions of the market for him to invite me and my visiting kids along on one of his shopping excursions. On the agreed upon morning, we caught the first Odakyu out of Kugenuma Kaigan and transferred over to the Tokaido line, to meet Yoshi-san on the last car of the 5:07 am (or somesuch ungodly hour) train to Tokyo. I can't remember exactly, but I'd say we had to change lines at least once; that's the beauty of the Japanese rail system. As long as you can figure out where you want to go—not always a given with hapless Gaijin—in the Greater Tokyo area, you're never too far from a train station. And it rarely takes longer than about ten minutes for the next train.

Finally we arrived at Tsukiji, this vast, sprawling city block, alive with frenetic activity; I was going to say, it's a beehive, but a hornets' nest might be more apt. I was glad we were along with Yoshi-san, who'd done this hundreds of times before. The trick was to stay close at hand but out of his way. There were several access ways to this otherwise enclosed collective life form, and through these portals watchful people entered, and left. To these people, being agile and attentive were survival requirements in this largest fish market in the world, for if they were careless, if they let down their guard, say, by failing to see one of several motorized freight movers, the warrior wasps, come barreling down the lane, maybe a thousand pounds of steel and other heavy, hard material, times twenty mph in a collision with a not very attentive and suddenly very sorry human—165 lbs, composed of materials not at all hard—well, the result of that collision would be a pretty good chance for outright, or within 48 hours, transcendence from the corporal realm.

These power carts are similar to American fork lifts in that they are powered by propane, and have very small wheels covered in hard rubber—meaning they are only good on reasonably level concrete or asphalt surfaces. Otherwise, the Japanese version is not all like the Western forklift. The local rig is a flat deck, perhaps a meter and a half wide by two and a half long, by 50 cm high, for transport of crates of marine delectables. The operator stands at the pointed front, like a captain at the prow of his ship. He controls steering as well as power by means of controls attached to the steering wheel at the top of a vertical shaft. This shaft goes through a heavy steel bracket mounted to the front of the cart, then on to a set of wheels mounted on either side of the base of the shaft. Finally, the propane-driven motor is mounted to the side of the shaft so that it swivels as the steering wheel is turned. This motor pulls the deck and its cargo over a pair of wheels on a common axle; the frame looks like a triangle.

It looks like a fairly bizarre contraption at first, but these carts haul ass up and down the corridors, always at top speed, maybe 20 mph. These cross-hatched "roads" connect the main portals with all the subcontracting dealers, one proprietor in particular, a giant, cigarette-puffing *kaeru* (frog), squat and a pallid gray, croaking out to one and all: *Irashai!...rashai!...rashai!* Welcome! Right this way... over here... this way!

These cart drivers understand that the road sides must be maintained as safe areas for pedestrians, most of whom are here to negotiate purchases of piscine carcasses, the *raison d'etre* for their collective presence, after all. OK, so it looks bad running down the customers in the act of paying money, especially if they were transacting in those "safe" buffer zones alongside the freight access roads.

But the center of those transport byways presents a different narrative. It is unquestionably open season on people who forget where they are and wander into the already fairly narrow and indistinct roadway. If they are not very light footed, or very lucky, they are apt to be hit. Yoshi-san was quite clear of the danger these vehicles' drivers posed to the unwary before we arrived at Tsukiji, and it didn't take long for me to understand the extent of the threat. For one thing, these drivers often go flying by each other, just like automobiles on the nation's highways, except in this case, there are no designated lanes for these somewhat arbitrary roads, no traffic signals at the intersections. With no traffic management, no signals, it is borderline chaos all the time, and the slow-witted observer should not have come, for s/he has become a personal experiment concerning the theory of natural selection.

Yoshi-san must have stopped at eight, maybe ten fish-monger shops where he personally selected the oysters, scallops, and several varieties of clams and sea snails, then on to the next vender who specialized in, say, the tuna family of sleek, dark-fleshed fish, halibut, and so on. He'd sign chits for the order, to be delivered to his restaurant by late morning. When he'd made his rounds and completed his orders, we took leave, where outside, dawn had finally committed to another sunrise. Before heading back, if memory serves, we went into a neighborhood noodle shop for a hot bowl, to warm us up for the hour-plus nod on the train back to Fujisawa. I was glad to have gone; it was definitely a unique experience. You never saw so many different denizens from the sea, all purported to be edible! To tell the truth, though, I was glad to get out of there, too. I was getting a little shell shocked, a bit twitchy/jumpy at sudden motor noises nearby. The perils that might befall my children seemed a little more likely inside Tsukiji, than outside, where the borders were more distinct, the crowding not so acute, and the motorized threats not so omnidirectional.

Editorial update at time of publication: At the first auction of the new year, 2016, a prize *Hon maguro*, the over-fished and endangered Bluefin tuna, weighing in at 441 pounds, sold for the staggering sum of $117,000, or $265 per pound (according to "The Washington Post," bylined in "The Oregonian," +/- 1/16/16). A staggering tidbit! To make a substantial meal from this fish, say you were having some friends over, could necessitate you to taking out a sizeable mortgage on your house.

Kujira (whales)

The issue of whaling, and the world's reaction to Japan's annual hunt, came up from time to time in current issues of conversation classes. On several controversial issues, I have felt I was able to represent a particular interpretation as to why, from an outsider's point of view, something should, or should not be accepted as policy. Regarding *Kujira*, whales, however, mammals from the Order of *Cetacea*, I feel a certain amount of ambiguity.

123

That is to say, I understand and empathize with at least a portion of the argument that each side seems to represent.

From what I know of the Japanese position, whaling has been a centuries-long tradition, one aspect of harvesting the oceans for the bounty they offer, not unlike seafaring cultures the world over. Kimiko cites the belief that had Japan not been whaling in the recovery time following WW II, many people would have suffered from lack of protein. She asserts that back then beef and pork were so scarce that they were only available to the rich. That, had whale meat not been made available to children through the school lunch program, there would certainly have been higher incidences of brain damage due to severe protein deficiency among school-age children. Generally, nutrition was a hard-scrabble concern in those days, and eating whale meat mitigated the dilemma significantly. One of my students reported that as late as 1962, 30% of meat consumption nationwide was whale. This gentleman said, in terms of whale hunting, it was not a question of "good" or "bad," but what was expedient in delivering adequate protein to the most people.

I think it is safe to say the opposing view would like for the hunting of all marine mammals to stop. That's all whales, dolphins, porpoises, seals, walruses, sea lions, and so on. The reasons are complicated, but run something like this: It is bad enough for the environment to devote so much of the earth's surface to raising domesticated animals for food, but it is wholly unjustifiable to continue to raid wild populations for the meat, and other non-critical resources, they provide. We humans came very close to hunting to extinction several species of whale. Since the bans, initiated by international agencies in the last century, some of the species have recovered quite well—a victory for all—but some remain on the endangered species list; these have not recovered sufficiently to approximate pre-hunting populations.

Interestingly, the people who make the argument against the continued hunting of whales don't seem to express the same concerns as to the rest of sea life as potential food. To be sure, generally we are in accord when facing the human-caused extinction, be that the Blue Whale or the Bluefin Tuna. To knowingly drive a species to extinction for any reason cannot be condoned, and for those who relentlessly pursue this result for profit, well, let's hope this degree of greed assures its perpetrators a secure berth in the very lowest spirals of Dante's Inferno. Otherwise, it feels to me like there's an implied

124

kinship based on fellow Mammalia membership that we simply don't feel with fish, say, or squid, or crabs. Another part of this bias is the widespread acceptance that members of *Cetacea* have a sophisticated intra-species language permitting them to plan group strategies, practice the pelagic equivalent of the "barbershop quartet," and try out pick-up lines. Whales are like us! We shouldn't eat creatures that have brains/thinking processes that resemble ours. But it's ok to gorge ourselves on cows, pigs, chickens, and sheep with any semblance of native intelligence bred out of them over the centuries in deference to faster growth, and more flesh per unit of food.

The anti-hunting argument would have us sharply curtail our current war on the rest of the biosphere, with patient and deliberate management, in the hopes of us collectively surviving another century. Vegetarians can make the argument that we should back away from our consumption of *any* animal protein. Protein from animals, in many ways, is not as healthy as grain/legume-based protein, and requires far more acreage to produce meat protein than possible from grains and legumes. This I get. But I just don't see the argument of fellow meat eaters that it's ok to raise and butcher cows and pigs, or hunt deer and elk for the meat, but not ok to hunt non-threatened sea-going mammals for food.

To Kimiko's point that whale meat came to the rescue of a generation of children facing health-threatening protein deficiency, whether true or not, those conditions do not apply to the current social wellbeing of the country. Japan's economic successes over the last 40 years have catapulted her to the top tier of the food chain. So, no more argument for consuming whale based on need; now it's a matter of taste, often a very expensive taste. Fair enough, the Marketplace dictates that for every demand, (within human possibility) there will be a supply. But this marketplace view of the globe now needs to be contingent on a caveat, a rather critical caveat, it turns out: *Thou shalt not eradicate a species* for profit, or any other reason. Even though we humans have clearly demonstrated that we have the power, we absolutely do not have the right to obliterate all the members of a distinct way of life, having evolved over hundreds of thousands, if not millions, of years to occupy their own unique niche.

I've heard this referred to as the Noah Principle, where the Biblical Noah was the gatekeeper as to which species could board his Arc and which would be denied, thus facing extinction in the Great Flood. We are not God, and God did not give us (if *us* includes *me*) permission to consume to *exhaustion* vast realms of the biosphere. Or to plunder the mineral resources, the birthright of all generations, in the scope of a few generations, through blind consumption and greed. This is us, the short-lived Anthropocene epoch, hurtling toward another mass extinction.

With this universal prohibition of species-cide firmly established, it ought to be possible, based on good science, to hunt modest numbers of wild species, including non-endangered whales, as far as I'm concerned. I am not a vegetarian, though I consider vegetarians as occupying the moral high ground in conversations of how we *should* consume Earth's resources—in health as well as moral terms—and how to provide high-quality protein most efficiently (grains and legumes over animal protein by a land-use factor of one to ten). But is there a case to be made for a moderate flesh eater? For those of us who grew up guiltlessly enjoying the flavors, aromas, even the texture in masticating a slab of flash-broiled albacore tuna, or maybe a juicy ribeye steak, just on the rare side of medium—it's not an easy adjustment to accept complete renunciation of creature-based foods. Perhaps the best I'll be able to manage is to moderate my indulgences, including meat—and in terms of health, this is not a bad idea for all of us.

I probably held forth on this general topic (blowhard that I am, given any encouragement) in one or more of my conversation classes, invariably in support of Japan's right to harvest international waters like other countries do—always with the proviso not to fish or hunt threatened/endangered species. I am told most of Japan's annual harvest is from Minke whales, one of the smaller whales that number in the hundreds of thousands in the Antarctic region. I'm reassured, further, that the few non-Minke whales hunted are not from threatened or endangered species; I hope I am not being naïve in this instance.

A couple of my students from my "Amazons' Class" (so named for their strength of character and intellectual ferocity), Masako-san and Sumino-san, tested my alleged willingness to eat a meal where whale is the whole show— as opposed to a tiny morsel from a sashimi tray. They invited me to a lunch at a well-known whale restaurant near Shibuya, one of the hubs of Tokyo. Knowing how rabid many Americans have become on this issue, they might

126

have wanted to see for themselves that I was as flexible and moderate on this subject as I had made myself out to be. You bet, I was/am open to eating whale—altogether now, *just not from an endangered species.*

This restaurant served—besides the trappings that accompany every self-respecting *yu gohan,* the afternoon/ evening repast (rice, clear soup/*miso shiru,* pickles/*oshinko,* and tea/*ocha*) —kujira. And nothing but kujira. We had sashimi whale, tempura whale, thin sliced, lightly grilled whale; we had it baked, and it was served in a *nabe,* a stew with lots of vegetables, sometimes noodles; we had it served in every conceivable manner. Some two and a half hours later, we waddled out of the place stuffed to the gills. *Oishikata!* Excellent, a supreme culinary treat! The texture of beef infused with the aroma/flavor of the sea. I shudder to think what the tab came to, but I was their guest; I was not to ask.

<u>August 9:</u> One of the highlights—no pun intended—of my kids' month-long visit was for us to be invited along with the Yoshida tribe to climb Fuji-san, 3776 meters/12,389 feet. I'd climbed it by night two years previously with Tommy Ogawa. Before that, I had climbed the South Sister, Oregon's second highest peak at 10,500 ft. or so, but I don't think my children had done any climbing resembling Fujisan. This time we'd climb it by day; early, as in dawn. Dr. Yoshida drove us the evening before to his *beso,* vacation house in rustic setting, on the shore of *Ashinoko,* Lake Ashi, in the foothills of Fujisan, making a dawn departure a lot more humane.

Eight of us made the ascent: Yasuo-san, the *futago,* twin boys, Keiichi and Satoru, at Loren's age (eleven years old), their cousin, Naoko, my three mountain goats, and me. I don't think anything unusual happened either on the way up or down, for which we are grateful, to be sure. At the outset, Yasuo-san bought us all hiking staffs, octagonally-cut poles 1 ½ inches thick and about five feet long. After reaching the summit, about six hours from setting out, we had some lunch, rested, and signed each other's hiking poles before hiking the hour loop around the caldera. Then, it was a 2 ½ hour descent to the van at the Fifth Station. The only downside to the whole adventure was Lorenzo getting nauseous from over-exertion and *hypoxia,* systemic oxygen deprivation, we surmise. After such exertion, we all should have been hungry, so back at the *beso,* we all ate. I don't think Loren over-ate, but his body was

127

still struggling to adjust to the severe conditions it had just been exposed to. The poor kid was a sick puppy for a few hours. Impressive projectile vomiting was the featured event.

Here's *Onei-chan*, elder sister Petra's retrospective of the day:

I remember the day we climbed Fuji-San. We set out very early in the morning, at first light, as I recall. The climb was really a hike—steep in some places, and in other places not so strenuous. There were about ten of us hiking together that day and the challenge for the grownups was to keep an eye on all of us kids. No telling how many other people ascended Fuji-San that day, but we passed others along the trail many times. And this is something that stood out to me from this experience.

Almost every time we encountered another party making their ascent, they would speak words of encouragement to us. Now, maybe that's just because we were gaijin, and they knew it was special to have foreigners climbing their sacred mountain, but I really do think it was the common practice to greet all fellow mountaineers with, "Gambate, ne?" Or, "Gambate ma sho!" (Let's work hard).

In the US, while on a hike, I am accustomed to greeting others with a "hi" or "hello," but never have I heard "keep working hard!" as a greeting. As I reflect on that right now, I wonder if climbing Mt. Fuji is a tiny microcosm of the Japanese society as a whole, wherein you have a group mentality, a "we're ALL in this together and we're ALL going to make it" kind of thinking. Thus, greeting a complete stranger on the trail with, "Keep working hard!" (And its appropriate response, "Hai, Gambaro!" -- "yes, I will work hard!") is an encouragement and a reminder that working together we will accomplish a great task.

We did accomplish a task that day—we both summited and descended Mt. Fuji in one day, and the memory of those experiences will stay with me for the rest of my life.

September 2: We Americans are prone to using nicknames in place of formal names for friends and ordinary people, especially in casual situations, which frankly, is most of the time. The name I normally go by, Tony, is itself a diminutive for Anthony, one of the names that appears on my birth certificate, but I have never gone by Anthony, or Carl, the other given name on my birth

128

record, since I am Carl III. After all, my father answered to that name and he had seniority. Anyway, somewhere along this time I decided to call Kimiko by a nickname, not because I found her given name unappealing or difficult to pronounce, but simply to personalize our relationship. It seems to be a predilection of mine. I could have settled for "Honey," or "Sweetheart," or "Darling," I guess, but they felt too generic and treacly for me. Over-the-top sticky, and cringe inducing, or so I thought. But what to call her remained an issue.

My impression is Japanese husbands and wives don't really address each other by given names—it's more of that *ishin denshin* inter-awareness, I suspect. Anyway, this casual search coincided with my discovery of Paul Simon's 1986 musical masterpiece, "Graceland." Inasmuch as the music from this album-Compact Disc is a collaboration with South African musicians, most of the songs have an exotic if not haunting quality about them, but I was especially intrigued by the lyrics to "You Can Call Me Al." There were several allusions within the lyrics that seemed to match my circumstances. I accede to the reader's imagination as to an elaboration:

> *A man walks down the street*
> *He says why am I soft in the middle now*
> *Why am I soft in the middle*
> *The rest of my life is so hard*
> *I need a photo-opportunity*
> *I want a shot at redemption*
> *Don't want to end up a cartoon*
> *In a cartoon graveyard*
> *Bonedigger Bonedigger*
> *Dogs in the moonlight*
> *Far away my well-lit door*
> *Mr. Beerbelly Beerbelly*
> *Get these mutts away from me*
> *You know I don't find this stuff amusing anymore*
>
> (Chorus) *If you'll be my bodyguard*
> *I can be your long lost pal*

129

I can call you Betty
And Betty when you call me
You can call me Al, call me Al

A man walks down the street
He says why am I short of attention
Got a short little span of attention
And wo, my nights are so long
Where's my wife and family
What if I die here
Who'll be my role model
Now that my role model is
Gone Gone
He ducked back down the alley
With some roly-poly little bat-faced girl
All along along
There were incidents and accidents
There were hints and allegations

(Chorus)

A man walks down the street
It's a street in a strange world
Maybe it's the Third World
Maybe it's his first time around
He doesn't speak the language
He holds no currency
He is a foreign man
He is surrounded by the sound
The sound
Cattle in the marketplace
Scatterlings and orphanages
He looks around, around
He sees angels in the architecture
Spinning in infinity

He says Amen! And Hallelujah!

(Chorus) *If you'll be my bodyguard...*

(Words and music by Paul Simon, from the "Graceland" Compact Disc, copyrighted 1986)
The little lady has been "Betty" ever since. /Beh/ and /ti/ conform flawlessly to Japanese phonology, but alas, the single English syllable /Al/ does not (since Japanese does not permit a final /l/, or /r/, for that matter). The closest Nihongo permits would be the two syllables /Ah/ and /ru/. Thus I have remained "Tony." Except for the occasions where I'm to attend to something serious or immediate; at which time, it's *Oi!*, roughly translated as, *Hey you! Hop to it!*

September 28: *From a letter to my children:*
A few things are different since I've been back. The most obvious is that it's actually cool. We left for our 20-day visit Sept. 2nd*, and you can best believe it was as you'd left it: sweltering, gasping, sweat-drenched days, with little relief during the feverish nights—How could you forget? Well, cross my heart, it's already jacket time. Last night I needed two blankets for most of the night. One hears a lot about the splendors of four seasons, and then there are places like Hawaii (and maybe southern Florida?) with basically one season in terms of temperature range, with rainy and non-rainy variants. But this is the only place I've lived with two seasons, the shift taking place in about three weeks. The poor Plant Kingdom is in shock, and us hominids shuttering all the windows, and reaching for our coats, wondering aloud, Wasn't it just last week I was walking around in a T-shirt trying to keep cool? As a side benefit of the cooler weather, the gokiburi (cockroaches) are noticeably slowed. Yesterday I snuffed two in one blow.*
Another change since youse left, within a week of your departure, that charming dog two doors down from me disappeared. Before you jump to conclusions, rest assured that I wouldn't stoop to such nefarious deeds. Actually, the whole family seems to have pulled up stakes. I kind of miss the beast; he was always there to "greet" me after the long train ride home from some far-flung class. To say nothing of his rousing morning sendoff. Then too,

131

he used to inspire the ogre in me; just the right amount of stimulus to induce the Jekyll/Hyde transformation. Now and then one appreciates—no, craves—such a catharsis, doncha think?

Petra, what do your friends think of your "Ducks parad street" shirt?* Maybe that you are a little stranger than meets the eye? A worthy impression to strive for, and one of my operating credos. Keep 'em off guard, or put another way, try to preserve the mystery. It's a fine line and sometimes difficult to maintain. Clearly, in most instances, it's counter-productive to come across as a full-fledged, wild-eyed, frothing-at-the-mouth looney. What we should strive for is just a mote of finely tuned weirdness to spring on the folks about the time they're sitting back in their chairs, confident they've got you completely pegged. A little skew, a modicum of tilt, will up your stock and will keep them slightly off guard at the same time.

(Ah, timeless words of wisdom from the sage paterfamilias!)

*While perusing a whole department store floor of teen fashion, my first born seized on this particular cotton pullover as a suitable example of Japanese fractured English.

August, or early September: The Interrogation

In this timeframe, m'lady and I decided to make public our relationship by announcing our engagement. Before we could do that, however, we would have to present ourselves in formal supplication before the assembled Morikawa council of elders, ten or twelve of them, to seek their approval. Stories had been making the rounds, troubling accounts that I had abandoned a former wife and three children to pursue their fair princess; other lurid accounts were whispered. It was beyond dispute that my potential father-in-law, Morikawa Keiichiro, and his seven younger siblings were to a person emphatically opposed to this unholy union.

Here's a *kotowaza*, proverb, appropriate to the occasion:
Jishin, kaminari, kaji, oyaji.
"Earthquakes, lightning, fires, and fathers" (14)

132

Of all the natural disasters to be encountered on these shores, the most feared is the senior male family member of a Japanese household.

Supporters and advisors in our camp explained we needed someone who could testify from personal experience as to the integrity and steadfastness of my character, and the quality of my life-goals and intentions. (*Asking a lot, wouldn't you say?*) This person would have to pack some social clout; he'd need to bring some stature, some gravitas. To my unbelievably good fortune, such a person existed! Furthermore, he volunteered for the challenge! Iwata-san had both the public presence and the willingness to preside as our initial match-maker, or go-between (*Nakoudo-san*). For years, most Tuesday evenings from 7:30 to 9:30 or so, in wide-ranging discussions we got to know each other pretty well. He understood how I thought, and we shared many interpretations of the human condition. So, he was willing to go to bat for me, willing to speak on my behalf. As icing to the cake, Iwata-san is a well-known actor. His stage name is Taguchi Kei, recognizable over the years primarily for his performances (stage, cinema, and TV) in Edo Period *chambara* (samurai sword fight) dramatizations. Needless to say, the Morikawa clan was excited to watch this fading celebrity work out, eager to see if Taguchi Kei *sensei* could make the case for this marriage.

This auspicious event took place on a Saturday afternoon, when most people would be available; Iwata-san and I arrived about the appointed time to find the family primed. As I recall, we were invited into the family conference room (12 *tsubo*, or 24 *tatami*s in size) and bade to sit in the center of the room, a couple of *zabutons*, floor cushions, indicating the place. We were served tea and everybody made small talk, gradually yielding to more substantive colloquy. The interrogators were arrayed in a huge semi-circle, father (*Otoh-san*), grandmother, the matriarch, and the uncles nearest in age to father sat in front of us, while younger uncles, aunts, and spouses spread to the outskirts of the half-circle, to our sides. None of Kimiko's twenty or so cousins were to be seen. One supposes they were occupied out in back heating the tar in a big caldron. And collecting the feathers.

For upwards of an hour I sat there and tried not to look ridiculous when at best, I could understand three in ten words. I concentrated on maintaining composure, presenting a polite smile and feigning equanimity with the world while studiously avoiding eye contact with the glowering uncles. What I really felt, however, was miniaturized to half my normal size, stripped of my clothes, and bound to a brightly-lit table, arms and legs shackled outstretched. The Morikawa family, all thirty or so adult members, would then be invited to follow up on any questions they might have for me. They would be encouraged to poke and prod my anatomy with sharp and jagged surgical and dental instruments—not to mention a Dremel tool with a complete range of fittings—in case there were any lingering concerns. They might, for example, feel emboldened to test my tolerance for pain: *Was I... sure... I didn't have... something... to confess?* Under such provocation, I suspect I'd readily spill my guts, metaphorically—reveal my deepest secrets, tell you anything you want to know—in a groveling attempt to avoid the literal event of spilling my entrails.

Incredibly, despite the Torquemada Inquisition imagery haunting me, what first sprang to mind was how embarrassing/embarrassed I'd be, a total wuss as to sensitivity and endurance of pain, screaming my head off for mercy, or failing that, a quick, humane dispatch.

I couldn't attest to the specific content of the interview. When we finally left, the family decision concerning our marriage was left somewhat in limbo, but the clear sense was that Iwata-san had calmly deflected all the barbs the family could muster. Our ace in the hole was Kimiko's feelings. Regardless of the family-succession obligations, her desires had to be considered— especially since there was a strong implication that Kimiko was prepared to marry me, with or without their approval. This could very well have been a bluff, but fortunately, the senior clan members counselled against continuing the opposition, and I was immensely grateful not to have been the source of a family schism.

The surprise in all this was Kimiko's grandmother, who supported us from the beginning. Mother didn't get a vote; she didn't matter, but *obaachan*, grandmother, was the one, next to Father, you might expect to be a traditionalist with strong feelings about preserving family rites as she had always known them. She had lived through the Great Kanto Earthquake and the dire conditions of the Second World War. She bore nine children, the first four during wartime. I don't suppose there are records of how tall she was as a mature young woman. Over a lifetime of severe hardship and deprivation has reduced her to brittle, paper-thin skeletal structure. Standing up for the old gal is a permanent bend at the waist. Her height now is about 3 ½ feet. She virtually raised Kimiko and her sister, so she understood Kimiko's true feelings. I had spent some time with this august relic, always with a smile and a twinkle in her eye for me. I was enchanted. It took a while for the reality to sink in, but once it did, some weeks later, the family was all in.

Iwata/Taguchi-san was unable to be our *nakoudo-san* at the wedding (April 3, 1988) as he had already committed to be part of a stage performance in the Kansai area for weeks around that date. After some hemming and hawing, Yoshida-san—actually three or four years my junior—agreed to serve that role on the arranged date; we had already contracted with a Fujisawa wedding hall, a mere five or six minute walk from the north side of the central station.

The Eighteenth First Born

From time to time, Morikawa Kiichiro must have pondered the strangeness of his life. He was the eldest, the "princeling" among eight siblings from a well-established family. As a result, he was coddled, pampered, and spoiled in his youth. But by the spring of 1945, as WWII was winding down, this 17-year-old, heir apparent to the local Morikawa dynasty, was called up and groomed to take that one way ticket, use his flying machine with its weaponry and his life, to try to stem the American Maritime advance. Japan was just about out of munitions, out of manufacturing capacity, and crucially, just about out of manpower. The homeland dipped deeper and deeper into reserves. It had come to this; Japan would use its barely trained *Kamikaze* (divine wind) aviators in their Mitsubishi Zeros as flying bombs to protect the homeland from the barbarian invasion. Before that could happen to Kiichiro, however, Hiroshima and Nagasaki were obliterated with thermonuclear weapons of mass civilian destruction, and then the war was over.

As far as enemy occupations go, Supreme Commander of Allied Forces in the Pacific, General Douglas MacArthur's regime turned out to be better than virtually anyone expected. To be sure, the Japanese had grounds to be

135

apprehensive, given their own predilections in occupying conquered lands. In short, there are standard military-issue invasions and occupations, and then there are those of a more humane sort. The *Bakafu* (military regime) of MacArthur, during the seven-year occupation, was benign and populist, by most standards. He instituted land reform, broke up large land holdings and distributed smaller parcels to the people; he dismantled the *Zaibatsu,* cartels of vertically integrated mega-corporations (Sumitomo, Matsui, Mitsubishi, and Yasuda) acting in collusion for control of the economy. His administration also instituted the so-called Peace Constitution, which prohibited a standing military (later interpreted as allowing Self-Defense Forces); and last but not least, the general spared the Showa Emperor, Hirohito's life by making him exempt from prosecution—for his part in promoting and supporting the war. This absolution recognized this man as an important symbol of national identity, and restored some dignity to this devastated country.

Japan permits, or tolerates, multiple US military bases on its soil in exchange for being a *strategic ally* under the US defense umbrella, originally as protection from Stalin and Russia's expansionist inclinations. America's post-war military *protection* had the immediate benefit of freeing up Japan's economy to pursue value-added innovation to non-military products, for sale to the consumers of the world (for an interesting contrast, see Tokugawa Dynasty, below). To its credit, Japan has not been reticent. One of the few stunning anthropogenic changes to have occurred in the four decades since the end of WW II has been the Japanese "economic miracle," having catapulted her from a nation in ruins, to the world's second largest economy. The Japanese people's ability to bring focus to the common task of rebuilding the country through productive employment for all, one could argue, is unique to the cultural makeup of Japan.

But for Kiichiro-san 43 years later, oh, the bitter pill! He would have to submit to his daughter's marriage with one of these latter-day blue-eyed devils.

<u>September 30</u>: The Emperor has been ailing of late; not so remarkable for a man of 86, but it's giving the country the jitters. For the record, he seems to have suffered from a blockage in the small intestines near the duodenum. He

136

is responding to treatment, we are told. His condition is said to be not cancerous. Because he is like a sweet, cuddly, old granddad he is fondly—if possibly irreverently—referred to as *Ten chan*. The *ten* from *Tenno*, meaning Emperor, and *chan* as a diminutive suffix, initially used to denote a cute girl, gradually extending to youthful, usually unmarried women, and finally applied to conspicuous figures in an ironic, if not a subtly derisive way, e.g., *Ya chan* referring to a *Yakuza* hoodlum.

This Showa Emperor has reigned for 62 years, longer than any other monarch in history, except for Queen Victoria of the United Kingdom. The Japanese calendar reckons the years according to the rule of the current Emperor, hence Showa 62. I imagine the old boy is getting a little weary of all the minutia of protocol the *Kunaicho,* the Imperial Household Agency, requires of him minute by minute, hour by hour, throughout every day of his life. Then, there's the fawning obsequiousness he has to put up with. He'd doubtless prefer to chill with some music videos on TV, pop down to the neighborhood 7-11 for some chips and brew during the 15-minute commercial break. Cop a feel from the wife... He's only the third emperor since the royalty was restored to a governing role in society, when the 15th Tokugawa Shogunate relinquished authority for "governance" of this newly defined "nation-state" to the Meiji Emperor.

The Tokugawa Dynasty, *Edo Jidai*

As Heraclitus observed more than 2500 years ago, "The only constant is change." Everything changes, all the time. But most of the changes occur incrementally, piecemeal, at a pace that is imperceptible to most people—if it were not thus in large measure, if things behaved randomly despite our best effort to understand them, we would lose any sense of predictability and our world would exist in chaos. By stark contrast, however, once in a great while a profound change happens, everything pivots on one discrete event, and thenceforward the world is forever altered. Such an event happened to the world of the Japanese at *Sekigahara*, a site of wooded hills, a wide expansive plain, and tree-lined creek bottoms, in latter-day Gifu Prefecture, on September 21, 1600. On this date what came to be known as the Armies of the

East met in mortal combat with the Armies of the West. By day's end the fate of Nippon for the next two and a half centuries had been decided.

During those warring decades leading up to Sekigahara, each fiefdom was controlled by one regional lord, the clan leader (daimyo), and his clan allies, until being displaced by another, with the emperor serving in Kyoto as Mikado continuity and the figurehead for ceremonial occasions. With the defeat of each daimyo and his local *Bakafu* (military administration), the conquered land would be confiscated and parceled out to the victor and his loyal clans, the size of which was determined by the relative strength of the lords and their fighting force of loyalist samurai. But all that would soon change with the new Tokugawa Shogun in the new capital of Edo, the name of this modest regional town situated on the bay near the confluence of three rivers in the Kanto Plain, soon to be the military, political, economic, and cultural capital of this newly and conclusively consolidated "country."

On this occasion Tokugawa Ieyasu finally took charge of the fragmented, warring clans once and for all. Without his decisive victory there would not have been an Edo Period, and no assurance of two-and-a-half centuries of "peace," though this period of calm and stability, this cessation of warfare, was imposed by the conquerors. In short order, a single generation, it became clear to one and all that fealty to one master, the Tokugawa *bakafu*, was vastly preferable to the unpredictable series of warlords the average vassal had faced for centuries up to that point.

Sekigahara! How did Ieyasu manage to achieve this all-important victory? After all, he was the underdog. At the outset, he commanded fewer forces than his opponents, and the Western Forces had the previous day to build defensive fortifications and wait for the arrival of the Eastern Forces. Furthermore, this battleground was closer to the home turf of most of the clans that made up the Western Forces. It was a simple matter to construct the narrative that Ieyasu and the clans that made up the Eastern Forces were the "invaders," the "usurpers" of what should rightfully have been the authority of the Shogun delivered to Ishida Mitsunari, Commander of the Western Armies, and Regent for the son of the recently deceased Toyotomi Hideyoshi. Hideyoshi had earned the mantle from his predecessor, the assassinated Oda Nobunaga, the first to consolidate a semblance of country-wide power, shaky though it was, in over a century.

But Ieyasu had served under Oda Nobunaga as a loyal retainer, as well. In fact he was the senior clan leader loyal to Oda, and as such, had legitimate claim to lead the country out of the power vacuum that existed following Toyotomi Hideyoshi's death. Wikipedia (search "Sekigahara") estimates that between 172 and 190 thousand combined forces met on the field of battle that day, perhaps the greatest number of combatants in history to clash in one blood-drenched event until Napoleon's campaigns, two centuries later.

Consider for a moment, the logistics of providing for this many troops. Most of them were foot soldiers. The Eastern forces would have marched to this place on the main road, the Tokaido, from Edo and environs through Hakone Pass, Tanzawa Mountains and others. Would their clan lords, the daimyo, feed these men? Tend to their minor wounds or injuries? Forget about shelter. These warriors would have to shelter themselves with what they could carry, in addition to their weapons and armor, but they could hardly be expected to carry more than a day's rations. This suggests there must have been hundreds, perhaps thousands of non-combatants bringing up the rear of this train primarily to prepare the staple ration, rice, one *masu* per warrior, per day. A *masu* is a wooden cube with an open top, about 3 ½ inches on a side. This unit of measure was doled out to every *bushi*, warrior, marching under your banner. Presumably logistics provides this amount of rice already cooked and still warm. In terms of weapons of the day there would have been archers with perhaps 50 arrows each; a contingent of cavalry, some thousands of horsemen and their mounts; lancers each packing 10 to 12 foot lances and halberds; and the backbone of the infantry, the thousands of swordsmen, each with a 32 to 38 inch *katana,* and a shorter, foot-long *tanto* for very close quarters. Also, guns had become a part of warfare during the previous thirty years or so, and both sides had contingents of artillery.

So how did Ieyasu (at 58, an old man, for those times) manage to prevail on that fateful day? It's safe to say that every clan had its own intelligence network, "spies" in the common vernacular. With Ieyasu it was a combination of knowledge of the activities of his allies as well as his enemies, thanks to his superior intelligence-gathering network, and his refined skills as negotiator and diplomat—from the school of Machiavelli. All these skills were honed and refined into this ambitious and ruthless leader. For months in advance he courted, bribed, and cajoled many damiyo as to their loyalties, in

139

the event of conflict. Ieyasu had made his pitch to the fence sitters, as well as to some who had initial opposition: rewards for covertly supporting Ieyasu's campaign—or assurances of bleak and swift reprisal should the Eastern Forces win the day without the support in question. The caveat was they would have to start the day putatively in the Western camp, and demonstrate their true allegiance after the battle had commenced.

The Armies of the West initially had 120 thousand warriors pledged. As it was, 16 clans initially participated on the West's behalf, but six of them defected, with a total of 23 thousand men, switching sides to fight alongside Ieyasu's forces. The Eastern Armies had pressed the advance and engaged the enemy before the arrival of Ieyasu's son accompanied by 35 thousand additional men approaching on the Nakasendo, a more circuitous route through the central mountain chain from Edo. Starting the fray at 8 o'clock on a chilly morning, the fog was just dissipating, and the enemy positions were coming into focus. At that point Ieyasu had only about 75 thousand warriors in the field. Two hours into the pitched battle when there was no clear-cut momentum established, the show could've gone either way. Fortunately for Ieyasu, the betrayals began. One War Lord, Kobayakawa Hideki, with between 15 and 16 thousand warriors, occupied a small hill overlooking the plain where the main forces were in the throes of battle. Ieyasu, seeing this inaction, ordered his artillery of 400 small cannon (hand-held *Arquebuses* of Portuguese design), to fire a volley to *stimulate* Kobayakawa into participation. It had the desired effect, and ultimately it turned the tide.

Once the defections started, it became the domino effect; the rest quickly followed. Not only did this numerical switch have an impact on this front of the battle but Ishida Mitsunari and the remaining daimyo had to have been deeply demoralized. The momentum had shifted, and by another few hours the choice was to flee, or stand and be slaughtered.

(Needless to say, many details of this historic battle have been left out: which daimyo in what sector prevailed at what cost, and which forces succumbed; the mounds of heads that were inspected for identification purposes before being cleaned, then buried, allies and foes alike. Though compacted for brevity's sake, I believe my account is faithful to events in the field.)

All's fair in love and war is a common expression in English—apparently, Miguel Cervantes de Espana, in the 16th century (he of "Don Quixote" fame), said as much. Even so, I have to say I felt a little disillusioned in my research of this momentous event. I was laboring under the white-washed archetype of the Samurai, the sanitized version of the noble warrior, as a disciplined and virtuous servant of his master. Implicit in this standard, the higher the level of authority all the way to the top, the more Zen-like and honorable in dealings with one's fellow man. In my naiveté, this was the upshot of my expectation. Well, as for integrity, Ieyasu was a back stabbing, double crossing, devious, slippery-tongued demon who prevailed by making and breaking pacts to suit his own agenda. One of my students, by way of "justification," pointed out that the Japanese board game Shoji—roughly parallel to Chess—permits a move of duplicity/ betrayal as a legitimate means of winning… Clearly, there was a lot at stake: not just Ieyasu's life and that of his extended family, but the future of a "united" Nippon was his to connive, contrive, and finagle. He won simply by being more ruthless than anyone else around him.

That said, from a particular perspective, the fact that there *was* a decisive victory, securing a united country under a single banner, may have been the real benefit of Sekigahara, and less so as to which set of forces defeated the other. The reality of no more internal battles for conquest or territory created a profound shift in how the traditional social stratification was valued. For 265 years the Tokugawa dynasty oversaw the longest period of peace Japan has ever known—before, or since. This simple truth resulted in tossing the Japanese social structure on its ear. Society had been organized since time immemorial, pre-Nara Period (710~794 C.E.) at least, according to the feudal caste you were born into. The long-standing hierarchy of social ranking was:

1) *Shi,* 士, or *bushi,* warrior, (leader)
2) *No,* 農, or farmer
3) *Ko,* 工, or craftsman, artisan, builder
4) *Sho,* 商, or merchant

I guess you'd have to say the priests, as guardians of the spiritual way, and aristocrat administrators, were above classification. It's interesting that these managers and message manipulators seemed to prefer anonymity and obscurity, when possible. At the opposite end, beneath the merchants, were the *Eta*, the untouchables, people without class relegated to society's dirtiest work: refuse collection and tannery work, rendering animal hides into usable leather goods.

The highest formal rank of society since the beginning of history had been the samurai, pledged to defend the lord, his high-ranking people, and the nobility, and only incidentally, the common people. Pre-Tokugawa samurai, depending on the relative strength of the feudal lord (daimyo) and the turf they occupied, could get embroiled *at any time* in kill-or-be-killed disputes. Pre-Tokugawa samurai earned their keep. By contrast, post-Sekigahara, within twenty-five years, a generation, three-quarters of the samurai came to be superfluous, and apt to get into squabbles with each other. By the third or fourth generation of the Tokugawa regime samurai could be seen as a drain on resources. Without an occasional border skirmish or rebellion to keep the local samurai on their toes, they tended to get a little defensive about their status, a little irascible, even. But the operative concept here is they still had the power of life or death over people of the lower castes. Are you feeling hungover, maybe a little surly toward authority? That would be a sure-fire recipe for losing your head! Gradually, samurai began to succumb to temptations: drinking, philandering, and gambling. In short, without battles to fight, without clans to support them, without clearly defined territory to defend, the social utility of this highest class of people fell significantly in importance.

Second in status were the farmers, those who work the soil. If the people can't eat, very quickly nothing else gets done, either. Recognition of the critical role our farmers play need not get any more complicated than this: No food, no work. In any kind of social organization, the importance of those who till the soil so that "all" may eat is, I trust, abundantly clear.

Below the farmers in social status were the craftsmen, builders, and artisans, those people (carpenters, masons, potters, clothiers, etc.) who make things that make our lives more civilized, and, on rare occasions, our festival lives more exciting. At the very bottom of the social hierarchy, in the pit, were the merchants, those trader middlemen between the producers, or manufacturers, and the consumers. In other words, *parasites*. People who profit from nothing more than facilitating the transaction between the growers/

makers of the goods, and the people prepared to buy the goods. In modern terms, we'd acknowledge that merchants are essential to urban life, but in early Edo their utility was just beginning to be apparent.

This sustained peaceful period may have been rough on the samurai, the traditional defenders from traditional enemies, now, warriors without a cause, but it meant the craftsmen and the artisans could evolve their skills more quickly and with less threat of disruption—provided that Tokugawa *bakafu* protocols were met, of course. However, shock and surprise, the class of people who made out the best in this prolonged period of imposed social stability were the low-life merchants! Those were the people who contract with the manufacturers, growers, shippers/transporters/importers, storage, distributors, all the way down to retail sales, especially in the burgeoning urban centers; those who put it all together in retail emporiums that drew in the crowds—and made the investor/owner families wealthy. Commerce! These businessmen became drivers of the economy. With the Meiji Restoration, by the dawn of the 20th century, in one generation the innovations of the coevolving business and financial sectors profoundly changed Japanese society.

This transition from the Edo to Meiji periods also ushered in authorization of *myoji,* or family names, for everyone, in addition to commonplace given names. Prior to this time, only samurai families had their own crests, *kamon*, and family names to go with them.

November 6: Last night on the news there was a brief account of Hirohito on his first perambulation in 45 days—more like staggering, than *tripping the light fandango*, it appeared. The topic of the emperor's condition came up in my class this morning, and somewhat hesitantly, I might add, since there are at least two war-time matrons in this particular circle. I shouldn't need to point out that the strongest identity with the emperor, nationalism, and "cultural purity" tends to be embraced by those most nearly approximating the old boy in age. To their credit, under careful, but discrete inquiry—so as to winnow out the merely *tatemae* from the *honne* (roughly, the distinction of the former saying what the audience wants and expects to hear, while the latter is speaking from the heart, one's passionate core, without regard to social consequences), each of these housewives professed gratitude that the emperor is no longer a living god. That in spite of being forced to accept this drastic change at the hands of the conquering warlord, MacArthur, these women say, it has rendered Japan vastly more humane, less authoritarian, less feudal and hierarchical, more egalitarian. Fujigasaki-san was in junior high school at the close of the war; she well remembers having to pray before the picture of the emperor, before entering school each day. She and Kawasaki-san both recalled the gravity with which an inadvertent act, like stepping on a newspaper photo of the emperor, was treated: Summary incarceration. If it was determined that the act was willful, execution was a real possibility. And no one dared utter such blasphemies as *Ten chan* in public, for there were chauvinists (nationalist fanatics) everywhere. It could only invite disaster. But the truly amazing thing is that this profound change was brought into existence by fiat, by decree, externally imposed, with virtually no resentment today—except in the hearts of the dwindling diehards who would have us believe that Western influences are corrupting *Nihon no kokoro*, the Japanese soul. (The noted author, Mishima Yukio was a conspicuous example of this latter camp.) To me, this suggests that the majority of Nihonjin accept the ruling based on the beneficial but largely unanticipated consequences—and regard the source of the ruling as relatively unimportant.

November 27: A letter to my parents:

Things are hunky dory with the little lady and me. Until the family business succession is ironed out, she is still expected to work at the family store selling rice, liquor, and other staples (six days a week Ugh!), but I make an appearance there now and then, and gradually the glacier is thawing. For everyone but father, the paterfamilias of the Morikawa clan. On her free day, K usually stays here with me. I'm invited (commanded?) to attend the gala extended-family gathering on the second day of the New Year's holidays— said event leaving me less than entirely thrilled, offering them, as it does, the chance for prolonged and detailed grilling. However, on occasions such as this, I stand ready, being made of stout stuff, thanks to you two. I'll let you know how it turns out. Provided I still have fingers to clutch a pen.

You asked about my opinion of the recent stock market "correction." It is and always has been a high-stakes, glorified gambling arena. The speculators who are not prepared to take a beating now and then shouldn't be there. District Court Judge Ginsberg's nomination to the Supreme Court is another matter. She may make a decent Justice (though any appointee by Reagan is suspect) precisely because she puffed the noble weed. As you know, I think there is a great deal of hypocrisy in America (and the world) about "drugs." Admittedly no one should abuse him/herself in any way. That said, most of us humans seem to fall prey to various worldly temptations from time to time, with brother Phip perhaps being something of an exception. By and large, we of the "advanced," industrialized nations don't seem to have the strength, fortitude, or self-discipline to sustain the pursuit of sainthood, while the bulk of humanity is too busy scrambling for shelter, clothing, and enough food—the real basics—to indulge the luxury of altered consciousness.

I'm neither condemning nor praising this tendency, this fall from grace, since, under the rationalization of wanting to experience life, I also have sampled here and there. Within reason and hopefully with discretion. Like most people cross culturally, and over centuries. I'm asserting that beyond survival focus, it is part of the human condition to want to change one's perspective once in a while. Being human is aspiring to perfection, whatever that is, but accepting our frailties when we fall short. If we're reasonably careful—and very fortunate, I've come to believe—we might succeed in the Journey, without any prolonged wallow in the abyss. Or too much of the cold and lonely vigil on the pinnacles. But my hackles invariably rise when some fatuous ass, who uses to the point of dependence alcohol, tobacco, caffeine, and often enough tranquilizers and/or sleeping pills, tries to tell me marijuana is justifiably classified with methamphetamine and heroin, in terms of harm to one's body and threat to society. I realize my position does not sit well with Nancy Reagan, but she and the Moral Majority have a lot of housecleaning to do before her credulity is restored.

As responsible adults, I think our most important task is to educate our youth as to the personal consequences of the indiscriminate use of drugs. All drugs. Not through threat, or intimidation of legal repercussions—that only encourages some to rise to the challenge; the concept of the "forbidden fruit" applies here—and certainly not through scare-type propaganda. Better, let's appeal to their imagination, their creative selves. By trying to give them something meaningful to live for, some identity more valid than self-indulgence. And even with our best attempts, tragically, we will lose some to

145

the hypnotic flow of the River Lethe. The point is the laws can't prevent self-indulgence, but can certainly make it worse. We delude ourselves to think otherwise. On this issue, I find myself firmly in the camp of the anarchists. We fail as parents, we fail as a society, and ultimately, we fail as a civilization if we substitute for communication, and meaning, and love, the threat of reprisal. Let's set up a timetable (say, five years?) to phase out all the drug laws—and in the meantime, work our butts off giving our kids some direction and hope for a sane future. I'll accept that I'm an idealist and a fool. Furthermore, I remain unrepentant.

Love,

December 15: I had a frustrating, vexing experience at the bank today. At one point, in a fit of pique, I nearly lurched across the counter at the leering Sugaya-san and throttled him on the spot. It all started some eight months ago (4/19/87) when I plowed through the not inconsiderable paperwork toward the purchase of a $3,200 so-called "demand draft"—what we would call a cashier's check. In any case, I surely did plunk down said amount (at ¥149 to $1, I might add) and did finally take possession of said draft. Which I then sent directly to Gina for purchase of the round-trip airline tickets for my kids to visit me, needed in full at least six weeks prior to departure time. Well, Gina *misplaced* the check. Gosh darn it all, she received the letter, realized she possessed the necessary check, then put it somewhere—perhaps in the "round file" along with the rest of the day's junk mail. Never... to be seen... again.

At this point I am able to put behind me any niggling rancor over this. Any possible, lingering disappointment—not a part of my outlook. I am likewise refraining from gratuitously psychoanalyzing Gina's subconscious for potential obstructionist inclinations.

I immediately went to the bank, whereupon Sugaya-san commenced the process to retrieve the money, after a careful accounting of the story (not an easy task, given *kare no eigo to boku no Nihongo,* his English and my Japanese), and the extensive paperwork requisite for such an undertaking. When pressed, Sugaya-san replied he did not know how long the process might take, as it was the first time it had happened in his branch of the bank. When asked for a "ball-park" estimate, he called the main office for consultation, then ventured "six months." In shock, I left matters where they stood. As of late November I made inquiry about my lost-in-the-works money. Sure enough, recently clearance had been granted by the correspondent bank—Chase Manhattan—for payment, but I'd need my guarantor's signature/*hanko* registered at the city office. This means that the quite-busy Dr. Yoshida had to take time off and go to the city office during business hours and sign this document. Which he actually did, bless his heart. So, I then took this paper back to the bank, and filled out the lines as dictated by Sugaya-san: Previous demand draft number, intended destination, and when I wrote out the original date of purchase, I started putting down a "4" (as in 4/19/87). I immediately realized he wanted <u>April</u> 19, 1987, so I crossed out the 4 and wrote out the month.

To make a long story short, by crossing out an item, *any* goddamn item, I have voided that particular application; we would need to begin anew. I felt this was completely unreasonable, and was unwilling to ask Dr. Yoshida to repeat the process. I left with the local *jefe*'s assurance that he would call me early next week after conferring with the bank muckymucks. Why I need my guarantor's involvement at all has not been adequately explained. It's not as if I were using Yoshida-san's money, or borrowing money from the bank. They had sequestered *my* money, *and* made 20 yen to each dollar due to the dollar's recent devaluation...

My frustration arises from not understanding crucial details, and not being able to tell Mr. Smiley what I'd like. Sample fantasy of our next encounter: "It's been a lot of fun playing *'Mother may I'* with my own money, sir, but I don't wish to play any longer, so the game's over. Here's what we're gonna do; if you want the form filled out letter perfect, you fill it out just like you want it, and I'll sign it where you tell me to. Then, within a very finite amount of time, say, 48 hours, you'll deposit $3,200 in my account. Or I will present to you and your bank a new, personal, and dramatic definition of the word *Yabanjin* (wild, unpredictable barbarian). You are to let your imagination conjure what that might entail." I don't know if this is his personal vendetta (for crimes I am not personally guilty of), over-zealous bank policy, or the Fates conspiring, but one way or another, I'm taking a bureaucratic hosing and the novelty has worn through! My patience "parking meter" is red-flagged.

Time's up. What's it going to be, Sugaya-san, a reasonable plan to give me back my money, or *"Deranged gaijin runs amuck in local bank. Finally subdued after ten minutes of pandemonium and terror"*? True, short of criminal charges against me, I would be summarily dispatched out of the country, my passport stamped *persona non grata*. Even so, it could not help but reflect badly on the bank.

It had always been my impression that banks have more sophisticated means of depriving you of your money.

Meishin, Superstitions

Doubtless every culture throughout history has had its own collection of peculiar customs and habits. To cite a couple of common-place examples in Western cultures, Europe and diaspora, the number thirteen has been considered so unlucky that buildings stopped acknowledging the thirteenth floor, or the thirteenth room. Building managers couldn't generate any commercial interest on the "unlucky" floor, so elevators started going from the 12th to the 14th floor, according to the references. I guess the floor doesn't exist if we don't acknowledge it. But my favorite example is, people continue to say, "God bless you," when anyone, even a total stranger, sneezes in your vicinity. As if we still believed the sneezer might actually blow her/his soul out of his/her body. So, 1) if you have a soul, and 2) if it could be blown out of your body in one quick spasm, causing concern for the soul-body connection, then 3) you must also believe that making the reflexive comment, "God bless you," would restore the sneezer's normal body-soul relationship. I am completely flummoxed as to what to say to that. To which, most folks might report, perhaps that was how the social acknowledgement came about; however, now it's just a politeness gesture. Chalk me up as rude and insensitive on this one. I'm just not going to ask God—who ought to have better things to do—to bless you solely on the basis of you having sneezed.

Japan is certainly one of, if not *the* oldest continuously autonomous culture (discounting MacArthur's post-WW II seven-year military occupation). There's a continuity of the historical narrative in the arts, spiritual practices, and rituals of common identity, some of which go back well beyond

1500 years. Plenty of time to develop a unique, rich, elaborated heritage, including superstitions. In no particular order, here are a few examples that many *Nihon-jin* observe and/or practice to this day.

1) Many people believe that one's <u>blood type</u> is strongly indicative of personality type. Since there are only four types (A, B, AB, and O), it follows that there are four distinct personalities preordained by blood—and *not* by gender, birth order, stability and well-being of the family, education, relative absence or presence of strife in life, or any other environmental influences. Me? I'm *O-gata*, O type, positive, the universal donor. Everybody's happy to get my blood. This makes me appreciated and a little part of everyone, which I favor on an intuitive level.

2) Not a few, especially women, place some degree of confidence in <u>Palmistry</u>, the revelatory pattern of lines on the palm of the customer's dominant hand. Important life outcomes are said to be revealed, as "read" by a gifted fortune teller.

3) The same <u>Astrology</u> that afflicts Europe and its offspring, as near as I can tell, operates in Japan, as well. The *location* of the planets in their orbits around the sun on the hour, day, and at the place one was born, is said to determine significant aspects of one's personality and temperament... I am struck dumb by our collective gullibility. Figuratively speaking.

4) The <u>Chinese Zodiac</u>: twelve animals (in order of appearance: the opportunist Rat, Ox, Tiger, Rabbit, Dragon, Snake, Horse, Ram, Monkey, Cock, Dog, and the Boar) that correspond to birth years on a twelve-year cycle. One's birth-year critter presumably dictates critical personality traits (16). This belief system has been around for a long time, since perhaps the Nara, or early Heian Jidai (794 to 1185 CE). There doesn't seem to be a direct connection to Buddhism, and, originating in China, it could have no connection to Shinto, suggesting this twelve-year cycle of animals is an independent means of knowing. Knowing *what*? You might well ask.

I was born in the Year of the Snake, and having been raised in the Southwest of the US—southern Arizona, to be exact—I grew up in the company of any number of lizards and snakes, actually kept snakes and large lizards as pets for a while, in a large, outdoor, walk-in "terrarium." As a result of such youthful familiarization, I am basically cool with reptiles, poisonous or not. As for attributes of a *Hebi doshi no hito*, Snake Year person, this book concedes that I "possess tremendous wisdom" (yet I am *Cassandra*, appealing to an audience of the deaf), that I am "quite vain," and "have doubts about other people's judgement... hate to fail at anything." Furthermore, I am "most intense," and "habitually overdo anything..."

Ok, I acknowledge that more than a *skosh* of the foregoing rings fairly true, though, these are highly subjective characteristics. Yes, I hate to fail, but seriously, who *likes* to fail? And under the right circumstances, who isn't "most intense"? As for "tremendous wisdom," that's just feeding one's vanity, stroking one's ego, what the con artists would call "setting the hook." Because all of us are vulnerable when it comes to being spoken of as tremendously wise, we are apt to be more disposed to accept whatever follows such ungrounded flattery out of the same mouth.

Yet, I wonder why this Snake Year personality synopsis doesn't mention my high level of skepticism for this and all other superstitions— belief systems whose efficacy cannot be demonstrated by empirical evidence. And one final cautionary statement: "Great care must be taken in the third phase of a snake-year person's life, for it is the last phase that is the worst." This all more-or-less fits, meaning, what, that I should pay that last bit of advice special credence? It's possible those attributes fit most folks. And in any event, they are sufficiently vague to apply broadly. The concluding advice for a Snake Year person was to marry an Ox Year or a Cock Year person. Kimiko was born in the Year of the Cock, but for the life of me, I can't seem to find much concordance of her presumed attributes based on birth year, and *not* her very own set of skills, outlooks, predilections, and interests that *nurture* has taught her.

There is another application of the Chinese zodiac, however. For some 1500 years up to the Meiji Restoration, and the widespread introduction of reasonably accurate time pieces, the 24-hour day had been divided into twelve increments also corresponding to the 12 zodiac animals. Top dead center, midnight, begins the new day with the first creature of the zodiac, *nezumi*, the Mouse, or Rat—though actually, the time between eleven pm and one am is considered the "hour" of the Rat. The time of the Ox fell between 1 and 3 am and the hour of *tora*, the Tiger references the time between 3 and 5 am, and so on.

5) One should <u>trim finger and toe nails</u> only during the daylight hours, so as to avoid or minimize contributing to one's parents' premature death. After the parents die, is it wide open as to nail-clipping occasioning, or should we continue to observe this nighttime prohibition on behalf of, say, aunts and uncles? Cousins? These concerns weigh heavily on us conscientious folk, anxious to cut loose without upsetting the cosmic applecart...

6) The <u>Seven Lucky Gods,</u> *Shichi fuku jin*: A collection of gods, some ancient and originating in India and China, some ancient and indigenous to Japan, each having his/her realm of influence, and generally not in competition with the other gods. In modern times (since Meiji Period, 1868), it has become customary to pray to them all together (17).

   A) Ladies first! <u>Benten-sama</u> is the only woman in the group. In one form or another, she was said to have originated in India. She has evolved to become the patron saint of the arts, including eloquence and music, which is why she is usually featured with a *biwa*, or Japanese lute, in hand. A nationally important Benzaiten Shrine is on Enoshima, walking distance from my abode in Kugenuma Kaigan, and my old stomping grounds.

   B) <u>Ebisu</u> is a perhaps mythologized real person of Yamato roots. He is said to be the god of wealth, good fortune, and candor, and perhaps most of all, the patron of "fair dealing." It's easy to see why this god would be popular.

   C) <u>Hotei</u> was a real person, Chinese name of Kaishi, who died in 916. With the passage of generations, centuries, the mythopoeia spirals out like a Fibonacci spiral expansion. Hotei-sama is patron of children, fortunetellers, wits, and bartenders (*I know, right? Who would've thought bartenders would justify their own special god?*)

D) <u>Bishamon</u> is a guardian and missionary for the Buddhist faith. Despite his warlike appearance, his role is defender against evil. So, what? You pray/make supplication to Amitaba Buddha *and* Bishamon to intercede on your behalf, and ward off any evil spirits that might be lurking in the vicinity, waiting for the opportunity to ensnare you in some vile scheme that cannot help but result in your pain and suffering... Isn't it enough to place your faith in the Buddha? Or, better yet, we might put our faith, along with our tax money, in education and the rule of law/law enforcement. Clearly, I am unable to sufficiently buy into the *Gaki*, hungry-ghosts, explanation of evil. If the spirit of Buddha is not up to the task of protecting his followers, why should we have any confidence in this Bishamon character? *Ah, but I'm committing the sin of being logical, here.*

E) <u>Daikoku</u> probably originated in India and underwent various transformations before being accepted in his present incarnation. He is said to be the patron of businessmen, farmers, and builders/craftsmen—three pre-Meiji Period social castes—with the exception of the samurai. *Hmm-m.*

F) <u>Fukurokuju</u>, according to legend, is able to raise the dead, and confer extended longevity. Indeed, if you can pull off those two feats, your reputation is set, no additional laurels necessary. I should probably be expressing my gratitude to Fukurokuju, "Lucky-sixty" sama, for helping me live as long as I have.

G) <u>Jurojin</u> has the reputation of being a heavy boozer, and fond of female companionship: the quintessential "dirty old man." Furthermore, he's said to be the god of Wisdom! Pinch me quick to prove I'm not dreaming; I think I have found my "lucky god!" (17)

7) When a <u>baby's upper teeth</u> fall out, put them under the house for the mice to eat. When the lower teeth fall out, throw them on the roof for the *oni* (demons) to eat. It's difficult for me to imagine the origins of this superstition.

8) From *Butsu metsu* to *Tai an*. In roughest outline, the days rotate through a six-day cycle, from the least lucky day, *Butsu Metsu* (said to be the day Buddha died), to the luckiest day, *Tai an*, with the other days, *Tomobiki, Senkatsu, Senpu,* and *Shako*, ranging from mostly lucky to mostly unlucky, in between the best and worst. Nobody I talked to ever acknowledged believing this setup. Still, people go to great lengths to avoid scheduling weddings, engagement announcements, or any other prominent elective event on *Butsu Metsu*, and preferably not on the days preceding and following the unluckiest of days. Nobody admits to believing there's an inherently unlucky day every six days, but that's the tradition. Very few people defy "the way it's done." After all,

> *Deru kugi wa*   The nail that sticks up
> *Utareru*   gets hammered down.

9) Thanks to <u>Lafcadio Hearn</u>, the reader has many hours of pleasure to look forward to exploring an incredible compendium of monsters, shape-shifting demons, goblins, and ghosts of all types (18). *Tengu, Kappa, Oni* (demons), *nue* (winged creatures), and *baku*, amorphous creatures that devour your dreams; what'll it be tonight? Do they fall within the concept of superstition? I'd say so. However, I'm willing to concede there are phenomena in human experience beyond empirical explanation. Still, it wouldn't hurt us in the West to ask what is gained by perpetuating the myth/superstition of, say, "the Tooth Fairy." Or even Santa Claus. (Uncle Sam?) Considering the inevitable denouement, what is the lesson we want our children to learn? That life is full of dashed expectations, and one might as well learn that lesson early? That our busy hi-tech lives preclude us from imagining richer, more relevant, more meaningful tales of beauty and fantasy?

10) If you see a lizard cross the road in front of you, it is imperative that you hide your thumbs, to avoid complicity in your parents' untimely death. *Say what?* I'm not making this up, *really!* Who knew one's genetic antecedents could be imperiled as a result of such trivial behavior on the

part of their offspring? This superstition was reported to me by an otherwise rational student, functioning normally, according to all outward indicators. Unfortunately, said student failed to provide me with any further account: *Why thumbs? What's up with the vulnerable parental units?* Let's say, your parents happened to have already departed this vale of tears; would it be alright to flash a little thumb now and then, when the mood was right? Or should one continue the ban on naked thumbs in the presence of lizards out of concern for the Ripple Effect: Other relatives— aunts, uncles, grandparents, cousins—might avoid lethal consequences of thumb exposure, but still wind up crippled, sclerotic, drooling, and cognitively out to lunch, not "present" in a meaningful sense. Oh wait, if we live long enough, we're *all* going to wind up that way… A pox on those damn road-crossing lizards!

11) A couple of Japan's uniquely endowed creatures bear special mention. They are the *Tanuki* and the *Kitsune*, or *Oinari san*, when it is associated with Shinto ritual. Tanuki is "Raccoon-Dog," a subspecies of the Asian Raccoon Dog. *Tanuki* is often mistranslated as "badger," but badger, he is not. Since the Tanuki is not native to North America, we are left with the image of something between those two creatures.

Over the centuries this real-live canid has given rise to mythical properties. The Tanuki of fable is considerably personified: He's friendly, laid back, and congenial. He's a big fan of sake and enjoys company when he drinks. Ceramic replicas of this original *party animal* are often displayed at the entrance of drinking establishments. He stands on his hind legs, has a straw hat held on with a cord under his chin, and holds a jug of sake. The only other distinguishing characteristic we notice are his gigantic testicles. Like a mature billy goat, we're talking *cojones* built for frequent action. The mock-Tanuki's penis is flaccid and proportional to his body size, but his testicles are dragging the ground. Kinda makes you suspect that this easy-going guy wants to get drunk with you (on your dime, of course) while he sniffs out any females in the vicinity. Like that foul-smelling ol' billy goat, you imagine this Tanuki's mere presence, and his potent pheromones, brings them into heat—er, I mean, elicits their arousal. Furthermore, there seems to be an interesting parallel with Greco-

154

Roman mythology: Dionysus/Bacchus, god of wine/intoxication, singing, dancing, and dramatic arts: *laisse les bontemps roulez*. Pan, and the Satyrs, whose upper bodies are human except for pointed ears and two horn nubs erupting from the forehead. The lower half of the body is the furry hindquarters on a male goat, complete with hooves instead of feet, a randy little billy-goat tail that gets waved like a flag in the breeze—and the testicular equipment to accommodate a mighty herd of nannies.

Kitsune is "fox" in Nihongo. Unlike the Tanuki where gender is prominently featured, with the Kitsune of lore, male- or female-ness doesn't seem to be relevant. *Oinari san* is also a fox, but more specifically the religious incarnation. This fox is the guardian of the cultivated fields and especially the storage building, *kura*, where the harvest is kept. Which is intuitive since foxes catch mice, among other small prey mammals, while the rodents, left unchecked, would increase exponentially, and in short order, do serious damage to one's grain stockpile, specifically rice.

In Kamakura there's a small shrine devoted to the honored fox, *Sasuke Inari jinja*. It's tucked away from anything else off in the woods, among the hills. The last 150 yards of the winding trail up to the shrine has thirty, maybe forty torii gates to pass through. Since these tori run the gamut from newish and clearly well-cared for, to derelict and slumped in neglect, it's plausible that each gate is sponsored by a separate family.

What is less intuitive is the ability of the *kitsune* to assume human shapes, especially women, complete with feminine characteristics. Thus disguised, the fox is able to lure drunk and/or otherwise befuddled men to their downfall, even death. It's never been made clear to me the moral of this outcome: Is the man fatally flawed owing to his indulgences and spontaneous desires, and therefore gets what was coming to him, his just desserts? Or conversely, is this a tragic outcome, the result of a capricious decision by a duplicitous fox performed on an unsuspecting and undeserving man? What's in it for the fox?

Incidentally, the fox (along with the coyote and the crow) features prominently in Native American folklore, as well. Why? Perhaps this creature is regarded across multiple cultures as clever, capable, and wily. In contemporary music, there has been a strong association of a fox with an attractive, young lady. Jim Morrison of the Doors sang of such a *femme*

155

fatale as a "Twentieth Century Fox," a play on the movie production company of the same name. And Jimi Hendrix had an enormous hit with "Foxy Lady."

I've endeavored to conjure descriptors that might apply to both the genus *Vulpis*, as well as young women in their prime. What occurs are words like *long, sleek, lithe, graceful*, and *nubile*—as well as *possessing a luxuriant pelt*. Maybe *wily, cunning*, and *shrewd*, as well, but case by case. Much of this speaks to a kind of hard-wired attraction of men for women in their sexual prime, cross culturally, thus hormonally driven. I'm guessing, precognitive, as originating in the amygdala, the limbic, or "lizard brain." And in most cases, subconsciously or not, women ply their natural "charms," relative to their specific culture's expectations, for all they are worth. In a looser sense, the "Christmas Cake" phenomenon, and the subconscious urge to play up one's sexual maturity in order to procreate, might apply to most women. It appears to be a hard-wired *pas de deux,* sometimes with elaborate protocols of courtship observed. Other times, it's the most basic of transactions: *My place or yours?*

A *kotowaza* that relates to this is:

Oni mo ju-hachi

Even a demon is beautiful/desirable at 18 (years of age).

Specify that the demon is female and you can sign me up. I've known a few *oni* in my time whose initial allure was an aesthetically knock-down gorgeous presentation. In addition to the kitsune/fox (noun) as a shape-shifting illusion intent on luring you astray—all for failing to be sufficiently virtuous *and* vigilant—we also speak of out-foxing (verb), or being out-foxed by, an adversary; being shrewder, more devious and cunning, than one's counterpart.

Think Tokugawa Ieyasu.

More *Nihon-glish* posted in public:

1) "Immigration service is working side by side on your heart" (on the highway approach to Narita Airport, a decidedly bizarre and chilling comment, to be sure).

156

2) "Smile and Heart" (Toyota sales shop). I can't seem to explain why these paired nouns don't work, but they definitely don't.

3) "Sugar Butter Sand Tree" (confectionary shop).

4) "Oops" (Dance studio name). That's how we all start out—at dancing, or any other skill, right? We try and—*oops!*—we fail, and our exclamation becomes acknowledgement of the failure. We try again and fail again, but some learning takes place. Soon, the failures are a matter of degree as confidence builds and competence develops. But at the outset? As the name of your studio? Well, might as well stick it out there, and get it out of the way. Or trivialize it. *Oops!*

5) "Neo Anti *Boo" (Hair salon name, complete with the asterisk).

158

<u>January 2</u>

Kimiko and I attended the Morikawa family's New Year bacchanal, an expected appearance, which in this culture, bears the equivalency of a command. Everybody was dying to get to know this *gaijin*, soon-to-be husband of Kimiko, senior member and leader of the next generation of Morikawas. Many of the celebrants had encountered me briefly prior (at the *Interrogation*), but this was our first occasion to get shit-faced drunk, while making chummy with each other. It was to be an interesting evening.

Early on, the women folk would have a New Year's toast with the group of men, and then soon head for the kitchen. For the most part, they hung out together in a smaller room off the kitchen. One imagines that the wives' preferences for a fun evening might not include sitting around a table getting blotto with their husbands, let alone with all his siblings and their spouses. Out of sympathy with the Morikawa womenfolk, Kimiko hung out with them and I was abandoned to my own coping devices.

I'll give you that alcohol relaxes the inhibitions; people feel more comfortable saying what they want when they are lit up, and alcohol is the only socially accepted way for Nihonjin to get loose. People have fun exploring their psyches in ways not available when they are sober. For a while. But when descending into one's cups becomes the routine, it's not a novelty anymore, just a quick slide to sloppy inebriation, and your only remaining friends are fellow drunks. I'm not saying any of my "uncles" are alcoholic, but that shoe just might fit in a couple of cases. For this family, to hold up under pressure while drinking throughout an evening, remaining relatively *compos mentis,* is a rite of passage and a serious challenge. Hospitality dictates that, just as you are about to put you glass of beer, *sake, shochu,* or whiskey on the table after a pull, one of your attentive neighbors will insist you permit them to fill it up again. Even with a lot of different snacks offered non-stop, you are still apt to get snockered pretty quickly.

It's every social drinker's intention to pace him/herself, of course, but people's tolerances vary widely, even within the same individual, from one event to the next. So, it is not at all easy to self-assess one's level of intoxication, and supremely easy to overstep it—owing to alcohol-induced cockiness—plunging oneself into the besotted abyss. But I was on my guard and managed to avoid retching on myself. Or anyone else (*since you were wondering*). I believe I understood, in terms of Morikawa inclusiveness, what a splendid idea it would be for me to avoid making a complete puking ass of myself, on that night, of all nights. Like a marathon runner, pacing oneself is crucial.

I'd have to admit that too many times, in my wilder youth, I have experienced alcohol-poisoning-induced peristaltic convulsions. The body savages the foolish brain for over-indulgence by spontaneously wrenching all the abdominal musculature, in an attempt to invert first, the contents, then the entire alimentary canal, from the stomach up, through the miscreant's mouth. The ultimate penance, as far as the body is concerned, would be vomiting oneself inside out. Ah, but not on this occasion.

During this plunge into general inebriation, one of my soon-to-be uncles, the second youngest and shortest, felt compelled to challenge me throughout the evening. We had drinking contests (*never a good idea!*) and arm wrestling. This guy had spent a 20-year career in the *jieitai,* Japan's Self-Defense Forces, and was doubtless in better shape than me. He was a pugnacious little Napoleon who was indeed stronger, I concede, wrestling with his dominant arm. He balked a little when I suggested we try with *my* dominant arm: *hidari,* or left side. But in the end, he pretty much had to wrestle me using left arms. Fair is fair, right? And the outcome was different, as you might imagine. All this is pointless commentary, except as background for the following: In one of his comments, this uncle wanted to emphasize how he saw himself a protector of his niece, my fiancée. As a result, he announced he would have to kill me if

A) I hurt <u>Kimiko</u> in any way? Nope.

B) I made <u>Kimiko's</u> life unhappy or miserable? No, but you're getting warmer.

C) I failed to make her evermore happy? *Bingo!*

I ask the reader to consider the subtle difference between marital failures B and C. B is low-down dirty, rotten behavior presumably prolonged over an extent of time. It is not to be condoned in any way. Still, this might not constitute behavior that rises to a level punishable by execution. But with C, you might as well shoot all the men who are married or in a committed

160

relationship, because in my limited, unscientific experience, it is flat-out impossible to provide your cherished one an uninterrupted and unwavering state of bliss, no matter what lengths you are prepared to go to… (*Husbands, guys, can I get a witness, here? Tell the truth; "always" is too high a bar, right?!*)

I nodded gravely at his besotted admonition, and made a mental note to consult with Kimiko as to the mental stability of this banty rooster of an uncle. It's never "just the booze talking," is it?

> *Ippai wa hito sake o nomi*
> *ni-hai wa sake sake o nomi*
> *sam-bai wa sake hito o nomu*

> First the man takes a drink
> then the drink takes a drink
> then the drink takes the man (14)

* * * * *

Pachinko

No urban center in Japan would be complete without at least one Pachinko parlor, a two-to-three story building exploding with flashing lights, within a block or two of the nearest station. The dazzling lights, along with the dull machine roar of thousands of steel balls clattering through a rigid maze and into metal bowls, is an attractant, it turns out, to many people who don't have a family to go home to. These people run the demographic gamut; that is to say, pachinko zombies are not age, gender, or level-of-prosperity specific. Pachinko is a kind of game people play to wile away some time.

One "rents" a bowl of steel Pachinko balls, about ½ inch in diameter, and feeds the balls into the machine you've chosen to throw your money at. In this vertical pinball machine you flip the balls, which then fall through a range of channels before disappearing. Sometimes a ball will fall through a special channel, which pays off in another 100 (or somesuch number) balls. "Winning" at pachinko means you redeem your won balls for cigarettes, or

161

soap, or other useful, everyday household goods. Banks of pachinko machines are lined up in rows, hundreds in a single brightly-lit room. When many of these machines are in use, it creates quite a background din. After the first twenty minutes, you've adapted; you've either accommodated the noise, or gone berserk. To counteract this almost soothing roar, the management has decided to *compete!* They play old martial music, strident marches from the '20s through the '40s at ear-drum rending decibels. Can't have anyone falling asleep in here. That and the fact that virtually everybody smokes; there's a gray haze hovering over the room. It is a mind-numbing, mesmerizing activity that you "win" at once in a while. The activity of the balls bouncing around in front of you requires just enough mindless visual tracking that you don't have to think about other things in your world. You can forget time, and then—lo, and behold!—it passes amazingly quickly. *What you thought would be a toss-off hour, late the morning of your day off, turned out to be eleven hours, the whole day shot. And at least ¥5,000 lighter.*

<u>March 18</u> (A letter to a friend):

Winter seems to have exhausted itself. It appears there are no more piercingly cold days left in the arsenal, so slowly, begrudgingly the cold weather is giving way to warmer, rainy days. It's a tossup: I'm tired of living in a refrigerator, but I don't much relish making my tutorial rounds on my 50cc motorbike in the sleet, either... Nothing like a complaint to get a letter off to a good start, I always say. Actually, I have little to complain about.

To serve the entree: Miss Kimiko and I are going to tie the knot! April 3, Easter Sunday, to be exact. And it's taking on all the trappings of a full-course blowout. Papa Morikawa resisted the idea for several months, but having failed to dissuade number-one daughter from her chosen folly, and in the face of growing family acquiescence, he's finally capitulated. From that point there's been no holding back—these folks are nothing if not thorough, especially among the honor-bound older generation. (Come to think of it, honor seems to matter less to the young of any culture, falling prey to the more immediate dictates of hormonal imperatives...) This marriage is seen as his last chance to show off to his family and friends, having fobbed off his only other offspring, Kimiko's younger sister, two years previously. To this end, he's pulling out all the stops this time. Weddings are a huge business in

162

Japan, and Papa is certainly going to do his part. A huge hall, used almost exclusively for such occasions, has been rented in Fujisawa. Up to 100 guests have been invited to the reception. The actual marriage will take place in a different room in the building immediately preceding the reception. It is a more exclusive event attended by some 40 family members, beginning at 10 am, with m'lady having to arrive at 8 in order to have enough time for elaborate hair dressing, facial make up, and the first of three costume changes.

The wedding ceremony takes about 30 minutes, including a Heian-Period (794~1185) bedecked Shinto priest shaking a paper-tufted wand at us by way of benediction, my reading a document in Nihongo from the aforementioned age (about as comprehensible to the attendants as Chaucerian English would be to us), and culminating with our drinking three successively larger, nearly flat bowls of sake. Then, it's off to the photo gallery for the formal portraits. Starting at 11, the three-hour reception commences, hosted by a professional Master of Ceremonies, and Dr. and Mrs. Yoshida, my long-standing guarantors, as go-betweens. Their roles are essential in coordinating the timed-to-the-minute stream of speakers and entertainers. Guests will sit at designated places around circular tables, and will be served a sumptuous combination-Chinese/ Japanese "lunch"—and at a cost of $85 per head, this lunch had damn well better be sumptuous! The go-betweens and we sit at this long table facing the guests on an 18-inch-high dais—as the main spectacle. At some point, we go from table to table lighting candles, permitting the tables' occupants to express ritualistic "best wishes," and a good deal of joking and needling the bride and groom, who bear the brunt of the humor graciously. Which is relatively easy on my part since I have no idea of what is being said.

Because Papa is a liquor retailer, we are to stave in a cask of sake for the further delight and dissipation of the assemblage. During the elaborate festivities, m'lady changes from a pure white kimono, to an elaborately decorated red kimono, and finally to a white wedding dress. I start out in a man's traditional kimono (haori and hakama), and finally inhabit a white tuxedo. I tell you, I feel less comfortable in the tux—feeling like a Tom-Jones wannabe in a Vegas revue, the lounge act—than in the kimono, strutting my stuff, slapping the folding fan (a prop) in the palm of my hand.

163

There is a towering plastic cake with a wedge of "real" cake inserted for us to photogenically cut—at the appropriate time, as instructed by the Master of Ceremonies. Toward the end of festivities, when the drunk family members have crooned their maudlin songs (Yes, karaoke is part of the billing!), and the speakers have all delivered their platitudes, I am to make a brief statement of appreciation—in two languages—and the event is finished.

As is customary, presents will be given to each guest: a set of ceramic plates and tea cups, a brandied cake, and an assortment of seafood, presumably dried, but I'm not really sure. Alcohol, especially Nihon shu (sake), but also whiskey, are selectively given. The monetary value of the gifts is approximately 50% of the money all the guests bring. Money, it must be said, is vastly more practical and convenient than toasters, wall clocks, and towel sets, a la the American style. Close family members can be counted on to cough up $400 or more, while more distant relatives and friends traditionally bring $200 to $250. Virtually all this money will immediately funnel back to Papa, who is somewhat land-rich but cash-poor, and would be seriously impacted by such a staggering outlay otherwise.

The following day we fly to London via Aeroflot, the Russian national airline, notorious for cheap flights and wretched service. The wedding is on Papa, and in a round-about way, the whole family, but the honeymoon is on us, so we sought out modest accommodations and transportation. Our round-trip airline tickets to Europe were significantly cheaper than the three or four hour rental(!) of one of Kimiko's outfits—the most flamboyant, red-patterned silk kimono—just to give wedding costs some perspective.

Our itinerary included a whirlwind pass through London: Albert Hall, Piccadilly Circus, Buckingham Palace, Kensington Gardens, and a huge chunk of a day wandering the halls of the British National Museum, mouths agape—acres of spoils, plunder from centuries of the biggest colonial power on earth—then, quenching a powerful thirst in a proper pub; and some English countryside-cum-Stonehenge. Amsterdam entailed Rembrandt, Van Gogh, and the ganja coffeehouses; Athens, the Acropolis and Plaka, my early '60s stomping grounds, and a Greek isle or three; the layers of culture in the amazing city of Byzantium/Constantinople/Istanbul; and a one-night layover in Moscow with a quick pass through Red Square, on the return trip. All in just under three weeks. Wooo Hoo-oo!

<u>Late April/early May</u>: Within a week of returning from the *keikon ryoko* (literally, marriage trip, or honeymoon), I was involved in a collision on my motorbike that nearly killed me. I was returning from my Nippon Roche pharmaceutical businessmen's class, on my way to Iwata-san's conversation-over-dinner class, when I collided with a teenage boy on a bicycle who darted in front of me from an alley way—no chance to break or swerve away from this sudden obstacle. The result of the collision was I did serious damage to his bicycle—the punk rider was virtually unscathed—but the handle bars of his bicycle nearly broke my neck, or crushed my larynx, at the very least. And I was wearing a helmet.

It was the only time (so far, knock on wood) that I needed to be transported to a hospital by ambulance, and while I didn't think then that my life was on the line, I did have difficulty breathing, or speaking clearly for some days. Also, the collision mangled my glasses, required some stiches on the bridge of my nose, and gave me a couple of bright purple shiners. Over the years, I've taken several spills on my trusty Honda 50cc bike, but this one was the worst.

Some weeks later when I'd pretty much recovered Tommy Ogawa, my comrade in the midnight ascent of Fujisan in summer of '85 and TEC stalwart, stood with me as interpreter and advisor in an arbitration meeting with the moron bicyclist and his father. They were lobbying for a bicycle replacement, while I would have liked some compensation for missed classes and revenue, and repair of glasses. I was a legitimate resident foreigner so all my medical expenses were paid for. The kid's father was quite pushy throughout the negotiation based on the implied responsibility of the bigger, heavier transportation device, a kind of Rule of the Road. For example, a car bears far more *a priori* responsibility in a collision than anything smaller, less powerful (motorbikes, bicycles, pedestrians) in part because of the assumed consequences from an accident between the two: the car might wind up with a bent fender, perhaps crumpled grill work, or a broken windshield—and no injury to the driver. The result to the motorbike rider, bicyclist, or pedestrian? All too often dead, crippled or maimed for life. The same general ratio would normally have applied in motorbike versus bicycle or pedestrian, only the results didn't run true to form in the case of the crazed teenage *kamikaze* bicyclist vs. the mild-mannered, sedate, law-abiding, nearly-killed motorbiker.

Since I can't remember the outcome of the negotiations, it must have been amicable. Or at least not antagonistic. And unlike the US, this situation had zero chance to become litigious.

A Tale of Two Dogs

Near Harajuku Station (one station out from Shibuya, itself third or fourth most important hub in Tokyo), Omotesando Dori is a very popular area for the youth, where mostly young teenagers congregate and squander their hard-come-by money and precious free time on utterly useless activities. An experience that seems to be all but irresistible to young teenage girls (12 to 15) is the "Snoopy Phenomenon." In front of Harajuku Station, some of the most expensive real estate in Tokyo (hence the nation, thus the world), is a rather narrow, two-story building called "Snoopy Town," crawling with an embarrassing throng of teenyboppers. It turns out that among all of Charles Schultz's endearing characters, Snoopy would be the one to carry on the legacy. Not Lucy, not Schroeder (my personal favorite), not the canary, not even lovable Charlie Brown himself, but Snoopy! Who knew?

A little disclaimer here; the reader deserves to know my bias pertaining to Mr. Schultz's long and successful career: *Shazzam!* I think he should have reduced or quit his output, or shown a good deal more selectivity with his cartoon satire over his last several years. I think he'd become fairly tedious and banal after decades of mining his cartoon community for material. That said, Snoopy in Japan is pure gold. Corporate product innovators must be working night and day to come up with novel ways to push products with the world-famous beagle logo on them. Because teenage girls can't seem to get enough of the adorable little dog. *Urk, gag!* Still, better a cartoon facsimile than the real creature, I suppose. Furthermore (under the rubric of "Social Engineering"), this is an infinitely better outcome than early sexuality, and way early parenthood. Perhaps any social phenomenon that retards identification with sexually mature womanhood, and emphasizes instead, prolonged girlhood, complete with dolls, could be said to promote a desirable outcome.

Ah, but the most famous dog in Tokyo is Shibuya's Hachiko. Legend has it—and that phrase should instantly trigger skepticism as to the complete veracity of the tale—legend would have us believe that a loyal Akita canine would accompany her owner to the Shibuya station every morning, seeing him off to work, then reappear to meet the Master's homecoming in the evening. Circumstances are vague, but at some point the humble, hard-working wage slave died. It seems the man had no local family, and with no one to take responsibility for the traditional Buddhist send-off ceremony, the local and prefectural governments expedited cremation of the body and liquidation of the assets... All of this of course was well beyond the cognitive capacity of Hachiko who continued to muster without fail every evening, waiting in vain for her Master's return. Until she succumbed to starvation? Was run over by a truck? Turned feral and was subdued in the act of chewing off the leg of a drunk businessman, waylaid on the way home late one night? Alas, the tale does not provide us any such meaningful hints.

This story was said to have taken place in the 1920s or '30s, a time when the powers-that-were may have been particularly eager to promote obedience, and loyalty to one's master, and acceptance without question of one's role in the grand scheme. This was a time of rapid expansion and control of colonized territory, as well as the harsh effects of the global depression, and the increasing power of the militarist/fascist regime, which broached no dissent at home...

It was entertaining, not to say instructive, to find a seat near the latter-day Hachiko, a bronze double-life-sized replica of an alert, cheerful Akita-breed of dog, on a plinth one meter cubed, doubtless designed large enough to prevent other dogs from raising a hind leg in salute *on*, as well as *to*, their famed forbearer. It is a renowned landmark and meeting place. It is also a terrific place to park a while and take stock of *les jeunes filles* mingling desultorily in mid-calf high-heel boots, exotic stockings, mini-skirts falling no lower than mid-thigh, and as often as not, in faux fur and hair dyed the range from a subtle off-black, dark brown, and auburn, to bleached blond, to say nothing of spiked pink, electric lime, or orange. Their swain counterparts slouch in purposely unkempt hairdos (too long to be short, and too short to be truly long), jeans with the pant-leg hems dragging in the street, over-large coats, the manufacturer's name/logo prominently displayed on all garments;

cigarette held languidly in one dangling hand, trying desperately not to look at anything specific, projecting a sullen countenance to the world. *Lookin' terminally cool, dude.* Preening in front of their audience. The essence of struttin' one's stuff.

In any given clot of manswarm, two out of three are engaged in reading or responding to messages displayed on the miniature screen of the electronic device, a proto-smartphone, clutched in front of them. No sign of economic hard times among this pre-adult demographic, at least in these celebrated locations.

Language considerations

I required nine years of on again, off again classroom education to receive my Bachelor's of Liberal Arts degree, when the norm was, and remains, four years. One could make the case that I am just a slow learner, but it might be closer to the truth to say I learned more broadly and thoroughly in contexts other than the classroom. So, after my first two years of hovering around the academic drain, I cashed in some investments and salable possessions, and went to Europe for just shy of a year. *To find myself,* the wags would say; hell, that was as good a reason as any, and at twenty years of age, a damn good start. Especially since academic pursuits weren't working so well at the time. A couple years later, my brother and I got in some quality travel time on an extended trip through Mexico, before he returned to Phoenix and an imperiled marriage engagement, while I continued south to Panama and back, something like six Central American countries, before returning to the university. Then in 1965~'66, I again suspended my academic studies, succumbing to wanderlust for an around-the-world pilgrimage in a year and eight months.

Did "learning" take place during these extensive excursions? I'd like to think so, though perhaps that learning—being assimilated for the most part without formal, orthodox interpretations to mediate, and being embedded in a flowing context—would be difficult to categorize, and hence, evaluate. However, one skill did get challenged and developed as a result of these journeys of discovery. I became a better communicator, at least *en español*. I'd taken a few Spanish classes around the time I travelled through eight or

168

nine Spanish speaking countries. You can bet that by the third or fourth month surrounded by español, *solamente español*, I got better at communicating.

Also, between my first trip abroad and my global circumnavigation, I wound up staying more than a year in Greece, working for an English-language newspaper, and falling prey to an *Ellenida*, a Greek damsel. By the end of my stay, without making much effort, I had acquired basic communication skills. I could make myself understood/understand others in simple Greek, *Ellenika*. Those who wish to communicate with basic grammar and vocabulary—and imagination—will create the means.

I'm *not* trying to call up accolades for my linguistic prowess—far from it; comeuppance for my hubris, my wholly unfounded pride, was soon forthcoming. What I am trying to say is some communication competence (with European languages) led me to feel I had some natural facility. I only bring this up to illustrate that he who soars high on language proficiency illusions, is soon to experience the dregs, the gutter, the abyss when said hotshot smarty pants linguist comes up against the abstruse, arcane, and labyrinthine nature of Nihongo, the very instrument by which to thrash that smug language arrogance out of you, as with a bamboo switch. A couple of serious *whacks* every day, when you least expect them, will soon teach you to forget you comprehended *anything* about a foreign language. If your hide is up to it, *you goan larn a li'l ree-spek.*

The following comprises a gratuitous and sketchy overview of Nihongo (the Japanese language), with special consideration given to bicultural/bilingual curiosities, some of which are covered more comprehensively, not to say, authoritatively, in other publications, by *real* experts in the field. *Exampli gratia*, the works of E. O. Reischauer (11) and, in terms of getting at *Nihon no kokoro*, the essence, or heart of traditional Japan, no one does it better than Lafcadio Hearn (18)—though of course neither are as *au courant*, or incisive as the treasured volume you now hold in your hand.

For a little historical landscape, during the 6th through the 9th centuries active trade took place between China and local seats of indigenous culture in what came to be called Nippon, the Land of the Rising Sun. At that time, China was seen to be the source of all things august and good, the origin of civilization. Pockets of stability and prosperity, and a burgeoning civil service in the Nara area (Yamato) and elsewhere, made it imperative that Japan develop a writing system. This was a time when *Bukyo*, Buddhism, was also flooding into Japan. It was easier to borrow the orthography from China, piggyback with *Bukyo*, than to invent a writing system of their own. It meant literate people could pretty much read Chinese and translate the text into the Nihongo of the day. Thus, we see the origins of *on yomi*, the kanji reading in fifth or sixth century *Chugoku go*, or Chinese. The trick was how to superimpose this imported script on the already fully-fledged, spoken language, or what was to become *kun yomi*. The best way the literati could think of was to invent the twin syllabaries: Hiragana, and Katakana—more on these shortly.

So what was this writing system that nascent Nihon was willing to accept? It is not a series of letters, like the Roman alphabet, abstract symbols, each representing its own phonological utterance, but no intrinsic meaning assigned. Nor is it a system of consonant-vowel pairs, or syllabaries, one step removed from letters. *Kanji* characters started out as stylized depictions of everyday scenes: *Hito* 人 looks like a person—ok, a pin-headed person with no arms, but you get the drift. *Yama* 山 looks more or less like a mountain, when you stand back far enough and squint. *Kawa* 川, with some imagination, resembles a river. Mastering the written form of one language in order to apply it to another completely unrelated language required a deep understanding of the meaning of each character in the original, as well as the native application. As a result, all kanji have at least two different readings; one set is *on yomi,* meaning "original, or Chinese reading." The other set is *kun yomi,* "country, or indigenous reading."

One of the simplest *kanji* characters takes two strokes with your writing brush: Starting from the upper right quadrant of the writing field (just to the right of an imaginary midway vertical line), make a stroke down into the lower left quadrant. Then, about half way between the beginning and the end of the first stroke, bring a stroke roughly perpendicular to the first stroke down toward the corner of the lower right quadrant:

In English, this character means "person" or "people"—since Japanese, like most Asian languages, does not explicitly distinguish singular from plural nouns. Among the pronunciation possibilities of this simple character in *on yomi* are

> *1)* *jin,* as in *Nihon jin,* "Japan person/people" or "Japanese," and its allomorph,
>
> *2)* *nin,* as in *ninki,* "popularity." Both are approximations of 5th-through-8th-century spoken Chinese.

Some common words for person/people in *kun yomi* are

> *3)* *hito,* as in *hitokage,* the "shadow of a person."
>
> *4)* *bito, koibito,* "lover."
>
> *5)* *uto, kurouto,* "an expert."
>
> *6)* *udo, nakoudo,* "a matchmaker, go between."
>
> *7)* *na, otona,* "adult(s)."
>
> *8)* *ri, futari,* "two people" (19),

and possibly others that I have no knowledge of, all pertaining to this very simple kanji. When to use one reading over another—from the eight or so choices of this one simple figure!—is the $64 question. The answer requires a quantum leap in culture and context awareness, and that does not come in 140 characters or less, a few paragraphs in Wikipedia, or getting the hang of ordering sushi at the local *isakaya.* And keep in mind, there are some kanji that require upwards of *25 strokes! For one fornicating kanji!*

So, you might well ask, along with this (at least) double reading for most of the 2000 or so kanji characters literate folks were expected to know, why in god's name would they want to pile on the two syllabaries, two written forms of the same set of 46 consonant-vowel syllables, including the basic vowels, /a/, /i/, /u/, /e/, and /o/, and the all-important, the sole, final consonant in Nihongo, /n/? An important use of Hiragana is to signal the function of the kanji in the sentence: Is this symbol a noun, an adjective, a verb, or something else? Take the idea of *Beauty*. The idea can be expressed as something/ someone to be enjoyed through the senses (taste, touch, sight, hearing, etc.): an objectified noun. It could also be an attribute of some experience, as in *beautiful* music, or a *beautiful* sunset. Finally, one can imagine engaging projects in order to express one's attempt to *beautify*, to contribute some aesthetic enhancement to life. Hiragana insertions here and there among the kanji (think of them as *post* positions rather than *pre*positions), signal to the reader the qualifiers of the content words, as well as the actors acting or being acted upon.

Furthermore, Hiragana acts as a shortcut to many native words. Take the basic word for leave-taking: *Sayonara*, which is written in Hiragana, not kanji. I'm told there is no kanji (and hence, no *on yomi*) for this most basic of leave-takings. I speculate that as of the 6th or 7th century, the Japanese had already established this word to signal "goodbye," "farewell" and chose not to adopt the *on-yomi* equivalent from Chinese. Katakana is a duplication of Hiragana; it replicates in a different script the same 45 consonant-vowel combinations, adding the final consonant /n/. Mostly, its use tells the reader the word is of "foreign origin" (interestingly, this pertains to Western languages, primarily; not Chinese). It is an approximation of the pronunciation of the word in its original language—as close a rendition as Katakana, and the phonemic possibilities of Nihongo, will allow. Katakana is also used as *furigana*, written beside the complicated kanji in small script, to give the reader an indication of the intended reading of the kanji in question.

Becoming literate in Nihongo is no frivolous task—have I flogged that deceased *equus* enough? True, the simplest kanji figures require just a few strokes. But the complicated characters can take 25 or more strokes of the brush to complete. When Nihonjin encounter an unfamiliar kanji in conversation, such as someone with an obscure name, the person with the unusual name will hold out his left hand flat and with his right index finger, will go through the steps in writing the imaginary character until the other person recognizes the kanji. The other statistic to remember is it takes knowledge of some 2000 kanji ideograms to read a newspaper—ok, exactly 1,945 kanji are officially designated as "Common-Use Characters,"(9) but then you have to add the two *kana* of 46 figures each. Compared to the 26 letters necessary to read and write English, and most European languages (with some variations), Nihongo is many times more complicated and difficult to read and write. And yet the Japanese literacy rate per capita is higher than America's. What's up with *that*?!? Social emphasis on academic accomplishment based on Confucian precepts inculcated *pre*-Buddhism?

My wife taught in the Japanese School of Portland for over ten years. This school taught almost exclusively Japanese kids living in the Portland area typically, for two or three years while the father worked at a Japan-Oregon business partnership. In international terms, this could be seen as an advantage or benefit for the students involved. Those who had such an opportunity, of course, attended American schools five days a week, and quickly got absorbed in new friends and the youth culture. "Overnight," they become age-appropriate bilingual and bicultural. But these kids *needed* to attend Nihon Gaku, the Japanese School, virtually every Saturday, in order to stay on top of kanji acquisition. This is no joke; fall behind on the relentless assimilation of kanji, and you are stigmatized for life.

The secondary function of this school is to teach mathematics to the students who are already learning grade-level-appropriate math in the American schools they attend five days a week. Asian countries, I think without exception, rank higher than their American school counterparts in Math proficiency. The consequences of falling behind your Japanese school age group—in either subject—brands the Japanese student as "strange," and "peculiar," one to be regarded with caution. Which is enough to cement your marginalization. Anathema! Too often, what should have been a benefit to these students—who have lived abroad and become fully acclimated—often brings stigma, and something of an outsider status at home.

Needless to say, arriving in Japan in my mid-forties, I was not a good candidate to become literate in Nihongo. After more than a decade I could read both *kana* and recognize 60, maybe 80 kanji. That's not a great achievement, but again, students paid me to help them improve their English, not practice my Nihongo; that message was made clear to me early on.

A major problem for English pronunciation by the Japanese is the phenomenon called *Katakana Eigo*. This is to say, most Japanese have learned to pronounce English by transposing all the sounds encountered in English to those permitted in Katakana—*ka, ki, ku. ke, ko; ma, mi, mu, me, mo; ha, hi, hu, he, ho;* and so on, for 45 discrete consonant-vowel combinations, along with additional diacritic marks to signal a change from unvoiced to voiced sounds: /s/ to /z/, /k/ to /g/, and /p/ to /b/, for example. And, to emphasize the point one more time, Nihongo has only one final consonant, /n/. Collectively, they comprise all the vocalized sounds necessary for the entire Japanese phonological range. A lot of English *does* work that way. Take the nickname, Tony, of my given name, Anthony. It has two discrete syllables in consonant-vowel combinations, /to/ and /ni/, which are perfectly suited to Japanese pronunciation. But there are a hell of a lot of words in English that end in a whole bunch of consonants other than /n/. Exampli gratia, my family name, Cole, is considered one syllable in English, but *Katakana Eigo* renders it into two syllables in order to make it pronounceable in Nihongo: Cole becomes *Ko ru*. An all-too-commonplace corporate name in English weighing in at three syllables, MacDonald's, becomes *six* when rendered into Katakana English: *Ma ku do na ru do*. If you say it fast enough, you get a stumbled-over approximation of the original, as if mumbled by an intoxicated person. With a speech impediment. A couple more examples as seen on the Odakyu Line—in katakana: *E ku su pu re su,* meaning "express," that's taking six syllables to approximate pronunciation of a two-syllable word in English. Then, there's *Shi ru ba shi to*, "Silver Seat," designated seating for the truly aged and or decrepit—provided you are able to dislodge the surly teenager invariably thereon ensconced.

Here's an example of built in, structural ambiguity in Nihongo that just barely has a counterpart in English. Homonyms are probably true of all languages: at minimum, two words, two identical sound phonemes that have different meanings, and different written characterization of the meanings, but are indistinguishable as to pronunciation. As near as I can tell, English has scads of homonym pairs. Also, there are a few triplets, such as *to, too*, and *two*; *rain, rein*, and *reign*; *do, due*, and *dew*; and *right, write*, and *rite*. There may be a few other triplets out there: *so, sew*, and *sow*; *sight, site*, and *cite*, but so far I've been unable to come up with a single English language example of a homonym quartet. Zilch. In fact, in terms of homonym triplets, nothing beyond the few cited above.

I commented to my wife, while taking a local train from her neighborhood station, Kobuchi, to Yokohama, that there sure seemed to be a lot of different ways to write a kanji for /ko/, each with its own distinct meaning. She nodded vaguely—well, of course *vaguely*; it's a cultural trait, right?

Not letting her squirm out of this, I asked point blank, "About how many?"

She shrugged in her charmingly evasive way, and answered, "I don't know, *lots*."

"More than 20, do you think?"

"Maybe. More than ten, anyway."

More than ten ways to write the sound /ko/ in kanji to signal a unique, distinct meaning! We don't really need to be more specific than that, do we? *More than ten* adequately expresses the wild, prolific use of homonyms in Nihongo. One might, at this point, begin to have some insight into Francis Xavier's pronouncement that Japanese was the "language of the devil," when considering the enormity of the task to compose a simple correspondence, even from one's familiar spoken vocabulary, if one is saddled with having to scrutinize a dozen or so ideograms for the one that signaled, say, "pleasant smile," and not the one that alluded to "putrescent stench." And little ol' innocent /ko/ could mean both those and a bunch more possible meanings, besides. A slip up like that could be socially irreparable—weeks in the doghouse, at least. And the thing is, I pulled /ko/ out of my hat. It's just one of a large number of phonemes, distinct sounds that are among the most common sounds in Japanese, in combination with other vocalized meanings occurring immediately before and after. But /ki/ is easily as common, and /ka/ is right up there. /Shi/, /to/, there are lots of them that could easily have ten, twelve, or more homonym variants. This would seem to be semantically ambiguous to an extreme extent in spoken Nihongo when compared with Eigo (English). It may be that the relative phonemic variation limitations in Japanese—only one final consonant sound, /n/, while perhaps 15 are possible in English—may have been a significant driver toward more extensive homonyms. Be that as it may, it seems to me, this phenomenon is a serious obstacle ultimately requiring large-scale kanji literacy before a broad comprehension, not to say acquisition, of Nihongo could be possible.

In significant ways Nihongo deserves the sobriquet of being "diabolical" to outsider acquisition in no small part because of the serious commitment becoming "literate" entails, even for the Japanese. But hot on the heels of literacy is the cultural sophistication required to know which social register, which manner of usage to use in everyday speech: Common vernacular, laden with slang, often the language of youth defiant of authority, vulgar, in part because they are already cast as society's second-tier citizens vs. formal, polite speech. I don't presume to understand more than the superficial outline, but considering formal/polite speech, Nihongo provides at least three "distinct" manners of speech to show the appropriate level of respect to the person with whom you are in dialogue, and in some cases, about someone else. Just wrap your Western, linguistically egalitarian mind around this, if you please!

Kei go, the category of "honorific speech," *belonging to or constituting a class of grammatical forms used in speaking to or about a social superior* ("Webster's Seventh New Collegiate Dictionary"):

1) *Teinei go*: This feels like the basic "polite form," the manner everyone should use to show basic respect to an unknown person. Let's follow a simple verb, "to come," *kuru*, in basic form—not particularly polite, but not impolite either—through the three honorific forms. In *teinei go*, *Sensei ga kimasu*, "The teacher comes/is coming."

2) *Sonkei go*: The speaker talks to the listener in a respectful manner, elevating him/her in social status relative to the speaker, in the choice and use of vocabulary. The focus is on the person being spoken to. *Sensei ga okoshininaru*, "The teacher comes/is coming." This has the same sentence construction as *teinei go*, but with a different choice of honorific verbs.

3) *Kenjo go*: In this case the speaker deliberately presents him/herself in a lower, humbler class in order to create an expanded, more eminent image of the interlocutor. The emphasis is on oneself, the speaker, and the choice of language is to show diminished status. *Watashi ga sensei no tokoro ni mairimasu*, "I come/am coming to the teacher." The meaning has changed in this latter sentence; *I* am the agent/actor in moving *to* the teacher, whereas in the two previous examples, the

176

teacher is the actor, coming *here, to me.* I can't see how they could both be literally true.

Typically, verb forms are chosen to reflect gender and status of those involved in the communication. Not only is there a verb-ending change, according to the circumstances, the entire verb stem is different, as in the above examples, depending on the politeness choice.

Furthermore, though I hesitate to reveal it for fear of shock and disbelief on the reader's part, there are at least two other specialized forms of honorific speech, god help us: *Teicho go,* and *Bika go.* The former would have us cultivate "Courteous speech" above and beyond what one might naturally assume, a la *Sonkei go,* for example. *Bika go* makes the case for beautiful words/language, much as I imagine some poetry to be. These language-choice distinctions, based on social circumstances, are beyond-subtle differentiations for speakers of most, if not all, Western languages. Formal, polite English— equivalent, I think, to *teinei go*—emphasizes respect for one's interlocutor, but I don't think the West Coast American vernacular is able to provide significant politeness distinctions beyond that. And I'm guessing that goes for native-English speakers, in general.

When we contemplate needing to learn these subtleties of register in order to be considered literate and educated *Nihongo de,* we begin to imagine we hear Francis Xavier's faint cry of despair, whispered in the breeze: *...e a lingua do diablo,* it's the Devil's language...

In addition to the above observances, women speak a different form of Nihongo than men (*wouldn't you know?*), though that distinction seems easier to adjust to than the honorific forms. Beyond gender, one is expected to quickly, automatically adjust to the appropriate register depending on the relative age and status of the person with whom you are speaking. This relative status is not immediately apparent between unacquainted *Nihonjin* on occasion, so the principle task of the communication, at least at the outset, is to gently finesse that information (relative age, family stature, home turf, educational background, gender, and place and level of employment are among the critical indicators)—all this is necessary *before* the proper register can get locked in and the real point of the conversation can get addressed. Assuming there is a matter to be discussed beyond one's social position, vis-a-vis one's interlocutor.

177

Referring to the cultural and lingual gulf between Japan and the West, Koizumi Yakumo avers,

...the underlying strangeness of this world—the psychological strangeness—is much more startling than the visible and superficial. You begin to suspect the range of it after having discovered that no adult Occidental can perfectly master the language. East and West the fundamental parts of human nature—the emotional bases of it—are much the same: the mental difference between a Japanese child and a European child is mainly potential. But with growth the difference rapidly develops and widens, till it becomes, in adult life, inexpressible. The whole of the Japanese mental superstructure evolves into forms having nothing in common with Western psychological development: the expression of thought becomes regulated, and the expression of emotion inhibited in ways that bewilder and astound. The ideas of this (sic) people are not our ideas;...their ethical life represents for us regions of thought and emotion yet unexplored, or perhaps long forgotten... Could you learn all the words in a Japanese dictionary, your acquisition would not help you in the least to make yourself understood in speaking, unless you had learned also to think like a Japanese—that is to say, to think backwards, to think upside- down and inside-out, to think in directions totally foreign to Aryan habit. Experience in the acquisition of European languages can help you to learn Japanese about as much as it could help you to acquire the language spoken by the inhabitants of Mars. To be able to use the Japanese tongue as a Japanese uses it, one would need to be born again, and have one's mind completely reconstructed, from the foundation upwards.... As for the literary language, I need only observe that to make acquaintance with it requires very much more than a knowledge of several thousand Chinese characters (21).

On the relatively rare occasion when a woman would need to refer to herself in the first person singular pronoun, *I*, in a familiar setting she would be apt to say *atashi*, or *watashi*. A man would say *boku*, or more casually, *ore*. Only in extremely formal circumstances would either man or woman use *watakushi*. The non-gender-specific suffix *san* is attached to either family name or given name, but primarily the family name. An adult referring to a male child would call him by his given name attached to *kun*, e.g., *Toshiro-*

178

kun, or more likely *Toshi-kun*. A girl would be called by her given name followed by *chan*, but youngish unmarried women can also be so called, e.g., *Hiromi-chan*, by her close friends and people of the previous generations. *Kun* and *chan* are usually used diminutively, but are sometimes employed ironically or sarcastically. (Under no circumstances should a gaijin use *chan* or *kun* casually as applied to another adult who is not an intimate.) And finally, *sama* is used when speaking to or about a person of clear superiority— in age, social status, public recognition, and so on, always with the family name. *Sama* signals deeper than normal respect.

For a few months, I taught two young daughters of a housewife who was also my student in a group of housewives. These two sweethearts, five and four years old, broke me up the first time I heard them refer to their mother, not as the normal *O-kaasan*, but *O-kaachama*, mixing the diminuitive, *chan*, with the deeper honor shown in *sama*. I'd love to know if someone put them up to that curious "contraction contradiction," or if they came up with it themselves.

On another occasion with a different class of young girls, the subject of the royal family came up, specifically the recent marriage of the Crown Prince's younger brother, Ayanomiya, to a charming young woman with the given name of Kiko—I'm sorry to report I don't know her *miyoji*, or maiden-family name. Through engagement to marriage, this has been the best public relations event to happen to the royal family in many a decade, due largely to Kiko's disarming, good-natured outlook. This group of girls clearly were in thrall of this cute *ingénue* bride, every one of them. She's around 23—half my age—and could pass for 16. So at one point I referred to this real-life princess inadvertently as Kiko-*chan*. I might have gotten away with Kiko-*san*, which is more-or-less standard respect, but the *chan* suffix speaks in some sense, down to the person referred to, or is satiric. In either case, it is grievously disrespectful to a (brand new) member of the imperial family, and these young girls knew it. They would have to set this ignorant gaijin straight. Without missing a beat, one of the brave souls piped up: *Kiko-sama, dayo!*

It's an interesting experience being taken to task socially by a group of seven year olds. Without a doubt, you can learn a lot about basic language, and culture, by hanging out with kids. *Why is that?* Perhaps, because they represent a simplified interpretation of the world around them. Maybe it's that child-like innocence and purity of vision—unclouded by much awareness of the relative nature of things, or the perception of consequences—all of which make it easier for the non-native speaker to comprehend and absorb.

Keeping track of nuanced relational distinctions is all-but insurmountable for anyone not raised in Japan, surrounded by the omnipresent but subtle interconnectedness of language and culture, as Koizumi sensei makes abundantly clear, above. Fortunately, the Japanese have no expectation of you mastering Nihongo, or the labyrinthine social code, and so make allowances for your gaffes and pratfalls, one after another. In public, the Japanese seem genuinely grateful that you make an effort to speak a politeness phrase or two in their language.

But let us native English speakers refrain from waxing too puffy on the straightforward ease of English language mastery. For better or worse, English is the product of an extravagant hodgepodge of origins, *n'est-ce pas*? Languages like Italian, Spanish, Portuguese, French, and Romanian can all claim to be direct, pedigreed progeny of Latin. That is not the case with mongrel English. Besides Latin, English is a composite of Greek, Latin filtered through French, and variants of Anglo-Saxon—and those are just the primary sources. As a result of our varied set of origins, spelling and pronunciation patterns of our lexicon are all over the place, a nightmare of confusion and incomprehension, even for the native speakers. Then, we have our regular vs. irregular verb forms, our transitive and intransitive verbs (raise/rise, lay/lie, set/sit), somewhat arbitrarily determined countable vs. non-count nouns (vegetables vs. fruit), specific vs. non-specific articles, and so on. And let us not forget the mystery of the dummy subject: What, pray tell, is the "it" in "It is warm"? Or "It's a sunny day"? (I submit that the time has come for us English speakers to learn to say, "A sunny day is. Warm is.") Since languages are inextricably linked to cultures, I suppose they are all ideocentric and at some level inherently illogical.

These and other anomalous-but-essential features of "correct" English were all surreptitiously and deviously conceived for the stated purpose of maximizing anxiety and confusion among hapless English-as-Second-Language learners. Not to mention, to provide a steady income stream for the world's intrepid, itinerant English peddlers. *Oops, did I just let the cat out of the bag?*

Beyond grammatical considerations, however, it seems to me English has built-in semantic expectations of precision and concision in normal speech, the "maxim of parsimony," beyond the ritual greetings, that are absolutely not evident in Nihongo—unless the language pertains to establishing or confirming relative dialogic status. In English, we would have you say what you mean; be as specific and explicit as you can—with the notable exception of the poetry genre. I see this tendency as polar opposite to the inherently *aimai*, or vague content, of everyday Nihongo. That, however, I concede the foregoing is dependant on the focus: Yes, English had built-in specificity as to nouns; is the noun in question countable, and if so, is it singular or plural? *And* is it unique or special in some identifiable way? Or is it ordinary, commonplace, and not central to the context? Is it *a* chair, or *the* chair?

Nihongo has no inherent need to imbue a noun with specific quality/quantity; Let the narrative carry that load. *Unless* the noun denotes a human relationship. In English, we say brother, and let adjectives et al. clarify sequence, if that is important. Nihongo makes the relationship explicit by encoding it in the vocabulary. *Oniisan* is older brother; *Ototo* is younger brother. It is not possible to say just "brother." Furthermore, if the communication should need to specifiy quantity, there are four or five distinct markers, according to

1) Living vs. inanimate: *Ii piki, ni hiki* (one, two living thing[s])
2) Cylindrical: *Ii pon, ni hon*
3) Round things: *Ichi mai, ni mai*
4) Flat things: *Ii satsu, ni satsu*

To my surprise, on more than one occasion, a student has approached me with the startling admission that English is, in some unclear way, easier, more direct, than Nihongo—the student's native language! It may be that in English one is freed to devote one's attention to the *content* of the discourse, and not have to attend to one's role in the manner of speech, vis-à-vis one's counterpart. Or such was my interpretation. Thanks to its multiple origins, English is a language rich, even vast, in descriptive, culturally varied language. This may be seen as more like an obstacle than a benefit to the second language learner, but at 75 (*2017, ed.*), I still take pleasure learning vocabulary and language usage.

September 30: Some thoughts on the imminent demise of the world's longest reigning monarch, the Showa Emperor, Hirohito. Nearly two weeks have passed since the Emperor complained of gastric pain, then vomited a huge amount of blood. Almost exactly a year ago he underwent surgery for abdominal obstruction—some would say, owing to an enlarged pancreas. This latest incident was caused by the same pancreatic tumor that was inoperable last October. As of yesterday, he's received some 3,400cc of whole blood (AB +) and 800cc of platelets, the latter in an attempt to stop the hemorrhaging. In addition, he receives oxygen when breathing becomes labored, antibiotics to try to bring down the fever. Of pain killers (narcotics) we are not informed. NHK, the national broadcasting network, gives us frequent updates, released three times a day: 9 am, 2, and 7 pm, provided by the Imperial Household Agency. It's no exaggeration to say virtually the entire country is drawn into this end-of-an-age drama. From the outset, the palace officials prepared a registry for the masses of well-wishers to sign. The newspapers report that these long lines of people, patiently waiting in the rain (in what has now been recorded as the wettest September in meteorological history—some would say, *namida ame*, or "God's tears"), at first numbering in the thousands, now well into the hundreds of thousands, gather "to pray for the Emperor's recovery." One wonders if there was a problem in translation. Is this somesort of euphemism for a peaceful death? What could we possibly mean by *recovery*?

The evidence is unmistakable that this time, the condition is terminal. The government has all but shut down. Important ministers have been called back from far-flung conferences. Only the most critical conferences abroad are attended, and even then, by less-than-senior officials. The Prime Minister is holed up in his residency; all is in a state of vigil.

His life may indeed be prolonged some days, even weeks, by artificial means, but the prognosis is zero. Are these assembled tens of thousands of people deluding themselves? Praying for a miracle to restore him to his former feeble, unsteady, 87-year-old state? Or are they, in some fashion barely perceivable to us Westerners, praying not for, but <u>to</u> his "Devine Eminence"? We should recognize that an unreckoned proportion of the population still revere this emperor as a (barely) living deity. The senior citizens of Japan endured the war and its humiliating consequences with this emperor. True, his divine status was formally eliminated by MacArthur's post-war Constitution. But one does not change attitudes accumulated over centuries simply by fiat. Especially so deeply held an attitude as to be central to national identity. Constitutionally, "officially," his role was reduced to figurehead, much like that of a European monarchy: confirming newly appointed Prime Ministers, affixing his seal to laws enacted by the Diet, the parliamentary assembly of Japan, entertaining foreign heads of state, and the like. Thus, he became the symbolic head of state, the much-needed focus for a war-ravaged society to rally behind and begin the task of rebuilding the nation. Judging from the reaction of my students on being queried about this delicate subject, a wide spectrum of meaning is applied to the symbolism of His Imperial Highness, with not a few representing the extremes.

* * * * *

Japanese is rich in repeated, or rhymed couplets, doubled up sounds that sometimes represent sounds in the real world. Here are a few examples my students have provided over the years.

1) *Achi kochi*: here and there
2) *Bara bara*: randomly placed
3) *Beto beto*: sticky
4) *Bisho bisho*: (to get) soaking wet
5) *Bochi bochi*: little by little
6) *Butsu butsu*: to mumble
7) *Dan dan*: gradually, eventually
8) *Doki-doki doki-doki:* the sound/feeling of one's heart pounding, owing to physical exertion—or emotional excitation
9) *Fua fua*: light and full of air, like a sponge, or like Wonder Bread, compressible to 1/8 the original size

10) *Goro goro*: one who loafs, lounges, or lays around
11) *Guju guju*: squishy
12) *Heto heto*: exhausted, dead tired
13) *Iro iro*: and so forth; the equivalent of *et cetera* (etc.)
14) *Jabu jabu*: the sound of clothes being scrubbed on a washboard, presumably having strictly metaphoric use for the last half century.
15) *Joki joki*: lumpy, not smooth
16) *Kotsu kotsu*: little by little
17) *Mah mah*: so so; maybe not terrific, but not so bad, either
18) *Mukashi mukashi*: long, long ago; once upon a time
19) *Naka naka*: considerably
20) *Noro noro*: slowly
21) *Nuru nuru*: slimey
22) *Pari pari*: the sound of something dry, crisp, or crunchy—like a cracker—being eaten
23) *Pera pera*: fluent, smooth
24) *Pika pika*: just brand new
25) *Soro soro*: occurring soon, appearing gradually
26) *Sowa sowa*: restless, nervous
27) *Sube sube*: smooth
28) *Waza waza*: expressly, considerably

October 5: *Ten no Heika* has received 5,400 cc of blood to date, and still the old boy hangs on. He's now been given half again as much blood as he started with—dribbled into an arm, to have it come gurgling out of his natural orifices. His jaundice is worsening, indicating liver malfunction. Some of my students mutter that their beloved emperor is being deprived a natural death, a death with dignity. Still, there is national paralysis. Schools, community and regional festivals have been cancelled, weddings postponed. The feeling is, had these various groups known he would hang on so long, they would gladly have continued their original plans, but no one, especially not the marriage celebrants, want to take a chance that he cash out on "their" day. The shame of it! What would the neighbors think? Imagine the conversation with their grandchildren 50 years later: "Yep, we tied the knot on the very <u>day</u> the Showa Age ended, plunging the entire country into gloom and dispair."

Kamakura

Nippon has had four distinct capitals throughout history: Nara, Kyoto, Kamakura, Kyoto (Part II), and Edo, which transitioned to Tokyo with the Meiji Restoration (1868). Nara, Japan's first capital city, was pitifully short-lived—less than a century. Kyoto's first phase as capital began by superseding Nara just before the beginning of the ninth century, corresponding to the supremacy of the Fujiwara clan. This powerful family maintained its preeminence by the simple expediency of marrying into the imperial family, thus sealing loyalties and alliances. However, history shows over and over again that entrenched power over time breeds corruption, which eventually gets challenged. Kyoto's initial term ended in 1185.

Among many things, Kamakura is a symbol of the dramatic end of the four-hundred-year Heian period, and the relocation of the military and political capital from Kyoto (where the emperor would remain) to Kamakura, the new seat of military and political power. *Bushi-do*, the way of the warrior, dictated that you put behind you the temptations, vices, and palace intrigues endemic to the Kyoto of the day. Minamoto no Yoritomo chose Kamakura for his new capital because it was far from Kyoto, home to the Emperor and the entrenched palace pomp and intrigue. Additionally, this new location was a place that had natural defenses against invaders. Nestled among forested hills with limited access, the main watershed was a valley perhaps two kilometers wide at the ocean and one and a half kilometers deep. At the back end of this open vale Yoritomo chose to greatly expand the shrine that his ancestors had originally consecrated, and though his efforts burned to the ground several times during the Kamakura age, it was quickly rebuilt, always larger and more elaborate. Today, Tsurugaoka Hachiman-gu, dedicated to the Minamoto clan's tutelary deity, is one of the most spectacular shrines in Japan, and every year end and the subsequent couple of days, *millions* of people make the pilgrimage to ask for New year's blessings.

Additionally, Yoritomo was aided in his decision to make Kamakura the seat of his new military government because the entire area was under the protectorate of the Hojo Clan, and his wife Masako was a Hojo (21). For the first time in Japanese history the entities of "governing" the land were separated into two parts; Yoritomo shogun would oversee the daily affairs of the public in accordance with the laws provided by the Kamakura bakafu, and the emperor would see to culture, ceremony, and continuity of the state. This system was to survive for barely 141 years, from 1192 until 1333.

This *monogatari* is Japan's second most cherished tale—after Chushingura, the story of the forty-seven *ronin*. It accounts the generational rivalry between two clans, leading to a decisive battle at *Dan no ura*, when the Genji clan (or Minamoto: it's that tradeoff between *on yomi* and *kun yomi* in choice of kanji pronunciation) finally vanquishes their age-old rivals, the Taira/Heishe. An appreciation of that victory requires some knowledge of Heian period history, so buckle up for the quickie tour.

From early Heian, the Fujiwara clan was the most powerful group, having submitted eligible daughters for marriage into the royal family over centuries. But incrementally over that period, the Fujiwara had become more arrogant and corrupt, creating animosities, even enemies, along the way. As a result, popular unrest became pronounced, precipitating a civil war, culminating in 1156 when the Heishe secured power unto themselves by defeating the Genji. At thirteen, Minamoto no Yoritomo was captured as an enemy combatant and nearly executed. The war lord Taira (or Heishe; see comment on Genji/Minamoto, above) no Kiyomori was prevailed upon by his own mother to spare the life of this little more than a child. Instead, he would be banished to the boondocks. Kiyomori and his coterie had seldom if ever left the capital Kyoto, and its environs. From their point of view, being required to live in Izu under the purview of a distant clan, the Hojo, would be *taihen iinaka*, deep country, far removed from the action in Kyoto—and out of the way.

The prophetic opening lines from the *Heike Monogatari,* "The Tale of the Heike," the rise and fall of this once mighty family, portend a common fate:

The temple bell echoes the impermanence of all things. The fading colors of the flowers testify to the truth that those who flourish must decay. Pride lasts but a little while, like a dream on a spring night. Before long, the mighty are cast down, and they are as dust before the wind (23).

186

Probably, every junior high school student in Japan has been compelled to commit this statement in original 15th century form, to memory, and perpetuate a commonly-held cultural trope of how ephemeral all human effort, all life, is. It's a bit of a morbid trip to be laying on the 14 and 15 year olds, doncha think? Couldn't we hold off until college with all this fatalism? Or at least, follow up with commentary to the effect that the time between birth and death is really all that any of us has. Since an end to all we know is a common given, what we have is the liberating, meaningful realization that one's specific lifetime is _the_ chance, our opportunity to create something good, or beautiful, or if you are lucky, something good _and_ beautiful—for however long, in months/years, we are permitted. And rising to that challenge makes life worthwhile.

Kiyomori's decision to spare Yoritomo's life amounted to one of those times when your act of compassion, your gesture of kindness—your _virtuous_ act—would come back to haunt you. To be regretted for evermore. It was to have dire consequences not for Kiyomori, but for the entire Taira clan including their child emperor Antoku.

By 1180 Yoritomo had married the daughter of the Hojo daimyo, thereby cementing the support of the dominant clan in the area, and set about raising an army to challenge the Heishi.

Minamoto no Yoshitsune was step-brother and nine years junior to Yoritomo. He too had been spared execution in defeat to the Taira in 1156, but in his case, it was an easier call since he was only four years old at the time. His banishment consisted of living in a monastery on Mt. Kurama, north of Kyoto, under austere conditions, including the rigors of samurai training. In this period of Japanese history several Buddhist sects—in stark contrast to basic assumptions most people have about Buddhism and practicing Buddhists—fought bloody turf battles as fiercely as the most bellicose daimyo, and it's possible Yoshitsune experienced hand-to-hand combat as a young teenager. Though slight of build, his one-on-one swordsmanship was peerless. However, his real genius was in planning and executing military battles; his tactical acumen was instrumental in the final battles over the Taira/Heishe in 1185.

There are several episodes pertaining to Yoshitsune's young adulthood, his winning the loyalty of Benkei, the giant warrior-monk, through his _bushi_

187

prowess; and ultimately, his futile attempts to accede to big brother's authority. They are all "true" in that they have historical data that constitute the backbone of the accounts. All our superlative anecdotes seem to be designed to support heroic attributes of the subject—the tendency of supporters of all our mythologized figures cross-culturally, our heroes throughout history, I suppose.

Yoritomo was said to be a cunning and capable leader, commander, and innovator, as in the creation of his new capital. You could say he earned the leadership role over Minamoto factions, the Hojo, and several other clans in political alliance with the Genji/Minamoto—made possible by their common opposition to all things Taira. However, what clearly stands out to me is his profound paranoia of plots, conspiracies, alliances bent of overthrowing his regime. Doubtless, some degree of wariness of the people around you provides survivor benefits, but his relentless pursuit of little brother, without a shred of evidence that Yoshitsune had ever compromised his loyalty to Yoritomo, is a fire engine scream of the corrupting, not to say maddening, influence of power. Paranoia driven to psychopathy—based in part from the subconscious guilt for surviving when the rest of the male population in succession to leadership of the Minamoto family was executed by Taira no Kiyomori. Ok, that's a stretch, but to my mind, it's plausible. He understood how incredibly fortunate he was to be spared execution. In any event, he wasn't going to take any chances. There would be no mercy for his adversaries, real or imagined—Yoshitsune, and Yoshitsune's infant son, with Shizuka Gozen—for fear of the same fate he had wreaked on the Heike. As a result, we have centuries-old sympathy for the injustice dealt the underdog, Yoshitsune: *Hogan biki*.

After some years in flight the fugitives, Yoshitsune and his loyal entourage, were finally cornered and killed/driven to suicide. Hounded to death. Now, no other Genji bloodline could possibly challenge Yoritomo's supremacy. Interestingly enough, Yoritomo did not have a long and fruitful reign. Seven years after initiating his new capital, he died from a freak accident at 52. He was thrown by his horse resulting in a slight injury to a leg, which became infected. He did not break a bone, nor did he experience arterial bleeding, but must have experienced scraped or punctured skin. Ten days later, he was dead. Could've happened to anyone. But let's just say, for the sake of argument, that a whole slew of his aggrieved ancestors, deceased spirits, ghosts (but at the same time, gods), saw their opportunity to respond to this ruthless warlord for his gratuitous brutality.

Staphylococcus works as well as a *katana* thrust into one's midsection (24). Dead is dead; to some extent how it comes about is incidental. His only two sons, Yoriie and Sanetomo, were later assassinated within a few years of each other, leaving no heirs (well, technically, Yoriie left two sons who were soon killed by Hojo operatives), effectively ending the not-quite-two generation Genji/Minamoto dynasty. However, Yoritomo's wife Hojo Masako proved to be very competent in managing the affairs of state through her chosen proxies. She must have been clever and innovative, indeed, since the organization she put into place—from Yoritomo's original plan—permitted the Kamakura shogunate to hold together for 130 years after Yoritomo's demise.

A combination of factors finally brought the era to its knees. First, the looming threat of Mongol invasions, attempted in 1274 and 1281, was a serious drain on the treasury of the Kamakura *bakafu*. Furthermore, the resentment in Kyoto of this rank upstart, this tiny, brash eastern capital never really went away. What did the trick was an attack by Nitta Yoshisada through the coastal *kiridoshi,* a narrow defile cut through the hill at Inamuragasaki in 1333. This battle is eerily reminiscent of the defense of Thermopylae by Leonidas and 300 Spartans in 490 BCE against overwhelming Persian hordes. In the fall of the Kamakura bakafu, according to legend Nitta, in frustration at being stymied by this impasse, uttered a prayer and flung his sword into the ocean. Which immediately receded enough to permit his warriors to walk around the blocked path. His force was able to overwhelm the defending forces, and continue on to the total capitulation of the bakafu, including hundreds submitting to self-immolation and/or seppuku... *It's that "instant low tide" bit that is problematic; Nitta does not show up in documentation elsewhere having demonstrated any special command over natural phenomena. In other words, this was a one-off for him; he wasn't characteristically "magic."*

What amazes me is the incredible construction of cultural icons built within the Kamakura *jidai*, a mere 141 years in duration: something like sixty-five Buddhist temples and nineteen shrines, most of which exist to this day in some form or another (22). Tsurugaoka Hachiman-gu is as impressive and aesthetically pleasing a shrine as any in Japan, owing to its landscaping and the fact that the background is a forested hillside, which along with most of the town itself, fosters the illusion that you are at the very edge of a wilderness area. The Dai Butsu, twelve-meter tall, cast bronze statue of Buddha is an impressive sight throughout the seasons. In its heyday, Zen Buddhism was flourishing, especially in Kamakura, so Kenchoji, the first big, dramatic temple was built in Kita Kamakura, soon followed by Enkakuji, another Zen temple, and Tokeiji accessed to the north by one of the most prominent of the seven *kiridoshi*, or narrow trails through the hills. Meanwhile, in this same timeframe, a messianic Buddhist prophet named Nichiren was finding new followers wherever he went owing to his charismatic, impassioned demeanor. *Whew! Those folks were nothing if not pious.*

I don't know where to begin concerning modern-day Kamakura. There are several good guide books to help the visitor navigate the locations of historical sites. I'll mention that, traipsing around this lovely city, one is apt to encounter brightly colored, liberated *koi* inhabiting the storm water channels alongside many of the major roads. They are carp, after all, a very hardy fish, able to endure ice in severe winter, and water of dubious quality.

At one point, my brother, Phip, and I were invited to attend a Zen meditation session at Kencho-ji, one of Kamakura's five great Zen temples, thanks to my TEC student, Endo-san.

Kamakura Haru (Spring)

New green of foreground
obscures serene Dai Butsu
smile: How precious, spring.

October 10: A bit of excitement around here is the Emperor, "Japan's longest reigning monarch," is about to keel over, and the whole country is all but paralyzed, waiting. All major events, from weddings to school outings, to community festivals, to government conferences, have been postponed, where possible, or cancelled outright. It's all a little morbid; we get these news bulletin updates several times a day—his vital signs: temperature, pulse rate, etc. How many CCs of blood got dribbled into his arm today (to date, he's received about double what he originally started with). Since he's hemorrhaging somewhere in the vicinity of his stomach, the entreating mind asks, How much blood has oozed out of both ends?

Nobody knows how to react. Hardly anyone was around for the death of the previous Emperor 63 years ago, and anyway the whole social landscape has changed drastically since then, especially post-war. The entire line of Emperors, some 2000 years' worth were living gods. And just as surely, gods in death. On paper, this Emperor, the Showa Tenno, is not divine, since MacArthur required the renunciation of divinity at the conclusion of World War II. Still, one gets the feeling not all that many attitudes have changed just because the Constitution has. So, the herd instinct—normal operating procedure here in Japan—dictates social behavior. In the three weeks or so since he fell ill, hundreds of thousands of people have waited in long lines to register their names and "pray for his recovery," as the papers report. Meanwhile, we're all gearing up for a massive show of inconsolable grief.

Sado, the Way of Tea

Ritualizing, even fetishizing, the preparation a cup of tea to drink, at the outset, sounds fairly unappealing to most Westerners, I'd guess. *Why go to all that bother?* we might ask. Well, consider this: there must be something to it, as the practice has been around since the days of Toyotomi Hideyoshi, ca 1580. Sen no Rikyu is credited with codifying Sado by the mid-16th century, and elevating the ceremony into the experience we see today, though there are at least three formal branches that have emerged from Rikyu's roots. Over the years, I've attended three, maybe four ceremonies, at least two of them, fairly formal affairs complete with the full-on *chashitsu*, or tea ceremony room. People who are serious about this experience build a six-tatami room, with a half-tatami square removed, and in its place, a sunken brazier. This room would be constructed completely by traditional methods and materials; straw, bamboo, mud, and paper are featured prominently. Ideally, the entry way would be Alice-in-Wonderland like, small enough to require the attendants to kneel in entering. Thus, everyone, from the highest born aristocrat to the lowliest wood cutter, bows in respect to the chashitsu, the tea house and its master/mistress. Sometimes *zabutons*, cushions, are available to sit on.

By tradition participants are to sit *seiza*, sitting on one's knees and ankles. I'll admit it is an efficient way to seat a large number of people in a small area, if one can endure the position. It turns out, the vast majority of Nihonjin of either gender, any age, can occupy this position for long periods of time, 45 minutes to an hour and a half, without any sign of acute distress. Alas, my skeletal-muscular configuration does not permit me from sitting *seiza* more than about 15 *seconds*. My knees begin screaming at me immediately upon the extreme stress of them bent this acutely, under pressure. But my contorted ankles, bearing most of my weight, constitute Geneva-Conventions-proscribed torture. Anything in excess of three minutes courts permanent damage to my ankles and knees. Invariably, my tea ceremony hosts have welcomed me, and treated my sitting aberration as if it were a perfectly acceptable alternative.

Under normal circumstances, three to six guests are served individually prepared bowls of hot, frothy *macha*, a powdered, bitter, intense green tea. The *Sado* sensei will have a fire going in the brazier, heating water in a cast-iron kettle while s/he takes a measured dipper of tea powder from a bamboo container, and places it in a tea bowl. With a generous splash of hot water, the powder is rendered into a creamy paste through the skillful use of a bamboo whisk. Then, water enough for the finished beverage is added; at this point the whisk is employed in a vigorous, rhythmical pattern until the surface of the tea is a mound of green bubbles. When the bowl is served to you, you approach the server, bow, and accept the bowl with both hands. Then, you retreat to your original seating position as gracefully as you can manage crawling on three out of four limbs, with the remaining dexterous limb clutching an exotic bowl of tea. Back in place, you support the bowl on an out-stretched hand, and with the other, rotate the bowl one circumference by turning it in thirds, three turns clockwise, being mindful of the subtle ways this bowl describes attributes of *wabi*, and *sabi*, the Japanese aesthetic of simplicity, harmony, and uniqueness that speaks to all beauty.

Having signaled your appreciation of the instrument of delivery, you now are to slurp the tea in three installments. In both hands, you are to bring the bowl to your lips for three deep, sucking inhalations, lowering the bowl to your lap between draughts, every gesture in slow motion. It took your sensei four or five minutes, with no real idle time, to perform the ritual of tea preparation. Every aspect of this experience is elongated, stretched out. You pay the utmost respect to your host(ess) and fellow participants by taking the event as the others do: slowly, methodically, quietly, with humility—and with an open heart and mind, being receptive to a sense of peace.

Think of it! Even back in the 16th century, the likes of Toyotomi Hideyoshi welcomed this simple, pure, unencumbered ritual, in part because it permitted an escape from the hectic day-to-day torment of leading, as acting shogun, over a precarious coalition of clans in volatile times. He had seized command following the assassination of Oda Nobunaga, first in centuries to significantly consolidate power, and seriously begin unification of the country. I'm touched that this Top Dog military man would submit to the same terms that any other guest would observe for some 90 minutes, with preparation and the afterglow, before returning to the slog of shogun *giri*, duty. Haggling with conflicting advisors over never-ending issues.

As I recall, during the phase of entering the room and settling into this exotic environment, there could be light banter—nothing serious, "political," or challenging—which would gradually give way to observant silence, as our host began the deliberate, methodical process of uniting us all in this humbling experience. Sitting there, having had your turn, or waiting for your turn, is a kind of zen meditation. Glancing at them obliquely, you take stock of your co-participants. You give the room a close going over: the semblance of a *kamidan,* or household shrine, maybe a *kakejiku,* or scroll, of a relaxing scene in nature, or perhaps a pithy sentiment captured in two highly stylized kanji, one above the other. Likely, a modest *ikebana* arrangement appropriate to the season, displayed in an understated, but stunning vase. You give your host (though more often than not, hostess) a careful but unobtrusive observation through at least one cycle of a tea preparation. At this point, try closing your eyes, and follow along with events by sound. These same sounds, tastes, and smells, essentially this same procedure in a space very much like this, could easily suggest tele-transportation back more than four centuries.

I can think of nothing comparable in the US.

Cremation

I once had the sad experience of attending a cremation ceremony— which turned out to be not so sad. My level of participation began just as the woman's remains were brought from the furnace, barely cooled, to a private room. The family and close friends lined up in order of closeness to the deceased. Each person in turn picked up a large bone fragment with a special set of *hashi,* chopsticks. This bone fragment was placed in the burial urn with 20 or 30 other pieces, to be placed in an extended-family gravesite. I was number ten or eleven in line to have that last, personal connection to the basic remains of a cherished friend. In retrospect, this whole experience of sharing that last act of transferring bones to the urn, permitted a sense of bonding with each other—because of and thanks to our dear comrade, Yuko.

American crematoria either heat the furnaces hotter, or leave the corpse in the chamber longer, because my sense is the remains you collect of your cremated loved one in the US is two or three pounds of uniformly gray, powder ash. Or such was the case with my mother. Whereas in Japan the remains are a mixture of small pieces of bone, a few medium-sized bone fragments large enough that you could imagine the part of the body they served—and powdery ash.

Afterward, most of the ceremony participants went to a restaurant for a sumptuous mid-day meal and lots of beer and sake. There was no presumption of group grief or sadness at this event. It's fair to say that alcohol lightens every social occasion in Japan, but this was more like everyone having as good a time as the setting would allow, and grateful to the deceased for this universally acceptable excuse to be absent from corporate or academic commitments. Not to speak of this opportunity to tie one on. But before we could enter this restaurant, we were bidden to toss a handful of salt, like *Osumo san*, over a shoulder—I've forgotten which shoulder, but you may be sure only one of the two will do—to ward off any malicious spirits who may have hitched a ride from the cremation site, hungry *gaki* eager to wreak havoc with some of their former acquaintances. Though complete strangers can get drawn into the mayhem, I'm told.

Did the attendants to this whole event actually believe there were malevolent spirits hovering around dead people, and that tossing salt would serve as protection? The question is irrelevant. It is far more important to see this as an example of a cultural norm. Belief in the logical justification for throwing the salt is so irrelevant as to be an undesirable distraction. Why would anyone want to violate so simple and harmless a custom? From my limited experience, I can assure the reader that a very high percentage of Nihonjin identify with, and want to be seen/ accepted as unambiguous, core citizens of Japan. It would take a Westerner, say an American like me, to seriously consider consciously violating the norm. The difficult concept to grasp for the Western mind is that one's personal whims and beliefs don't matter. Japanese people will perform this ceremony because it is called for by the protocols of the Shinto branch and/or Buddhist sect they were born (or married) into. They do it because they are Nihonjin, and this is what Nihonjin do.

October 12: As of the last few days, the Emperor's condition has been listed as stable, by which we take to mean "terminal" but the "slide" has been temporarily arrested. His pulse rate is up, especially when taken immediately on receipt of 200 CC of fresh blood (we are up to some 8000 CC by now). Of course, we are all *terminal*; some time or another we all return to the life-force we occupied during our time before acting out this being. I'm just a foolish gaijin, and therefore incapable of fully appreciating the Japanese culture, so I can say, in ignorance of protocols and norms, what I believe a lot of folks are thinking: Let him die! To what end are we artificially prolonging his life? Is it a matter of appropriate timing? For God's sake, just let him go. Bon voyage, *Sayonara*! By now, I'll bet he's ready; after all, his body has been trying to let go for weeks... This rather morbid frequency of comments about the impending demise of the Showa Emperor is a direct reflection of the public preoccupation with the daily reports.

November 8: Recently the Mayor of Nagasaki, Toshiro Motoshima, exercised his constitutional guarantee of free speech in stating publicly that the Showa Emperor shared responsibility—not that he bore sole responsibility, mind you, or was the chief architect—for World War II. Furthermore, had he surrendered even one week earlier, Hiroshima and Nagasaki could have been spared nuclear holocaust. Not such an unusual remark, really; in fact, patently obvious... In the case of the former claim, MacArthur and Hirohito's first meeting clearly documents his taking on full responsibility by way of pleading for compassion and mercy for the Japanese people. The reasonableness of the Mayor's comment is not really the issue, however. While the post-war Constitution guarantees freedom of speech, there is a much older tradition (or should we say taboo?), which dictates that those who disparage or denigrate the Emperor, or even the Imperial system, invite censure, even retribution. Thus, you might not be surprised at the outcry that has since occurred as if from one voice, calling for his ouster. He is widely vilified, and those thoughtful souls who happen to agree with him are biting their tongues lest they call down the same wrath onto themselves. "Sacrosanctity" is given new meaning when applied by the Japanese to their Emperor, and the Constitution be damned! To his credit, Motoshima added that he too shared war responsibility, presumably through his complicity.

In the thick of this kerfuffle a right-wing extremist shot this courageous man with a 22 at point blank range. Fortunately, the bullet did not hit anything vital and the mayor, after a two-week convalescence, is back at 'em. Still, the vast majority of the citizenry is too cowed to speak out against this threat to the single, most important right to speak one's mind, even if,... no, *especially if* it is an unpopular idea, under the full protection of the government. This incident causes me despair over society's willingness, not to say ability, to govern itself.

December 11: What a wondrous thing the state is! One marvels at its power, if not its sense of direction. We have on the one hand an old man whose body was ready to die 2 ½ months ago. If we give him the benefit of the doubt and say, initially, his conscious self wanted to continue living, it is altogether reasonable to assume over the ensuing months—before he became completely comatose—that he might have been ready to go; that he would welcome the release from pain. Needless to say, we common citizens have no way of knowing, and may never know his final thoughts, for all but the vital signs, and intake/sluicing out of blood (up to 26,000 CCs?) are veiled in secrecy. On the other hand, we have the state, in the embodiment of the *Kunaicho*, the Imperial Household Agency, which wants, for reasons we can only dimly fathom, to keep this frail, pitiful, disintegrating body alive.

196

It is said that the Taisho Emperor, son of the Meiji Emperor and father to this emperor, exhibited a poor sense of timing by dying in late December. Thus Showa 1 was scarcely one week long. Are we to have a repeat, like father, like son? Not if the marshalled medical forces of the country and the *Kunaicho* can help it.

December 28: These few days following Christmas are mostly free of classes, allowing me to catch up on some holiday correspondence—and a plethora of Samurai drama with lots of *chambara,* sword battles, on TV. I can rarely follow the dialogue, being archaic and formal Nihongo, but since these dramas all more-or-less follow historical events, I sometimes know the story. In any case you can tell the emotional content from the visual and vocal-tone context. Last week I was treated to a 7000 yen ($56) ticket to see the three-hour kabuki-like performance of *Chushingura,* the theme of which I'm reasonably conversant, since it is the single most popular drama in Japan, certainly for this time of year. Also, I've been watching a produced-for-TV series on the life of Takeda Shingen, a rather shrewd, powerful, and lucky *Daimyo* (regional lord) of the 16th Century who never quite put all the pieces together toward becoming *Shogun,* or Supreme Military Leader, Generalissimo, Commander, you get the idea. Predictably, he comes to a bad end.

Come to think of it, I can't come up with a single "Hollywood ending" in Japanese dramatic arts or literature. An individual, or Group A, feels a natural affinity for another individual, or Group B, but there is an obstacle (called *life*) that they must struggle to overcome, or find the means to cope with. Eventually, the two groups accommodate, sort out, or kill off the impediment, and live happily ever after.

Not to overstate the obvious, in real life at least as many "fail," on a broad range of socio-metrics, as "succeed." Post-War Hollywood tended to crank out movies whose theme was: Life is tough, so what? If you've got the pluck, determination, and a good outlook on life, you will succeed in the end. *Voila*: The Hollywood ending!

Sometimes Groups A and B fail in their attempt, and sometimes they succeed. In either case, as long as they were engaged in overcoming the obstacle preventing them from living nobly, with an eye toward benefitting the community, the participants were *heroic.* In consideration of those who lost the contest, especially for those who lost everything, they were heroic in their defeat. Japanese narratives tend to focus on the incredibly varied ways people lose in their heroic struggle. One comes reluctantly to the inescapable conclusion that the essential ingredient of the traditional arts in Japan is the sense of unremitting tragedy, grief, misery, disillusionment, sorrow, depression, futility, despair, sadness, heartbreak, profound loneliness, and death. (*What is that, the thirteen-horse posse of the Apocalypse?*)

Lots and lots of death. Via murder, mayhem, and suicide—singly, in pairs, or in groups. Reliable triggers for blood-letting are calumny, deceit, humiliation, treachery, vengeance, betrayal, and villainy of any sort. What a country! Of course, these sentiments get expressed in other cultures, and just as surely in countries of the European diaspora, as well. It is certainly not the case that American TV or Hollywood have given murder and mayhem a pass. For better or worse, these aspects do, after all, comprise a significant part of the human experience. One would hope, however, that they don't make up the core, the most important part of what it means to be human. And, god help us, coping with despair, while comprising a significant theme for the arts, need not be the *only* narrative worth exploring.

So, how is one to conduct him/herself in the face of this multilayered miasma of pain, sorrow and grief—fleetingly punctuated with unanticipated episodes of joy and peace—that permeates Japanese literature, folklore, *kabuki*, live theater, much of popular music, and the cinematic arts? Well, if you are Nihonjin, you are to face any and all hardship with patience, grace, forbearance, and quiet dignity.

1989

<u>January 7</u>: The Showa Tenno finally departs this earthly coil. And his timing is impeccable! He reigned for just 63 years, longest in Japan's history. The end of the Showa era signals the beginning of the Heisei era. By way of a eulogy, I wish to commend the Showa Emperor for having made some minor contributions to the science of marine biology.

"Frescorpo: space for relax and condition" (Scrambled English on a sign advertising a hair salon).

Contraband *Ji Biru:* Home Brew

San gatsu, March: Somewhere along this timeline I started making home brew in Kugenuma, in flagrant violation of the law of the land. Background: The kanji, 地, means "small scale, local." Biru would have to be written in *Katakana* since it is a word appropriated from English. *Biru* is the closest *Katakana Eigo* can come to "beer." There are four corporate breweries in the whole of the nation (Kirin, Suntory, Asahi, and Sapporo), each brewery producing a half dozen or more different brands, presumably satisfying the range of customer taste and name-brand differentiation. Furthermore, their corporate management teams like the legal situation just fine as it is, thank you. Don't mess with a good thing. *If it ain't broke, don't "fix" it.* So, to make sure there are no small scale competitors around to muck things up, these Big Four beer manufacturers, servicing upwards of 100 million citizens, "persuaded" their Diet representatives to see things their way, and enact laws to prevent hobbyists from fermenting alcoholic beverages. Even for personal consumption. No homemade, local beer permitted.

Well, I said to myself, *that's just corporate thuggery.* And what am I apt to do when confronted by an asinine restriction like this one? Why, flaunt the hell out of it; you betcha!

I'd been making a pretty basic recipe of home brew, along with occasional fruit wines, on a fairly regular basis since I'd learned the fundamentals as part of the commune I lived in during the late 1960s, and

201

continued to ferment right up to the time I came to Japan. In a pinch, I could ferment a five-gallon batch of wort to a nearly finished state in a week, bottle and cap it in 20 quart bottles to "repose" for another week—that's zero to drinkable beer in two weeks!—though it would be better to settle out the yeast for an additional week.

Basically, as soon as I discovered I could buy malt extract syrup at Tokyu Hands, I knew I could make bootleg brew in Japan. The next time I went back to Oregon I stocked up on the requisite supplies: An adjustable bottle capper that I found at a garage sale, $5; a gross of bottlecaps, $3.75; about seven feet of thin plastic tubing (for syphoning the finished beer into the bottles), $4; a small, foil-sealed packet of dried beer yeast, $.69; and a hydrometer, a sealed glass cylinder with a specific-gravity scale inside, $5. You need this device to predict the amount of alcohol your beer will contain, and more importantly, when your seething cauldron of wildly multiplying yeasts (consuming the sugar while excreting alcohol and carbon dioxide) is ready to bottle. Meanwhile, I could easily collect any number of standard issue, 633 ml recapable beer bottles, all cleaned and ready to be filled and capped. Also, Tokyu Hands would sell me a plus/minus five gallon/20 liter food-grade plastic tub. Clandestine Kugenuma *biru*; I was ready to go!

I make no claims to the quality of this quick-and-easy process, but frankly most of my students who partook during parties over the course of four years or so, were so intrigued by the notion of the possibility of getting ripped on beer you could make yourself, that they didn't seem to mind my fairly green, yeasty brew. Of course, I didn't hesitate to point out the law I was breaking in making the beer, and that in knowing this status and willfully drinking it made my students, my fellow Bacchanalians, *accessories* to my crime. Thus, they were co-conspirators, violators of the law, too.

Whoopeee! Pass the pitcher…

April 8: A banner in English on the side of a building on the way to a Chigasaki class:

AMERICAN DISCOUNT STORE
JUNK MARKET

A *sign* of the times?!

For Golden Week this year Kimiko and I went to Shanghai. The little lady planned the itinerary with my avid encouragement. We took the Shinkansen to Osaka for the night. Next morning, we boarded a passenger and freight liner; a posh first-class cabin and pretty decent food. Two days later we arrived at the famous riverfront Bund, built by Western "concessions" in the early 20th century, and were taxied to Jiang Zhen, this first class hotel—said to be the meeting site for the detente between Nixon and Zhou Enlai. Tasteful, chic, but… sterile. First Class is First Class, is First Class, the world over. With very little superficial difference, they are indistinguishable inside their top-ranking, state-of-the-art shell. The next day we transferred back to the Bund, and the landmark Peace Hotel for its faded elegance, for its '20s and '30s Asian expat haven ambience.

Our visit was right before Shanghai's economic explosion. There might have been one or two high-rise construction cranes visible on the skyline, harbingers of what was soon to come. Like Hong Kong, Shanghai is not an old city at all. Before being ceded to the Brits, and then in quick succession, the Americans, the French, in the 1850s, and finally the Germans and Japanese by the early 1900s, Shanghai was a nondescript fishing village on the Huang Pu, a tributary near the confluence with the Yangtze River.

That pre-economic-upheaval period was an interesting time to visit. We walked Nanjing Road away from the riverfront perhaps a mile, and back again. The most conspicuous means of conveyance over the entire course, the economic heart of the city at the time, was the plebian bicycle. Followed by the motor scooter, cycle, and the like. There were some buses, always packed, and a few cars and trucks. The department stores displayed goods inside glass cases, staffed by sullen sales clerks whose jobs were secure whether you bought anything or not. *Oh look, another bigshot tourist! Big fucking deal.* They didn't give a shit about you, and they didn't mind signaling that message. Compared to Japan, Shanghai felt post-WWII, but not by much.

The Sogo department store in Yokohama, largest in Asia, has 12 floors above surface and two or three basement floors, each floor featuring unique reasons to explore. Giant department stores in Tokyo/Yokohama, Osaka, Nagoya, etc. compete by offering cultural incentives, like world-class visiting exhibitions of everything from fine ceramics, stoneware to porcelain; to incredible painting and sculpture collections, both domestic and foreign. But they all have everything a fashion-conscious consumer could possibly want. Restaurants of all styles and ethnicities on most floors. Two basement floors of food, from soup to nuts, as they say, the raw ingredients to the ready to eat... Of course, China will get there. But right here, right now, the contrast is stark.

Within a decade skyscrapers and massive urban renewal would completely transform the city into something completely unrecognizable.

Shanghai played host to a lot of visitors from Hong Kong, and once in a while a Hong Kong woman would appear with a Caucasian escort. Kimiko was approached several times by curious locals as to information about our relationship. They took her to be Hong Kong*ese* and rattled away at her in presumably fluent Cantonese. When she could get a word in edgewise, she'd let them know she was Japanese and unable to speak their language. After a day or so of this, we learned to say our nationalities in Mandarin. *Wo shi me guo ren*, means "I am American person," which I didn't really need to say, anyway; one look at me told them all they needed to know. On the other hand, *Wo shi ru ben ren*, "I am Japanese," was a useful expression because it forestalled questions that assumed her local language competency.

Over coffee—at uber-rich prices—we caught the old swing jazz band at the Peace Hotel, heirs of a tradition that'd started in pre-WW II days. We watched scores of elderly people practice Tao Tai Chi along the Bund riverfront in the early morning. And on one of our walks we chanced upon a private park. That is to say, there was a fee to enter. The park had once been a race course for the French Concession; it was declared a public park in 1948 by Mao himself. The cost of entry was ridiculously cheap, about an American nickel each, but the notion of charging the citizens for access to their own public space, the commons, initially raised my hackles. You might understand how a purely dog-eat-dog capitalist society might sell off to the highest bidder the real estate that had any value. But wouldn't you expect a self-avowed communist country to know more than most (e.g., theocracies, monarchies, plutocracies, autocracies/ tyrannies, and fascist regimes), the value of the "people's parks," and monuments, as unifying places? This was tangible geography as nexus for one's collective identity.

Well, it turns out that a nickel has too many practical applications for most Shanghaians to enjoy some peace and relative quiet on a park bench, a range of well cared for trees and shrubs outlining the paths, and hardly anyone else around, unlike the other side of that gate where there is no place to sit, and even pausing in the midst of the manswarm is to create an obstacle. I don't recall how long we loitered in that unremarkable-but-for-its-location park—half an hour? Forty-five minutes? However long, I'd say we got our nickels' worth indulging our privileged status.

I think Kimiko would agree with me that our in-country dining experience was disappointing. We've both had exotic and exquisite Chinese dishes in *Chuka gai*, Chinatown, Yokohama. And while different in some aspects, Kimiko has come to appreciate various Chinese dishes from restaurants in and around Portland, Oregon, as well. But alas, the "real deal" was usually plain and uninterestingly presented. Bowls of vegetables, sometimes meat, swimming in oil. After a week we were ready to fly back to a cuisine that offered fresh vegetables (a fresh *salad*, anyone?) once in a while.

Confucius, Kong Qui, or Kong Fuzi (Master Kong) in Chinese, and *Koshi* in Japanese

This philosopher, or social engineer, lived from 551~479 BCE. One of the most pervasive, longest lasting *sub-rosa* influences on Japan—and China, and Korea, and much of SE Asia, *exampli gratia* Vietnam—has been Confucianism, a body of teachings on moral behavior, both for the individual and the social structure. Like Buddha, and later, Christ, virtually everything the man said or did was left to the interpretations of acolytes, often centuries later. Much ink is devoted to the cultivation of knowledge, which too often amounts to the revealed knowledge of Confucius and his codification of the hierarchy of the ideal social order. In the *Analects*, a compilation of Confucian aphorisms and sage pronouncements on how to live righteously, he emphasized strong family loyalty, ancestor worship, respect of elders by their children, and of husbands by their wives. For an aging man in a hide-bound society there is much to like in the Confucian system of beliefs. For just about anyone else in a more dynamic, flexible structure it is somewhat less appealing.

Essentially, Confucianism is the ethos of old men, reserving highest honor for the elders, those geriatric men who lay claim to positions of authority in society. It has led to a rigidly structured society, and codified behavior. In Japan it arguably reached its peak of influence during the Heian Period (ca 794 ~1185 CE), a relatively peaceful time when the imperial system was flourishing, and attributes of culture continued to be borrowed from China wholesale, especially those aspects of culture that supported and reinforced strong central control by sage leaders born to their roles, and fixed classes.

The Chinese have a tradition of conducting annual ceremonies commemorating the birth date of Confucius. This tradition was interrupted by Mao Tse Tung, especially during the Cultural Revolution in the 1960s, when the official position was that ancient traditions/culture acted as a millstone around the necks of progressive reformers. In order to advance, Mao thought it would be necessary to do away with the inflated trappings of history, which only held back social progress. Confucianism was regarded as feudal and reactionary in its attitude toward disparities in social status. It was seen as being fixed, anachronistic, and resistant to the needs of modern times. To a feminist, or a proponent of meritocracy, where age in and of itself is not uniquely a sign for veneration, Confucianism was and still is anathema.

So what do these teachings from 2500 years ago have to do with East Asia in general, or Japan in specific, nowadays? you may well ask. Compared to Western thought, with its emphasis on personal rights and prerogatives (especially since the Enlightenment and the Age of Reason with their advocates of Voltaire, Rousseau, Locke, John Stuart Mill, and even Thomas Paine, and Thomas Jefferson), Asia—at least that part impacted by Confucianism so long ago—*still* embodies the teachings of ancestor reverence, deep respect for one's elders, teachers (*thank you very much!*), and those in positions of authority, male dominance, and social roles that are difficult, if not all but impossible, to transcend. Social cohesion could be maintained harmoniously if the citizenry but follow these few Confucian protocols.

In Japan personal freedom has very little existential meaning. Perhaps more than any other country, in Japan the collective "good" is everything; *personal anything* could only begin to have meaning in the privacy of one's home, away from the primary, legitimate concerns of the community.

It occurs to me that we in the West consider intellectual conformity—group think, the herd or hive instinct—of very little premium, and I am certainly enough a product of my origins to agree. Some of the drawbacks to thinking and acting collectively include the stifling of unique, individual innovation. Said innovation can be applied to technological improvements which often yield benefits to the collective and profits to the initial risk-takers. But ingenuity also applies to the arts, I believe, giving form (dimension, texture, and rhythm) to the most direct, unique, and sublime expression of our godhead—the closest, purest expression of our (transitory) ability to tap into the universal, the continuous all-in-one. It is hard to imagine that blinding flash of creativity emanating from *nemawashi,* the consensus-generating protocol of a committee or group.

By contrast, agreement of the whole requires cooperation, patience, consideration, and a degree of commitment—a sharing in the decision to act together. If "acting" requires consciousness, then conformity of action is consciously working and playing, existing, together. There can be no doubt that there are considerable benefits to be had in a society where collective uniformity of purpose is the guiding principle. There is very little strife; on an international scale, Nippon consistently reports extremely low crime rates, while maintaining high quality and productivity—all by subsuming self in the sea of the social good. But it also follows that for any change to take place, a lot of group consideration must occur. *Nemawashi* is a sort of passing the subject around; each person puts a hand to it, attaches a comment or signs off as is, and nudges the narrative along. This process can be time consuming because the decisions ultimately have vast ramifications for a large institutional structure—public, or private—but the thing to remember is, everyone is involved, everyone has a stake, in the "identity"—neighborhood, school, corporate wage provider, or nation—under discussion. Japanese who are seen as unskilled at *nemawashi* are deemed to be poor candidates for management levels of the business world where cooperative decision making is critical.

A surprising body of research has been conducted looking at the social consequences of societies with a high degree of inequality, vs. societies with little inequality across a broad spectrum of measures. Researchers Richard Wilkinson and Kate Pickett, in *The Spirit Level*, documented in study after study how societies with little disparity between the richest, most powerful members, and their poorest, as in the case of Japan, also rate the highest in satisfaction and contentment (25). Whereas countries like the US, among the countries with the widest gap between the richest, most powerful, and the meekest, poorest members, rate very low in contentment, or satisfaction, *including the rich!* In one study conducted among 21 countries—all of them European, or European diaspora (The US, Canada, Australia, and New Zealand), with the exception of Japan—purported to show that "Health and social problems are closely related to inequality among rich countries." The vertical axis showed the relative health and social problems, while the horizontal axis displayed the relative income inequality. In this research Japan stood alone occupying the most favorable position of fewest social problems/lowest income inequality (with the Scandinavian countries of Finland, Sweden, Norway, and Denmark coming closest). In stark contrast, the US vain-gloriously occupied the opposite corner exhibiting the highest level of health and social problems, at the same time demonstrating the most extreme income inequality, Portugal appearing a distant second, and the UK third at double the distance of Portugal.

Another study specifically pairing income inequality with percentage of mental health, with slightly fewer countries than the previous research, found Japan, again, having the lowest income disparity, reporting slightly less than 8% of its citizens experiencing mental illness. And again the US is unique in its position of income inequality and degree of mental abnormality, reporting something like 27% mental illness, with Australia and the UK appearing with 23% mentally disturbed citizens. In unrelenting study after study, Wilkinson and Pickett establish a strong correlation between the relative wellbeing of a society's members and the degree to which these members array in a narrow spectrum of income "success."

A short list of other findings related to this general field of inquiry include: "Stress in early life affects physical growth, emotional, social, and

208

cognitive development…" p. 77 of *The Spirit Level* (25). "[W]omen's status is significantly worse in more unequal states…" p. 59. Income "inequality is associated with lower life expectancy, higher rates of infant mortality, shorter height, poor self-reported health, low birth weight, AIDS and depression," p. 81. And "living in a more equal place benefited everybody, not just the poor…at almost any level of income, it's better to live in a more equal place," p. 84.

The *kotowaza* that best captures this approximation of equal social status, and group identity is *Deru kugi wa utareru,* or "The nail that sticks up soon gets hammered down." In Japan it is very troubling to have to endure the swollen ego. Whereas in America, we are apt to believe something of the counterpart, "The squeaky hinge gets lubricated." If you don't complain, or call attention to the "flaw," the problem will not get addressed, and thus, *Squeak!* will only persist. *Sque-EAK!* And perhaps worsen: *SQUEA-AA-AACK!!*

There is a conspicuous constituency of people who act on the assumption that if you are not engaged in exercising your god-given right to state your opinion, which is often delivered in the form of a profanity-laden, affectively-dense complaint, you must be gutless, or stupid—meaning you don't have an opinion. These people thrive on adversarial contacts with the public, the adrenal rush of competition in one form or another. For them, modesty and humility are signs of weakness. There is a lot of broad-spectrum hostility.

In yet another contrast study, we learn that Japan, and most of Asia, are considered "high context" cultures, whereas the US, other English-speaking societies, and northern Europe are "low context" societies. This latter group tends to emphasize 1) individual values; 2) concerns for maintenance and preservation of one's individual "face" (i.e., status, reputation, and standing); 3) communicates in a direct, linear, syllogistic style; 4) meanings are coded in verbal messages, often with high affect; and 5) very little scanning of interlocutors for consensus-building.

The "high context" cultures rely on 1) group-oriented values and communication techniques; 2) sustaining mutual face; 3) indirect and circuitous style of sharing the message, permitting gradual accommodation and accord; 4) meanings are embedded in the context with essentially no affect; and 4) a high degree of scanning to assure consilience at each step of the dialogue.

A part of my identity continues to assert, as long as "I" inhabit this conscious "self," I want the right to express it, exult in it, even flaunt it, and never surrender to mindless mass conformity. Imperfect, mortal, often erring, often inarticulate, stumbling—one tiny, short-lived kernel of self-awareness in the cycling continuum/compendium—I nevertheless embrace my uniqueness, my sense of self, while at the same time conceding that it is sheer vanity, an expression of folly. I am acknowledging that the more I embrace my uniqueness, the harder it will be to let go.

Though it is inevitable over the long haul, I do not envision much letting go just yet. I still feel vested; I still have a stake in this game. Still hanging on.

* * * * *

I had an elderly student, Shimizu-san, who spent most of his free time fishing. He was sufficiently accomplished at it that he regularly caught fish. No doubt, over the years, experience teaches what places are best, at what time of day, or even the season. I never knew if his effort was a valuable contribution to the family's meals, but I rather thought of it as a kind of Zen meditation where you perform a series of routine, un-thought movements, and in so doing, permit the possibility of releasing your mind from the tyranny of Self—catching a fish in this context would be considered incidental. Anyway, this senior citizen was perhaps somewhat unique among his retired peers in that he was actually enjoying his life. Given that his health was more-or-less ok, getting out of the house and being involved in a cheap hobby was probably the best thing he could do. Additionally, the fact that his wife was delighted he had an interest that got him out from under foot was a significant dividend.

At one point, Shimizu-san showed me his small collection of *gyotaku*, prints he'd made of some of his trophy fish, allowing the fisherman to document his catch—and eat it too. I imagine most American sportsmen, hunters or fishermen, would prefer to have the very beast they conquered, life-like as rendered by the taxidermist's artistry, on display for all to see. The Japanese sportsman doesn't have vast halls or large dens in which show off lions, bears, wolverines, posed in life-like menacing stances, and even if he did, he'd doubtless feature themes that emphasize living in harmony with, rather than dominion over, nature. But in the case of this fish, I admired the quick and easy custom of slathering powdered-charcoal ink on one side of the fish and placing that side on a prepared surface—perhaps, some classy *washi*, hand-made paper where threads and other "imperfections" are clearly visible. Or the inked surface of the fish could be pressed onto a plain cotton sheet, like the one Shimuzu-san insisted I take. This fish, in stark contrast to the white background, is about 13 or 14 inches long, eight or nine inched tall, and we don't know the width/depth dimension, but may surmise she was narrow, perhaps even svelte, in relation to the other two dimensions. She looks like a salt-water bottom fish, but my knowledge of shoreline piscine biota is very sketchy. Besides this fish front and center on this white material, there is length and weight, as well as location she was caught, and Shimizu's *hanko*, a print of his unique identifying "signature" carved into the butt of piece of jade, ivory, or some other stone, and then inked, and stamped on the cloth. All in all, it was an attractive way to show this particular species of fish; you get natural history, art, and, assuming he rinsed off the ink and stuck her on ice— or a hot skillet—soon thereafter, a contribution to a decent meal.

America, 亜米利加, Be koku, Rice Country

In today's Nihongo, when dealing with foreign words, the normal pattern is to use katakana to approximate the word. Before katakana became popular in writing foreign words (probably early-Edo period), countries like "America" were written in kanji, in a process called *ateji*, not that it tells us anything. In this case, there are four syllables to be represented by four kanji, chosen not for meaning but for phonetic rendering of the word. The second syllable of

America, /me/ is presented by the kanji for rice, 米. It was necessary to add *koku,* country, on the tail of the full four kanji—*a,* 亜, come after, follow; *me,* 米, rice; *ri,* 利, advantage; and *ka* 加, summation—to help the reader comprehend what the hell these particular kanji were supposed to mean together. Then, in short order, it got shortened. To simplify and to demystify the process, reference to America, prior to the use of katakana today, became *Be koku*, Rice country. *Be* is an *on yome* reading, and allomorph of the 5th, or 6th century Chinese pronunciation of rice, /me/. So, the   selection of the kanji for rice had nothing to do with the association of the US with rice, and everything to do with the pronunciation of the kanji.

* * * * *

I confess to composing sentences that now and then poke fun at venerable traditions and institutions in Japan—for the purpose of humor and/or irony, only. With no malice intended. We humans are a sorry lot if we can't laugh at ourselves, right? I guess you could say I am, on these occasions, exercising my *Outsider*-ness. Coincidently, I managed to discover a fair amount of startling, illogical, and morally questionable material from my own culture/community while committing attention and ink to the curiosities uncovered in Nippon. Still, my hope is that my budding knowledge and experience, and mostly, my love of Japan are palpable throughout my narrative.

Having stated my preface, I wish to air a couple of entrenched religious/ cultural issues that I take exception to. Let me say up front, I understand that most social behaviors and beliefs are not based in logic, or at least not the logic we might use from an early-21st century perspective. A good deal of our belief systems and social behaviors are rooted in canon aged in millennia, so of course, there is not a lot of logic that we can associate with currently, though logic may be the wrong tool for the circumstance where tradition trumps everything else. But Japan has demonstrated time and again that when a policy shift results in lives saved, or life processes made more expedient, convenient, or less expensive, change can happen with stunning alacrity.

My first beef is with the Japanese aversion to organ donation. This is the opportunity for the living to choose to donate any and all suitable organs to the next needy person in line—at the time of brain death. My authorization is listed on my driver's license. This means is a good way to announce the authorization since so many people in the US give up living behind the wheel of a vehicle. Also, the state-issued driver's license has come to be a de facto identification source. Organ donation is my choice, so even if all my surviving relatives objected, my decision would prevail.

On the one hand, you've got the traditional belief that you should face the crematory furnace with your body as intact as possible, so that your (brief? 49 days?) time as a *Gaki,* a hungry ghost, or at any rate, in *Ohigan,* the Other World, you would still possess all your faculties, and thus, not have to hobble through eternity lacking, say, corneas harvested for a living person in need. Or a kidney. Or a heart, or a liver.

From the other perspective, we see the clear results on the part of the kidney-transplant recipient who can gradually return to a normal, productive life. These organ donation supporters should hire some clever advertising. Surely, if ever there was a case, this is the case where logic—and compassion—should prevail over senseless dogma. Assertion: No compassionate "god" worth its salt would punish throughout eternity a devotee for volunteering any usable part of his/her corpse, prior to onset of decomposition, to help a living person in critical need. If that statement is reasonable to you, and since you and I agree at this level, then we are permitted to have some confidence that god(s) is/are similarly logical and sensible. That said, please consider donating useful parts of you, upon your demise, in order to help our fellow travelers survive a little longer, and/or vastly improve their quality of life.

Secondary to organ donation is the issue of adoption in Japan. Many couples in Japan want babies, but are unable to conceive; some of them are successful through *invitro* fertilization, and some few through surrogacy. Leaving a large percentage of these couples unsuccessful, and unfulfilled as parents, while orphanages house children of all ages who have lost their parents and have no other relatives, with vanishingly few potential parents willing to step forward. Also, as I understand it, Japan has very strict laws regarding adoptions by foreign couples. This would seem to spring from the notion that it is better to grow up, even if this entails extreme hardship, perhaps living a shorter, more limited, compromised life—but maintaining one's Japanese identity—than to see that person go on to a potentially more "successful" life (more prosperous, comfortable, with more lifestyle options), but surrendering one's *Nihon no kokoro,* that hard-wired awareness of being *within* the Family. To the extent that might be the case, it's a fairly acute

213

example of ethnocentrism, never a pretty sight. I do not share this love of a mother country, but in a way, I understand: *We are superior to outsiders*, because in one form or another, cultures have been celebrating their own unique and special qualities over others since history's first recordings.

In the West, we trace this tendency back at least as far as the Ancient Greeks, who called all non-Greeks—defined as not speaking the Greek language—*varvaros*, from which we have "barbarian." These were and are uncouth, primitive, inferior beings, by definition. And then, of course, the Bible's Old Testament is awash in the blood of one group slaughtering another—presumably on God's orders.

The Navajo call themselves *Dineh*, the People. Suggesting only the hominids that practice the same customs, dress, eat, and especially, speak like they do, qualify as authentic People, another example of hard-core ethnocentrism. Despite this little side track attempting to demonstrate the universality of ethnocentrism, *us vs. them*, I don't really have an ax to grind as to Japan's official policy regarding Japanese orphans up for adoption by foreign couples.

However, my primary regret regarding social trends in Japan concerns the lack of non-relative adoptions. I don't have a clear concept of why Nihonjin almost never adopt an orphan unless there is shared blood. That's literally the dividing line: If the baby, child, or teenager is related to you by blood, you are obligated in some degree, *giri*, to help raise this person. The closer you are in relationship—aunt/uncle and niece/nephew—the greater the *giri*, the obligation. In that situation, the surviving extended-family members convene and settle the adoption arrangements, and presumably, the extent of the other family members' commitment. This decision would not have been made on the basis of who wanted, or didn't want such-and-such involvement, and the notion that one might refuse to accept the family decision would be inconceivable. Literally, *unable to be conceived, imagined, or thought*. Such thoughts suggest the person understands and recognizes his own personal desire in this social equation, and is willing to pursue that individual desire regardless of the will of the social matrix. First of all, such an event would be an exceedingly rare occurrence, and even then, it would never—I say with some confidence, *never*—end well. This is a set up for a classical tragedy, or some other catastrophe, as in the example of lovers who are prohibited from continuing their relationship by one or both families, owing to differing castes or other gaps in status, and thus, commit double suicide.

Still, my conundrum remains: What are the dynamics of Japanese couples who are deprived of biological parenthood, yet refuse to parent an orphan—need I say, much in need of caring "parents"—from the national database?

<u>July 7</u> *(Shichi gatsu nanoka)*: *Tanabata* is another ancient ceremony with Chinese origins. In this tale two star-crossed lovers find themselves on opposite sides of the great river in the night sky (earth's galaxy, the Milky Way). Orihime, a weaver of uncommon grace and beauty, lives with her family, and every night she pines for her lover, Kengyu, a cowherd, who lives on the opposite shore of this vast river (26). Only on the evening of the seventh day of the seventh month, *if* there are no rain clouds to obscure the earthly view, does a magical bridge of magpie wings form, permitting Kengyu to cross the river, uniting the couple in a night of wild passion, better left to the imagination. *Writhing, aching, clutching...*

Since the Meiji Restoration and the adoption of the western, Gregorian calendar, the seventh day of the seventh month falls smack in the middle of *tsuyu*, or the rainy season. So predictable is this climatological event that some people refer to *tsuyu* as a fifth season. In many years of living in Japan, I don't think a single July 7th has passed that was not completely covered in clouds, accompanied by a sufficiency of rain. You just know these separated lovers have to be mightily frustrated, having one chance a year to fulfill their carnal fantasies fade and disappear into the clouds. Literally. However, in the Chinese lunar calendar, the seventh day of the seventh month is considered a signal of autumn approaching; it occurs some five to six weeks later in the Gregorian calendar, when *tsuyu* has spent itself. It is a date reliably past the rainy weather, and the lovers have a better than average chance of reuniting. Alas, this has not been the case in modern, post-Edo times. Just another couple of casualties, Kengyu and Orihime. For 2000 years, a piece of Japan's literary foundation of Chinese-based mythology, Tanabata is now nothing more than roadkill, collateral damage, on the super highway to progress and modernization. *Take no prisoners!*

December 1: "Time flies when you're having fun!" the old saw goes. Time indeed has flown of late, but without much fun to accompany it, sorry to say. I find myself working more, which of course means earning more, while having less time to enjoy it. Classes are becoming stale and largely routine. There is less anxiety/nervousness, less challenge and, as a result, generally less interest or excitement. This also holds true for the state of matrimony. I'm becoming a drudge.

> *Nothing is worth noting that is not seen with fresh eyes.*
> Matsuo Basho (12)

* * * * *

December 14 is the anniversary of *Chushingura,* "A Treasury of Loyal Retainers," or more popularly, "The Tale of the 47 Ronin." It is Japan's best loved morality tale, hands down. It hits all the themes: A tragic injustice, sacrifice for the sake of honor and loyalty, and much hardship and suffering—and frankly, folks, if there isn't a fairly heavy dose of pain and suffering, the show's Japanese origins are instantly suspect. The plot concerns a suicide mission to the heartland of the Tokogawa Shogunate, Edo, to exact revenge, and there is devious, convoluted preparation with a year-long subtrafuge to keep Tokugawa spies off the trail. Finally, the plan is executed; we have sweet, short-lived success and vindication, then *Seppuku*, ritualistic group disembowelment. Furthermore, it has the sublime virtue of being true, a matter of public record, no doubt with minor embellishments here and there.

Not a year-end season goes by without an elaborate TV production of this tale getting retold. It's an unwritten rite of passage for each generation of thespians. Within a few years of the historical event, the successful vendetta, *Bunraku*, half-sized puppet theater, playwrights were already taking up the event as an exemplar of the conflict between *giri*, duty, and *ninjo*, those pesky ol' human passions and desires that always seem to insert themselves at the

216

least opportune occasions. The biggest task these playwrights faced, Chikamatsu Monzaemon in the forefront, was how to disguise the story to approximate events from an earlier age, in a different locale, with different protagonists—so as to avoid the wrath of the Tokugawa censors. The *Bakafu* bigshots were not going to permit public entertainment that would seem to condone a challenge to authority.

Let's set the scene: The precipitating event occurred in March of 1701, a whole century after Sekigahara, and the founding of the Tokugawa Dynasty, *aka* Edo Jidai (Age), and the fifth generation since that battle among samurai factions to determine who would consolidate the clans and lead the "country." But 100 years later, without a clear and present threat, *Bushido*, the way of the warrior, had lost much of its luster, to say nothing of orientation, through disuse. The fifth Tokugawa Shogun, Tsunayoshi, having no foreign or domestic wars to wage, occupied himself with trying to bear a male heir—ah, the weary task of being the leader! *Next!*—and permitted designated officials to organize and manage courtly protocol. Chief Chamberlain among them was Kira Kozukenosuke.

By the standards of rural daimyo, observing this rigid and demeaning courtly protocol was offensive and decadent. Bribes were openly solicited, and it became insufferable to endure endless, stylized rituals when Lord Asano Takumi-no-kami's real duty was to manage and police the clan turf he was master of. As a matter of principle, Asano had refused to pay the extortion that was Kira's going rate. The only authority Kira had over the visiting daimyo, required to live in the capital alternating years, was to insure they met ceremonial protocol, and through these means Kira required Asano to repeat menial tasks until they met his standard. Meanwhile, what had started as oblique references to his incompetency had degenerated to explicit slurs and insults as to his worthiness as a man. On one such occasion Lord Asano's patience gave way. He'd performed his last "practice" ritual, and he'd certainly endured his last insult. In an explosion of delirious rage, Lord Asano drew his *katana* and slashed Kira, superficially wounding him.

The Ako Clan was modest in size, but had a strong history of support for the Tokugawa Shogunate going back to support for Ieyasu at Sekigahara. However, the rules were clear-cut on this matter: Under pain of execution, no one was permitted to draw a weapon in anger within the palace. Since some extenuating circumstances by way of provocation of the crime were understood to be present, Lord Asano was granted the only honorable death for a samurai: *seppuku*, or ceremonial self-disembowelment.

Meanwhile, a good deal of back story takes place in Ako Ken (Prefecture), near modern-day Hyogo Ken, some 380 miles (612 kms.) from Edo, ten to twelve days' trek in the nine-to-ten months of the year it was possible to traverse the mountain ranges.* That's nearly two weeks—under optimal conditions, hustling on foot every day—to transmit the news of Lord Asano's calamity, and one day later, the ultimate consequence. Chief Retainer Oishi Kuranosuke, tasked with managing local affairs during Lord Asano's absence, now faced surrendering the local castle to Tokugawa officials, which he did without a hint of resistance, hoping that total disintegration of the Ako clan might yet be averted. When this hope proved to be futile, however, Oishi called a clandestine counsel and polled the Ako clan samurai as to their future course of action. They were *ronin* now, warriors without a master, the worst possible outcome for a samurai—because it meant they had no specific turf to defend, and worse, no patron to support them.

Everyone urged revenge, *adauchi*, against Kira for his shameful and treacherous treatment of their Lord; a large contingent, especially among the younger men, argued forcefully for an immediate strike. Oishi reasoned that such a rash move would be doomed to failure since the Tokugawa Bakafu would be expecting it. His advice was to carry on their new "normal" lives until suspicion of their motives died down, and their covert effort would have a better chance of success. They were to find work, settle in, and bide their time.

In order to throw off the Tokugawa spies from their avowed purpose, some of these once proud samurai indulged in a life of philandering and dissipation in the pleasure quarters of Gion (Kyoto). Oishi, in particular, called ridicule unto himself by his frequent, drunken public antics, bringing dishonor to the clan and his family, and making himself a laughingstock. At long last their ruse worked, according to their own Edo informants, and the group, now shrunk from about seventy initially to forty-seven, began their preparations. This involved surreptitious plans to smuggle weapons through the immigration gate, the *sekisho*, at Hakone Pass through the Tanzawa Mountains and into the Edo Plain. From early in the Tokugawa *bakafu* security forces were determined to thwart any coup attempts by closely inspecting anyone leaving, but especially entering, Edo at this all-important check point. We don't know *how* they smuggled weapons and Ako clan insignia, only that they did, because Oishi and his band of intrepid men all made it to a safe house in Edo where they could reconnoiter Kira's compound for themselves and fine-tune this final act of retribution.

*I've been advised that Edo jidai runners have made the journey on foot between Edo and Kyoto via the Tokaido in *three to four days!* I concede that is possible if runners are staged at each station along the road, a kind of stretched out *ekiden*. These runners would then rush the message at top speed to the next station, and so on. The only agency I see financing such a "Pony Express," this expedited communications system, is the Tokugawa *bakafu*. If the urgency of the message were in the interest of the central government, they might be persuaded to send it.

On the other hand, there could be a regional accord to contribute runners to waystations in one's area, and thereby gain from the speed of information. It seems too fast for information specific to a small rural *ken*, a distinct, multi-clan-dominated area, but if somesort of communications cooperative were to set up, say, a daily relay of the "latest information" baton in both directions, then it certainly would be possible; I've simply not heard of such a system. I remain extremely skeptical that such a system existed, especially at that time.

A couple points of clarification before we pull out the stops of the drama, sending it to its crescendo, its apotheosis: Literal historians prefer to call the story, "Tale of the Forty-*six* Ronin," and exactly speaking, they are correct. Only forty-six certifiable, dispossessed samurai, including Chief Retainer Oishi's 16 or 17-year-old son, Chikara, took part in the year-and-nine-month subterfuge: the gestation, preparation, and ultimate fulfillment of their collective duty not to rest until they slayed the man who so treacherously brought low their master, the lord of the domain. However, another loyal servant of the Ako clan, from another caste than samurai (craftsmen/builders?), had been a co-conspirator from the beginning, and was clearly as committed as his comrades. Thus, he was granted honorary status to participate in the attack—*as if* he were a samurai. In this case, to do the right

219

thing meant *create an exception to the rules*. Somehow, calling the story, "Tale of Forty-six Ronin and One Member of XYZ Caste," strikes me as being unwieldy for the title, and too academic and pretentious for the audience. Thus, the common preference, and mine, for "...Forty-*seven* Ronin."

The second contextual point I want to clarify concerns the climate/weather to be expected at certain seasons of the year—as calculated by different calendars. The assault on Kira's compound, a walled area of some open spaces and several interconnected buildings, took place on the 14th day of the twelfth month of the Chinese lunar calendar—which would put the event at the end of January/early February of the Gregorian calendar, the Western standard since the late-16th century, and the Japanese model since the Meiji Restoration. The Pacific Ocean rarely brings snow to the Kanto Plain where much of the land is just above sea level. It is rarer by another magnitude—the proverbial *hens' teeth*—to have respectable snow (25 to 30 cm.) on December 14 of the Western calendar.

But the historical narrative is clear that a significant snowfall had taken or was taking place during the breach of the walls, throwing open the gates, and disarming, neutralizing the sleepy guards and family members who failed to put up a significant resistance. Everything went pretty much as planned; on the Ako Clan side there were no fatalities, and only four or five minor injuries. A precise tally of casualties on Kira's behalf are vague—it's not their story, after all. The sense is there may have been a few. The problem was, there was no Kira to be found. They were completing their second search, this time giving it a minute inspection, but it was looking like they were coming up empty handed again. Oishi understood time was not on their side, in the event the neighbors, hearing the commotion, might alert Kira's allies in the area. They would not be able to hold off a sizeable opposition for long; it was imperative they find their despicable enemy, the focus and sole purpose of this whole prolonged endeavor. After, the chips could fall where they might...

Then, they did find him, huddled in the woodshed. He was brought before the group for final comments before summary execution by means of decapitation—the swift separation of head from torso. Posterity does not record Kira's final remarks, but they very well may have entailed disparaging and unsavory references to the bestial nature of the ancestry of his captors.

220

Their final duty to their lord was to present Kira's head to Asano's tomb, on the grounds of Sengaku-ji, in Shinagawa, the outskirts of Edo. After its summary separation, the head was cleaned—they would have let the blood drain out as much as possible, then removed any external blood, likely, by rubbing it in the fresh snow.

They wrapped the head in a plain *furoshiki*, a broad, multi-purpose scarf, and tied it to the business end of a pike, where it would swing to the walking stride of the person carrying it. One imagines that these proud *ronin* took turns carrying this reviled trophy all the way to Shinagawa, some eight or ten miles. It would have been a precious burden.

This brazen act sent shock waves through Edo. These 47 ronin were immediately placed under house arrest by two sympathetic clans where, by some accounts, they were celebrated lavishly. The deed was unprecedented in Tokugawa history, so Tsunayoshi Shogun took his time and consulted many advisors and Daimyo. Finally, some six weeks later, the judgement was rendered; there had never been any serious doubt. They were permitted to commit *hara kiri* (same kanji, same meaning, as *seppuku*), tummy slice, auto abdominal vivisection, and join their master at Sengaku-ji. Disallowing an exception to the rule, for example, by showing leniency to these honorable men, assured there would be no awkward precedent to be exploited later.

It is possible to visit Sengaku-ji and its famous graveyard today in Shinagawa, a short train ride from central Tokyo. If you go, be prepared for a humbling experience. Incense billows in thick clouds seemingly unabated, affirming the triumph of loyalty—said to be chief among the Confucian virtues. Life is short, but virtuous devotion, especially in so pure a form as loyalty, is eternal. Or something like that.

Also, it needs to be said, the somewhat fading reputation of the samurai was at once restored to heroic stature.

* * * * *

Mamonaku, yon-ban sen ni, kakoeki-tesha ga mairimasu. Abunai des kara, kiroi-sen no uchigawa made osagari kudasai.

"Soon, on track number four, a local train will arrive. Be careful and stand behind the yellow line, if you please."

This canned announcement, or slight variations thereof, depending on the train line, is made a full minute before the arrival of the next train; that's hundreds of times daily, counting both sides of the platform, same station, averaging every twelve minutes, times 20 hours a day. My elder daughter Petra Cassiopeia, unprompted, committed this announcement to memory, one can only assume, by waiting on one too many train platforms.

Note to the Teacher part of Father: *Let's please find this child more to do, something more challenging and rewarding than memorizing programmed train-arrival announcements.*

1990

Wabi and *Sabi* (not to be confused with *wasabi*) are essential concepts pertaining to the core aesthetic of the Japanese. *Wabi*, 侘, a sense of unassuming elegance, *sabi*, 寂, the special nature of the experience, together refer to an artistic sense that expresses the essence of elegant simplicity and, in its uniqueness, an undercurrent but omnipresent wistfulness, maybe even loneliness. As an illustration, in *Sado*, the tea ceremony, sometimes the tea bowls—bowl-shaped "cups" without handles—are often unadorned and crudely made earthenware with a glaze of earth tones, and be worth many thousands of dollars, based on the *wabi/sabi* characteristics these cups manifest. A far cry from High Tea in English polite society: Some Earl Gray? A spot of Darjeeling? To go with an array of scones and marmalade, or perchance, crumpets, all served on Wedgewood "bone" china, fine porcelain really, exquisitely decorated, and so delicate the cups are translucent.

February 14: St. Valentine's Day, a day young marriageable OLs (Office Ladies) are supposed to spend a lot of money buying fancy, boutique chocolate for all their colleagues and their seniors at the office—to send what kind of message, do you suppose? That they recognize the gender counterpoint nature of the relationship? That they have romantic feelings towards these men? Feelings of lust? Alas, probably not much more than the sense if *giri,* duty, responsibility to do the expected thing. By the way, the event is known as *Saint* Valentine's Day in Japan, though I believe the Catholics have long ago acknowledged there was no behavior associated with this individual that qualified as remotely saintly.

This inter-gender imbalance is cleverly addressed with the 100% corporation invented…

March 14: White Day! On this occasion, all those men who were acknowledged one month before with the bestowal of rich and varied flavors of dark chocolate by their feminine acquaintances and colleagues, have been programmed to reciprocate, as dictated by the equal-and-opposite principle. Only this time, the style *de rigueur* is white chocolate. Even though everybody knows this whole chocolate pretext is literally an invention of the

225

Valentine card manufacturers, chocolatiers, florists, perfumeries—retailers of all stripe who tap this vein—nevertheless, most folks follow along, again, through *giri*.

November 12, Monday: A national holiday on the occasion of the enthronement ceremony of the Emperor Akihito, or *Sokui no rei,* even though it's been a year and 10 months since the (official) death of the Showa Emperor Hirohito, and the beginning of the Heisei Era.

Dignitaries from some 150 countries are in attendance, it is said, many with their hand outstretched—the Japanese Overseas Development Assistance having been recently acknowledged as the largest in the world, and is therefore, much coveted by developing nations. Estimates of more than 37,000 police have been mobilized as security from the avowed threat of the radicals who have pledged to disrupt the proceedings. Costs of the ceremony, which in itself took all of 20 minutes, were in excess of $95,000,000. Seven banquets are scheduled, sometimes two a day for the next few days, so that the local and visiting VIPs/dignitaries get a shot at hob-nobbing with His Majesty, many of them hoping for some aid.

It has been a bit of a banner week for me, too. From Nov. 4 (Sunday) through the 10th (Saturday) I taught 41 hours of classes, earning a grandslam 19 *man yen;* that's 190 thousand yen—apologies for that blatant lapse into wanton greed. Of course the income is important, critical even, but I don't have to let it take center stage. The week also included three dinners: Tuesday evening with the Iwatas, Thursday evening with the Yoshidas, and Friday evening with the Tabatas, and one class with lunch. I'm a regular English-education generator!

I can't seem to put the notion of Japan's economic clout behind me. Let me start with some off-the-wall statistics. One *tsubo* equals 3.3 square meters. 45 tsubo = 20m x 25m. In the Tokyo area, the purchase of 45 tsubo will cost ¥180 million, or $1.38 million. Japan is estimated to be about 1/20th the geographic size of the US. Saleable assets of Japan are reported to be worth four times the saleable assets of the US. The land comprising the imperial palace in Tokyo is said to be worth the value of the entire state of California. (*How on earth is "value" measured so that a small piece of Tokyo real estate might be worth the whole of California?*) And though I don't see the explicit connection, my residence tax is ¥40,000 per month, or plus/minus $365, just for the privilege of living here every month—but providing me full health insurance.

Sumo

I am fortunate to be living in Nihon during the active career of Chiyonofuji, "the Wolf," a living legend in the world of Sumo. At 36, he's definitely approaching the end of his career, but the man has won thirty-one tournaments—several without so much as losing a match—and 807 individual contest wins, third in all-time wins in recorded history. And sumo has been around for a thousand years, so this is a big deal. Plus, the guy is absolutely svelte compared to most of the other hippopotami. My guess is he's in the range of five feet, seven or eight inches tall and packs no more than 240 pounds of sleek muscle. Like an NFL linebacker, or a punt returner—quick on his feet, and able to deliver a full-body slam when needed.

There are six formal sumo tournaments (*basho*) throughout the year, each lasting 15 days. That's one match a day for each participant for 15 days, times six *basho*, or 90 matches a year. Nobody wins all the time; there are just too many sly moves one's opponent can play on you to get you to over-commit. With a quick sidestep, the bull goes charging by, seeing the error in the last moment, but unable to alter his direction in time. Each match can take five minutes of formal preparation for battle. From the introduction of each *sumotori*, we proceed to the two preliminary acts of ritualistic purification. These are warm up exercises, raising first one leg, head-height off to one side, then the other leg; the psychological event of staring each other down; then scooping up a handful of salt and tossing it out onto the *dohyo*, before the *tachiai*, or official launch. After such an elaborate build up, the main event can almost be an anti-climax; it has been known to last two or three seconds. They rarely run more than 20 seconds. Whether in victory or defeat, it is *summary*, resolved without delay. If, by chance, the two gladiators lock onto each other's *mawashi*, the brightly colored silk sash, for a temporary stalemate, the official is apt to call out, *Nokota, nokota, nokota*, to spur them on to more effort.

227

Elaborate rules dictate the whole pageant, who stays in the Juryo division, the lower ranking, and who is promoted to Maebashi rank: a majority of wins vs. losses, and/or how many consecutive wins. An *Ozeki*, the second highest ranking after *Yokozuna*, can be demoted for failure to win a majority of matches two *basho* in a row, but a *Yokozuna* mut retire if that happens.

This raised fighting surface, the *dohyo*, is a pressed sand hill some 30 inches above surrounding grade, with twisted rice-straw rope serving as berms. According to Shinto precepts, it is a sacred place. The official in charge of judging these contests is himself a kind of Shinto priest who consecrates this field of intense struggle. According to sumo lore, this is the last unapologetic bastion of male dominance. So, when the *Diet*, the national government, decided to commemorate the Sumo Association with a scroll or plaque on some occasion or another, the complications began. It turns out a Ms. Moriyama was the designate from the relevant bureaucratic agency to make the commemoration speech—from the *dohyo*. Well, the Sumo Association was delighted to be honored, complimented, and praised, but in no uncertain terms could/would the presentation take place on the *dohyo* in any capacity with a female. In this regard, all women are impure. Furthermore, this is part of a tradition of many centuries, so don't even think about trying to change it...

I don't recall how this dilemma got resolved. Maybe parliament changed its mind on the award. Or Ms. Moriyama did the expedient thing and stuck the plaque in the mail. These things command a little ink in a two or three-day news cycle. A week later, it's all but forgotten, obscured by the latest scandal or tragedy.

Three Yokozuna in full Sumo regalia: from left, Hokutenyu; the "Wolf," Chiyonofuji; and Ononkuni

Edo period writers

Ihara Saikaku was arguably the most prominent prose writer of the 265-year period. One of the Big Three proponents of the literary arts, along with the famous haiku poet, Matsuo Basho, and the playwright, Chikamatsu Monzaemon, one of the earliest to produce a thinly disguised dramatization of the Chushingura story. By a mere forty years later, the tale had become renown throughout the land.

The central theme of Ihara's compositions is eroticism, with the significant sub-theme being homoeroticism. To give you an idea, one of his books is entitled *Glorious Tales of Pederasty*. It is hard to imagine a mainstream publishing house in the US today being willing to publish a book with that title, even given this "enlightened" (or "decadent," depending on one's point of view) time. Nor, for that matter, would publication be any likelier in mid-18th century America, at the time it was published in Nihon.

Meiji, up to wartime writers

Natsume Soseki was one of the promising scholars sent abroad to absorb culture, and in his case, the task was to master English. He spent a miserable two years avoiding his classes, avoiding almost all human contact, teaching himself the language by pouring through volume after volume of classical English literature. On returning, he assumed the English Department Chair at Tokyo University, following in Koizumi Yakumo's footsteps. The problem was his professorial life was not that fulfilling. Or to be more blunt about it, he was not particularly good at teaching, didn't like it, so his lectures were boring and interminable. In short order, he was able to transition to a professional writer based on the Asahi newspaper paying him to serialize his satire of contemporary society through the savvy persona of a housecat. This success led to a long, productive career writing wry commentaries, somewhat tortured reflections, and an attention to minutia that doesn't tell us much of anything—having absorbed the European literary zeitgeist during his years abroad, an urban life that never seemed to go anywhere. (*I'm half tempted to launch into a critique of Soseki's "Mon," "The Gate," to give the Western reader a sense of how unrelievedly mundane and stultifying this writer can be,*

230

but I'd bore you to stupefaction. The reader this desperate enough for reading material may certainly pursue Soseki with my blessing.) I have given this scribe four or five chances, out of something like 14 novels—because I'm a masochist for literary punishment. But Natsume-san has not only failed to impress me, he can barely hold my attention, and I am acutely interested in the Meiji Period, his heyday and milieu. As it is, with a little luck, I might never have to read him again. The face of the ¥1000 bill, Natsume Soseki is considered the *"father* of modern Japanese literature," though *slightly twisted uncle...* might have been a more suitable choice.

From two collections of short stories, I'd say Akutagawa Ryunoske was a gifted story teller (27). Tragically, he seems to have been too burdened by life, despite having a wife and children, to endure beyond the age of 35. Those had to have been some serious demons!

Koizumi Yakumo, Lafcadio Hearn, a foreigner, is the exception in this list. He was born on the Greek island of Lafkada in 1850 to a Greek mother, and an Irish father. As a child, he moved to Ireland to enhance his educational options, but soon Mama got left behind. As a newly minted graduate, he sailed for the US to seek his fortune, found work as a Cincinnati newspaper reporter, from which he spun off some longer pieces, wound up living in New Orleans, and the Caribbean, for a decade working for another paper, and dabbling in ghost tales. Then, he finagled a New York paper in 1890 to subsidize his trip to Japan to do a series of articles—and he never looked back. In the 14 years until he died he must have written at least a dozen books, all on Japan. He is widely accepted as the gaijin most successful at capturing *Nihon no kokoro*, the spirit, or essence, of Japan. His work of course was all written in English. Having come to Japan at 40 (in my case, 43), it was too late for either of us to begin amassing the +/- 2000 kanji to achieve literacy in Japanese. It's no disrespect, however, to say he's a trifle outdated in some of his "contemporary" insights—inasmuch as he's been dead since 1904.

Post-war writers

Kawabata Yasunari, Tanizaki Junichiro, Abe Kobo, Dazai Osamu, and Mishima Yukio are all writers I have perused—some, extensively. Mishima is arguably the strangest, most eccentric person/persona to emerge in post-war Japan. I suppose I'm obliged to defend that emphatic assertion, so I'll offer a couple of episodes of exotic detail of the life of this complicated, very gifted man. The first is a glimpse of his childhood, and the other, an aspect of his death.

The nitty gritty: Mishima's paternal grandmother, herself a bored, widowed aristocrat, and absolute termagant of the house, took over raising the boy from infancy until he was twelve. It is said he slept *in the same bed* with this temperamental woman well into puberty. For years she prevented this bright, inquisitive boy from engaging in normal play with other boys. He was rarely allowed outdoors at all. Eager for any social opportunity and desperate to escape, even temporarily, the cell of his Grandmother's room, Mishima would play with his younger sister and her friends (28). *Hmm-m, I wonder if such an upbringing might torque a child's psychosexual bearings...*

Fast forward to 1970, his forty-fifth year: He'd achieved virtually every literary award Japan has to offer, narrowly missing selection for the Nobel Prize in literature, in deference to Kawabata Yasunari. Mishima was a media darling, appearing on TV talk shows at will. He was married with two daughters. And his literary output had been prodigious. The guy cranked out plays, novels, critical essays, poetry, screenplays, performed in movies and just for fun, wrote at least five modern *No* plays and one *Kabuki*—in period vernacular.

I read his *No* plays, and thanks to Donald Keene's introduction, I was able to follow the general idea of this highly stylized, symbolic drama. The original performances from the 14th century had no dialogue, while the protagonist wore a fixed masked, giving the audience no opportunity to read an affective dimension from facial expressiveness. Beyond the plain mask of a woman, in one instance, the performer is completely covered in a kimono; the only flesh visible are the hands. The audience had little else to go on but the dance these masked characters enact. Most of the hour-long event is this long, drawn-out dance fraught with symbolic gestures that only the cognoscenti are privy to; anyway, the subtle dance steps and hand gestures were mostly lost on me—a crude and coarse gaijin. *What's that you say? The next generation of Nihonjin don't really see the point, either?*

Thankfully, Mishima doesn't subject his audience to extended dances by fixed-expression characters, but he does focus on a specific point of human desire, exclusively from 15/16th century precedent, and takes it to the absurd. Given that *No* is such an abstruse, limited genre, I cut Mishima some slack. I thought he did a decent job at creating contexts for human irony and absurdity:

There's no way to make a madman like you understand the futility of human existence (from "Kantan," *Five Modern No Plays*) (29).

Throughout his lifetime, he demonstrated a flair for mixing and blending Art—a representation and interpretation of Life—and Life itself, the *source...* of awareness, meaning, purpose, desire, and passion. Over the years Mishima had developed an ardent nationalist streak; he came to believe Western influences were corrupting Japan's essential values and, as a result, he formed his own militia (+/- 100 members) with the stated goal of preserving the sanctity of the emperor and the imperial system. Ultimately, he commandeered the Self-Defense Forces Headquarters, and exhorted the cadets to join him in a *coup d'état* of the overly West-leaning government, the lap dogs of Western whims and orientation. (The worst of it was the wholesale capitulation of Japan to Western pop culture, particularly American movies and music—*rock and roll; the Horrors!*) When the cadets mocked, and made fun of his ridiculous exhortations—as he anticipated they would—he went back into the commandant's office and, along with his lover/second in command, committed *seppuku* (28).

Here's a grisly detail the squeamish reader doesn't *need* to know, but since I am somewhat haunted by it, I'm going to share. Mishima and his four hand-picked cadets had many times practiced their plan, from beginning the takeover of the *Jieitai* (SDF) commandant and the headquarters, to the final *hara kiri*. When one of the four noticed a small packet of cotton wadding in Mishima's personal briefcase on the morning of the event, he explained he would use it to insert in his rectum a sufficient amount to plug up the anus, in anticipation of his anal sphincter inevitably relaxing—soon after *kaishaku*, the severing of his head.

I have to say, I'm impressed by that thoughtful touch, that consideration for the poor schmucks who would have to haul his bloody remains out of there. There was no point in making their lives more miserable. A thoughtful guy, that Mishima. But here's a follow-up consideration: If a person commits ritualistic self-disembowelment, if he stabs himself in the lower abdomen with a long knife, his foot-long *tanto*—and attempts to drag the knife, slicing across the abdomen from one side to the other—there is no way, even from the first jab, he could have avoided slashing his intestines. He would die knowing he would not embarrass himself from anal leakage, but he was sure as hell going to "leak" out of his self-inflicted wound. He was going to spill some of himself on the carpet, and stink up the place, in spite of himself.

A little slide into the macabre, there. *Gomen nasai,* sorry.

Of these novelists, I came closest to "enjoying" Kawabata, and his ability to evoke a simple, straightforward story in engaging settings. For a while, I wondered if the translator(s) had failed to render nuanced but essential connections in these authors' narratives, leaving me adrift in a sea of ambiguity. However, by the tenth or twelfth translated work—by eight or nine different translators—I had to concede that the translations were likely to have been reasonably faithful to the original intent. Japanese literature and I were just not operating on the same wavelength. I suppose I'd been culturally disinclined to see a different style as just that: different. Not better, not worse, but *otherwise* in orientation. Operating from different assumptions as to how to interpret the world. Making judgements based on different standards; for example, *affect*, except in the case of rage, seems conspicuously scarce in Japanese literature. Or so subtly hinted at, so blithely alluded to that a gaijin potato head would have no hope of divining the passion.

I admit it's tough letting go my own culture's literary standards of story setting, plot, character development, use of humor, but if it's not too much to ask, once in a while might we have a wrap up, a summation—dare I plead for a *conclusion*? *Oneigai itashimasu,* my humble request.

* * * * *

米 : *Mai, Me, Be, Kome, Gohan*: Rice

It is fair to say that the Yamato race, the Japanese language and culture, the foundation of what we experience today, could not have flourished, and

234

perhaps, not even survived, without having domesticated rice and mastered the simple means to cultivate it. Rice as seed start, in all likelihood, was introduced with the early Asian immigrants, four or more thousand years ago. To the Japanese, rice is sacred. Each fall the Emperor performs an elaborate ceremony of gratitude to the Shinto spirits for another bountiful harvest of rice.

Gohan means meal, but it is also another word for rice. *Kome*, but usually with the honorific, "O," attached: *O-kome*, is honorable uncooked rice. Then, there is the rice that was used as a standard for taxation purposes in Tokugawa days: How many *koku* of rice a region was responsible for as an estimated percentage of the area's rice growing capacity.

The rice that virtually everybody in Japan eats is a polished, short-grain variety, *haku mai*. The crown jewel is *Koshi Hikari*, the "Sunbeam of Koshi" (a renowned local landmark in Fukui prefecture, where the strain was developed), nowadays a specialty of the Niigata area. The second most popular strain of rice is *Hito me Bore*, "Love at First Sight." It is a specialty of Miyagi Prefecture. Then, there's *Sasa Nishiki*, hybrid from two other varieties in 1963; it is the pride of Sendai. There must be at least ten nationally popular varieties in Japan. My wife claims she can discern the various regional variants, one from another, like in a "blind" wine tasting, but I am frankly skeptical. She can probably rank four or five varieties highest to lowest in quality, determined by agreed-upon criteria. On the other hand, who knows what a Nihonjin's nose and taste buds are capable of?

When many Americans hear the word rice, they reflexively think of "Uncle Ben's 3-Minute Rice." Most Americans would rank grains in order of carbohydrate consumption: wheat, corn, oats, barley, *then* maybe rice. Potatoes, as a non-grain carb, would also rank higher than rice.

The parallel for Europeans and Americans is wheat, the staple of Western Civilization. There must be a half-dozen different varieties of wheat, according to the intended use: Hard Red Spring is prized for bread; less glutinous Soft Red Winter is cultivated for cakes, pie crusts, crackers, and breakfast cereal. Hard White is good for brewing, in addition to bread (Wikipedia: "Wheat"). Also, we have Semolina, another wheat variant, the source of pasta.

Rice distributors usually have whole grain/not-yet polished *genmai*, brown rice, but they seem to think you, or a family member, must have a severe gastro-intestinal condition requiring it. Otherwise, why would you consume it? Even fully cooked, *genmai* requires more chewing, and most Japanese are chewing adverse. White rice doesn't really require any chewing. It's not uncommon to see people in a hurry inhale a bowl of rice as quick as they could paddle it with chopsticks into the intake orifice and swallow the lot. It's a little like the issue of denatured, bleached, white, tasteless flour—but more profitable, owing to its hugely extended shelf life—most Americans "prefer," but let us not careen over the edge with that rant for the moment.

Another interesting rice product is *mochi*. It is high-gluten-content rice that is scooped steaming into a large wooden basin, ideally, a tree stump, or the likes, in a year-end, typically rural event called *mochitsuki*, the mochi-making festival. This scalding-hot rice is pounded with a heavy wooden mallet until the sticky starch is converted into sugar by getting bashed by willing participants in turn. In 15, maybe 20 minutes of practiced, continual beating and turning this still hot, five-kilo, gooey mass, it is no longer identifiable as rice. Syrup-like, it is then poured onto shallow trays to harden as it cools. I find it fascinating that by slamming this cooked, high-gluten rice, the nearly pure rice starch could be "shocked" into changing to sugar, a slightly different molecule—and that some Japanese farmers figured this out, how many centuries ago.

It's only been the last couple of generations that Nihonjin could even conceive of building a meal without rice as an essential ingredient. Wouldn't you know it, these days it is cheap, tasty, convenient, and fashionable "fast food," more appropriately known as "junk food," as the alternative to traditional meals built around rice. This is one aspect of the Japanese following Western trends that is not such a good idea. In America, junk food is associated with obesity and diseases, such as diabetes, heart disease, and various cancers.

December 15: From a Christmas card to a hard-scrabble couple in Oregon on their consideration of a visit to Japan:

Well, another joyous holiday season is upon us—ready or not. Frankly, I'm not, but then nobody consulted me. I don't know about youse, but a little forced gaiety and group cheer go a long way, as far as I'm concerned. I trust you are both hale and bearing up under the vicissitudes of the season. We're holding our own, as they say. Phip is here (though about to go back to Novato for a couple weeks' vacation). He's adapting to the rigors of life in Japan better than I expected. He's teaching a lot and seems to be well liked, thanks to his background. He plans to stay until May, whereupon he'll resume life on Small River with his newly acquired nest egg.

Kimiko says Howdy, and remembers fondly a sumptuous meal you all prepared for us, coincidental to rendering us catatonic—or was it hebephrenic?—with truly Bacchanalian amounts of wine and other mind alterants. No doubt, her youthfulness allows her to recall such details.

We are already plotting your visit to these shores. We have sights to astound you, restaurants to tax your culinary imagination, e.g., partially fermented squid entrails, Shio kara, *and creamy sea urchin gonads,* uni, *yum! The inscrutable East awaits you. And we, your eager (if also somewhat inscrutable) hosts, are beside ourselves in anticipation.*

Ed. Note: They never came. They begged off. A change of financial status? Appalled and/or repulsed by my gustatory figments? We've remained close friends for many years, but I never found out why they changed their minds.

The end-of-year phenomena: *Omisoka*, December 31; *Sho gatsu*, New Year's; *Ganjitsu*, New Year's day

Oseibo, obligatory end-of-year gift acknowledgement from an understudy to one's patron, student to beneficent professor, employee to one's boss, *kohai* to *sempai,* you get the idea. Is the man to be curried known to enjoy drinking? Then a bottle of high-class sake, or some fancy whiskey would be appropriate. It could be a necktie, or some other token of appreciation, but frankly, every adult male office worker over the age of forty has more than enough neckties to last the rest of his life.

(*Ochugen* is the corresponding middle-of-the-year equivalent; that's twice a year the younger, less prestigious, and less powerful acolyte or apprentice, by long tradition, must pay a token acknowledgement for the gratitude felt by Junior for Senior's solicitude.)

Bonen-kai, end-of-year parties where an entire office department will gather at a drinking establishment for some food and lots of alcohol—beer, sake, and whiskey, often serially. The Japanese are often socially inhibited, and booze is the universal lubricant. It is the only socially acceptable outlet from the daily pressure *kaisha-in* (or office workers) experience. Of course, these parties can and do occur throughout the year; it's just that the waning days of the year provide more opportunities than usual to celebrate. The object seems to be to get shit-faced as quick as possible, and tell the boss (or whoever the authority figure is at the time) what you really think of him. Nobody takes it seriously; he/she doesn't really mean it since s/he is *sugoi yoparai*, really drunk. Late at night train station platforms, and sometimes the train cars themselves often bear witness to the excesses of alcohol. Japanese society takes a benign attitude toward public drunkenness because of the recognition of the personal release alcohol provides. I suppose there is the hope that the pain of recovery—the hangover—will serve as deterrent to future alcohol excesses, but it never really seems to work that way. Anyway, this end-of-year event is the one to let it all hang out.

If someone asked you what you thought the counterpart was to the year-end excuse for a big drunken party, how might you answer? That for the next month or so, you'd like a return to the comfort a predictable routine brings? Well, the way the Japanese usher in the New Year—after *hatsumode*—is to celebrate with a bunch of <u>Shinnen-kai,</u> or New Year parties! They are not nearly as prominent or as wild as the year-end events, probably because people by then really are trying to recover from the binge and return to a sense of normalcy. During one New Year, I remember attending six *Bonen-kai* events over a four-day period; that is two nooners and four consecutive evenings, paying serious homage to Dionysius. *Oh, my poor liver!* It takes a lot of stamina to sustain a series of these parties.

Osechi ryori is elaborate year-end food preparation, days in the making, requiring no refrigeration, a la the old days when none existed. Various kinds of fish and cod roe, cooked black beans, and *kombu*, or eel grass seaweed, are part of the preparation. The cooked, sweetened beans, *mame*, at this time of year, are symbolic of diligence and ambition. The cod roe, *kazenoko*, indicates fecundity, propitious for many children, doubtless more appropriate for a bygone era. Lots of salt and/or sugar and/or vinegar are used to cure these foods, to be snacked on for the first three days of the New Year when the housewife finally gets her vacation from housecleaning and meal preparation.

238

In fact, custom, also known as *meishin*, superstition, cautions that no one is to sweep the floors these first three days lest all the good luck be swept away.

The younger generation seems to be forgoing this elaborate and time consuming preparation, but fortunately, this special food can be ordered from area department stores and delivered to one's home—for upwards of *ni man, go sen yen,* or two hundred twenty dollars! *Ozoni,* New Year's morning clear soup served with a large lump of *mochi*--hot gluten rice pounded until the starch is converted into sugar, winding up in a kind of white, sticky candy, like taffy. Starch or sugar, *mochi* is a high-energy snack, but every year some people choke to death trying to swallow too big a chunk before adequately masticating and dissolving the *mochi*.

Ko haku is the five or six hour TV performance New Year's Eve. In the run up to midnight and the New Year, two teams of musicians "compete" for the TV viewers' rating: The Red Team and the White Team. These performers are primarily aging singers, sometimes truly ancient crones, evenly matched with young talent groups (*tarento*) on both teams. The old timers, men and women, have applied mascara with a plaster trowel, and tend to sing old, traditional ballads of unrequited love (*Enka*) with grotesquely exaggerated vibrato. The first song or two, you're curious because it is different from what you are used to. But by the fourth or fifth song, you've had enough. As descriptors go, "dreary," "mind-numbing," and "gloomy" spring to mind. *Mensch,* if you weren't quite ready to swallow the poisoned pill yet, suck on the business end of a gun, or step off the platform as the train comes roaring into the station—but had given some languid thought to it—a long evening of this kind of entertainment in the slightly surreal final hours of another year could put you right over the top.

Nengajo, New Year's post cards sent to all of one's family and associates, sometimes including personalized art signaling the new year's zodiac animal (2010, the dragon; 2015, the ram; 2020, the rat); each card featuring a specific number automatically entered in the mega end-of-year lottery.

Otoshi dama, the elaborately enveloped New Year's monetary gift senior family members are culturally obliged to give to the youth of the family. Kimiko offers ¥1000 each to the next generation of attendees at the

Morikawa New Year's bash (+/- 12 kids). I'm embarrassed to say how much I was given....

Hatsumode, the first visit of the year to a shrine (or temple) to ask for blessings, divine support for a son or daughter to persevere and do well in academics; in finding a good job; in pursuit of a husband or wife, and good health for family members. It occurs to me it's possible that *Hatsumode* represents a subconscious desire to show solidarity with the other 60 million folks participating in this culturally unifying tradition on these couple of days.

Omikuji, one of ten fortunes for the New Year one purchases (for ¥100) at a shrine. Mine was relatively low ranked but oddly enough, that in itself is considered auspicious, since the possibility of upward achievement is high. *Kyo* is considered bad luck, and *kichi* is just average, neither-good-nor-bad luck. I guess the logic is, if you've got *Dai*（大）*kichi,* meaning big, large, great fortune. You've had your summit and have nowhere to go but down... People tie these harbingers of luck for the upcoming year onto wire racks placed for the purpose, and sometimes to the branches of nearby bushes and trees. By such a means the breeze wafts your prospects throughout the spiritual world. Or so they say.

Ekiden is the relay race that takes place every January 2 through the 3rd. The race begins at Nihon Bashi in downtown Tokyo, and continues to Hakone/Ashinoko, at the foot of Fujisan on the Western edge of the Kanto Plain, a distance of some 65 miles. Then, back again, in two long days. The runners are exclusively from Japanese university teams. Some twenty relay teams from around the country, with some international participants, run for the trophy. Even though it's broadcast live on NHK TV, tens of thousands of people line the race course by the hour to cheer on the runners. It's all about solidarity.

* * * * *

I stopped keeping track of events in my journal around this time. By 1991 my time to wax contemplative with a pen and paper about how things appear, had pretty much evaporated. Time is a great luxury one is apt to take for granted, until it is no longer available. The occasions in the previous year that I chose to record tended to be exceptional events; I didn't seem to find the time to explore other imaginings. Since marriage in April of '88, most of the time I wasn't teaching, in transit to and from, or sleeping, was involved with Kimiko. The chance to write became even more a premium than it had been, and the journal became an unfortunate casualty. But Kimiko and I continued living in that same house in Kugenuma until May, 1995, when we moved to Portland, Oregon.

The following are anecdotes, many of them longitudinal observations, the product of a protracted view, starting with an overview of my children's visits.

My three children, Petra, Ariel, and Loren, visited me on three different occasions, always in the summertime, and always for at least a month. The first visit was in 1987, and it was distinguished by our climbing Japan's highest mountain, Fujisan, with the Yoshidas. The last visit was in 1991 or 2, and the middle visit must have been in 1989. There is precious little I can associate with a particular year, though the farrago of events could have happened in any of the three visits. I recall an experience I thought at the time was a notable contrast: On the day following our ascent of Fujisan, some Chigasaki housewife students of mine hosted us for a picnic on the beach. One day you are struggling to climb a 12,389 foot high mountain, and descend in one piece, the next, you are paddling your feet in the ocean, still recovering from the climb. And maybe that same visit we went to this swim resort on Oiso beach where you pay an entrance fee and have access to some five aquatic opportunities, a water slide, a giant swimming pool, a diving pool, and a giant loop of a pool where there is a constant looping current, like swimming in a river. Way cool.

That same visit I think we stayed overnight with a family in order to get up and watch a bunch of liquored up men in loin cloths, shouting, *Wa sho! Wa sho!,* carry this *omikoshi* ("portable" shrine) into the ocean for its annual cleansing as the sun rose. On the evening before, the host family and we sat on *zabuton* at a long, low table, and were treated to a 12 or 14 course meal. Of course the standard fare was provided, the staples of a civilized Japanese meal:

1) A cup of *ryoku-cha*. A fairly bitter, lightly-toasted green-leaf tea for household consumption and hosting guests.

241

2) A bowl of *miso shiru*, a clear soup flavored by a dollup of *miso*, a small chunk of tofu, a small leaf of *mitsuba*, a dash of *dashi* (dried, grated bonito), sliced daikon, and a pinch of cilantro—or just about anything laying around. There are as many subtle variations in the final product as there are cooks to make it. E.g., my wife likes to make *miso shiru* with a handful of tiny clams, when they are available. By the way, this "soup" is just as prominently served for *asa gohan*, morning meal/breakfast, as it is for *hiro gohan*, mid-day meal/lunch, and *yu gohan*, dinner. There is no major distinction as to types of food to be served/consumed among those fortunate enough to eat three meals a day.

3) A bowl of steamed, white, or polished, rice. Here too, it is not unusual to be served rice for every meal.

4) An assortment of pickled vegetables. The most prominent vegetable is *daikon*—an all-white, giant, carrot-shaped, tangy flavored root—but the Japanese pickle other vegetables, such as carrots, turnips, eggplant, and cabbage, as well.

In addition to these staples of *wa shoku*, or Eastern/Japanese-style cooking, our host also offered an impressive array of *sashimi*-ed (raw) seafood, a rich variety of *tempura*-ed food, an assortment of sea food and vegetables dipped in a batter and coated in special crumbs, called *panko,* before being grilled or fried. And a curious little savory custard, *chawan mushi,* with a tiny sprig of tangy mitsuba, and/or cilantro, one ginkgo nut, a small shrimp, sometimes a chunk of chicken, or a boiled quail egg, served warm in a Japanese cup—no handle—with a cap on it.

I felt immensely proud of my kids that evening. They'd withstood one cultural shock after another, scarcely having time to absorb or discuss together the strange events they were experiencing, when it was on to the next mind-bending event. And here they were facing *the Test*, in terms of full-run, up-scale Japanese cuisine. The hosts had really pulled out the stops on this meal. The question on their minds was, will this adult and child-to-teenager quartet be able to eat Japanese food? My impression is all three ate virtually everything placed in front of them. They might have been tentative at first with stuff like raw jellyfish, raw salmon eggs, or squid. And then there's *yamaimo*, taro, a wild, starchy root; I don't know how it is cooked, steamed or boiled I'm guessing, then served in a cup. It would have to be classified as a liquid, though it is so viscid and mucilaginous, that I suspect most Westerners would object to it, not based on objectionable taste, which is very mild and inoffensive, but solely on texture. *Are you ready for your cup of snot? We've warmed it up for you...*

In any event, I don't recall any specific refusal to eat anything. No doubt, the fact that they were ravenous—with the options worse than dismal—aided them in overcoming a certain natural inclination to treat intercultural oddities with trepidation. Particularly when those oddities were supposed to be eaten. Nothing quite like having the stomach gnaw on the backbone to lower the bar to the floor, as regards the presumption of edibility: *These people eat whatever this is. As long as we are able to stifle the gag reflex, we can eat it, too!* It boils down to the existential question, *How hungry am I?* In my case, my digestive tract seemed to be impervious to "strange" aspects of *Nihon shoku,* Japanese cuisine (relative to standard Western cuisine), so perhaps my kinder had enough confidence in me to trust my role behavior on this score. But, of course, the question isn't, *Is this food safe to eat?* It's *Am I hungry enough to eat it?* And to be fair, most of the food was not that far from "familiar" food, though perhaps never before so elegantly presented.

Here's Loren's take on the Japanese cuisine: *Food—the essential ingredient for a growing boy (not to mention plenty of sleep)—was another culture shock I remember well from out trips to Nippon. Dad was so well respected that we were treated to some of the best food experiences available. We had really high quality sushi and sashimi, Kobe beef, curry, escargot. Hard not to like these incredible delicacies. Unusual doesn't even begin to describe the likes of corn and shrimp on pizza, nasty gooey <u>nato</u> (fermented soybeans), raw egg cracked on a bed of hot rice for breakfast, or smoked/dried fish for breakfast. Onigiri have a story all to themselves.*

(*Onigiri* are the original, portable Japanese meal. They are thick rice triangles, maybe two inches on a side, an inch thick, partially wrapped in a thin, dried sheet of seaweed. The center of this triangle could be a pickle of somesort, *umeboshi*—a pickled plum with a sour punch—or a chunk of smoked salmon; the possibilities are vast as to what your *onigiri* might contain. Ed.)

We climbed Mt. Fuji on either the first or second trip to Japan. The Yoshida family were integral to the execution of the journey, and brought along onigiri for light lunch along the way. The pickled and heavily salted morsels in the middle were sure a surprise. Well, that wasn't the last surprise from the onigiri. Late that night, after a really terrific trip up and down Fujisan, I woke with a colossal headache and upset stomach. That night was my first experience with projectile vomiting. From my sleeping arrangements on the top bunk, I painted partially digested onigiri chunks on the ceiling and walls. Good times!

Despite the negative experiences with Japanese food, I still gravitate towards it. My all- time favorite food is sushi and sashimi, and I know my oneichan tachi (older sister, plural) feel similarly.

During their second visit I bribed them into learning *Hiragana* and *Katakana*. I figured it would empower them to be able to read signs and the names of train stations, which are always given in Kanji prominently, and in smaller Hiragana directly under. This was, I thought, the single easiest way to a limited degree of practical literacy. All three resisted the task to some extent, but learned most of the figures in spite of themselves. I think the "reward" they received was $100 each, which they'd figured out they were going to get, no matter what.

On another occasion we went camping somewhere near the base of Fujisan, except the notion of "camping" extended to sleeping in cabin dormitories and eating in a mess hall. There must have been 200 kids. I'm guessing there was somesort of campfire with skits, sing-alongs, and other team competitions. My few memories of the event include *rajio taiso* (radio calisthenics). At dawn we assembled in an open field, made to pace off a full arm's length away from the next person, and engaged in warm-up exercises mostly of swinging our arms back and forth to a somewhat strident radio broadcast.

Breakfast consisted of green tea, as much as you want, a bowl of *miso shiru*, clear soup, a bowl of plain white rice, a raw egg, and a small packet of three or four sheets of *nori*, dried seaweed. If one is sufficiently hungry, one cracks the raw egg into the rice, stirs it with the *waribashi,* or throw-away chopsticks, adds soy sauce at the consumer's discretion, and deftly picks up cold gobs of this gelatinous goo enfolded in the dried seaweed, and without

244

further thought—lest this sticky mess drip down one's front—shove it into the fanged maw. *Now, there's a Breakfast of Champions!*

The night before, by some luck of the draw, my second daughter Ariel and I wound up on camp dish-washing detail. It went pretty routinely until we got to scrubbing pots. Discouraged, I thought we'd never get the burned-on food off the bottom of those six-to-eight-gallon caldrons. I can't recall whether I expressed that sentiment or not, but I could have. I was not particularly known for my reticence, so I could have manifested a stunning paternal example of how I react to hardship. Whereas my tenacious little thirteen year old, without so much as a peep of a complaint, hacked, scraped, and scrubbed until those pots gleamed.

I didn't really know what to expect early on with my kids' visits, so I was quite surprised and grateful that so many of my students organized events to include us all. Many of my students went to no little trouble or cost to host us for special occasions. The Yoshidas reserved a big table on the top floor of an Enoshima banquet hall with a view across the causeway to the Katase beach where Fujisawa's annual fireworks display was to take place. Lavish events.

On another visit Kimiko and I took my young 'uns to Kyoto, where we bravely—or foolishly—perused the central city sites/sights by rental bicycles. Just another group of gaijin, in a city used to non-stop tourists, darting in and out of traffic without spilling a bike or rider. I don't think there was so much as a skinned knee, not to speak of a horribly mangled body as a result of a brush with, say, an eleven-ton bus. We five *kamikaze* bike riders lived charmed lives that day.

Memory is capricious, fickle, and does not always serve chronologically. Lately I recall that we arrived in Kyoto by *shinkansen*, mid-morning, put our over-night bags in coin-operated lockers, and caught the next local train for Nara. Less than an hour later we had arrived at this early capital and first truly urban center, at the beginning of an emerging unified, core identity. We mostly walked to the oldest wooden structure in the world. We walked to the largest enclosed Buddha in Japan, *Todai-ji,* or temple. Along with everyone else, we were charmed by the tame deer on the grounds of *Suchandso-ji.* We probably failed as Classical-Kyoto/Nara-period scholars—

245

except to note how shockingly short the Nara period was: 84 years; from 710 to 794. It was a lot to take in, returning in time for check in at our Kyoto hotel, and find some place to eat. Despite having traveled more than four hours by train that day, we'd also managed to traipse around Nara several miles, or so it felt.

Of course we fell prey to the tendency of visitors 'round the world to a renowned location for a short stay: we crammed in as many temples, fortresses, and shrines as humanly possible. As a result, we suffered sensory overload—the phenomenon that kicks in after about two and a half hours (*Whoa, who am I kidding? For most folks, no matter how whoop-dee-doo and ultra, mega, super-special the collection may be, ninety minutes is a long time of reasonably intense concentration to the art displayed in any self-respecting museum*). You had better take that exposure to world-class art, architecture, or what have you, ve-e-r-ry slowly if you have any hope of creating a personal, meaningful experience to remember. Us? In Kyoto, we assailed at least five World-Heritage temples, and shrines, and *Nijo-jo*—the castle the Tokugawas built for their own pleasure and protection, but finally turned over to the imperial household—before we called it a day. Each of these marvels was undeniably wondrous, spectacular, and unique. Alas, taken all at once, you've incapacitated your *New-Material Receptors* through the sheer magnitude of serial bedazzlement. Cognitive-Sensory overload. *Geap?!*

Here's Ariel's 15-year-old interpretation of the Ryoan-ji experience: *It was an area of gardens and ponds. One rock garden, called Ryoan-ji, was very famous. It was man-made by a Zen priest in the 16th century. It was very simple, with fifteen large stones in about five groups, surrounded by white rocks* (coarse gravel? ed.). *From anyplace on the platform, you could not see all the rocks. Fifteen symbolizes completeness, or all, and only God can see all of them.*

Other than that explanation, they give none. It is up to you. Many people think it is some mystic, meditation place. They think the builder was a genius. I think it is very peaceful, and if it makes people think about God, or help nature, great, but other than that, I tend to think it is a 'cosmic chuckle.'

The following day, we bussed to a temple noted for its mossy grounds on the outskirts of town. American landscape gardeners tend to treat moss as the enemy of all that is holy, and go to great lengths to eradicate it, including the use of some fairly serious herbicides. At this temple the monks allowed it to grow freely. It is quite beautiful, this green carpet beneath the maple, pine, and cedar trees. Coincidentally, this temple was holding somesort of a campaign to promote "world peace," a normally safe theme among most folks. There was a sign-in log where the guests were encouraged to register their hopes and prayers, or just comments. We could view the comments of folks from all over the world, occasionally in English, but also most European languages as well as unintelligible scripts, such as Hindi, or Farsi, or Hangeul. Petra, my eldest, imagined that signing the log book meant she would be performing an act of sacrilege in praying to a false god: Buddhist temple, Buddhist "world peace" log. I don't suppose it would have had any practical effect one way or the other, in view of the fact that the world is still not an especially peaceful place all these years later, but I believe she finally came around to seeing that her prayer for peace was to whatever God *she* chose, and therefore her participation in this event did not put her in any real danger of having her ticket punched: the one-way descent into the eternal lake of fire. But then, my opinions regarding religious matters were suspect from the outset, since I was, and remain, non-religious, while they are emphatically Christian.

Again, Ariel has volunteered her diary of the day, July 13, '89. ...*[W]e took a short journey to Sanzen-in. To get into this Buddhist Temple, we had to copy over sections of sutra. Still Petra, Loren and I were offended so we added a little of our own (such as 'John 3:16' and 'Christ Rules!'). The grounds were very beautiful with many rhododendrons all in bloom.*

It was an adventure, a learning experience for a somewhat estranged father and his three children.

A Train Platform Encounter

This particularly salient memory took place on a Fujisawa Tokaido Line platform, probably during my kids' first visit. The four of us were waiting for a train when out of the blue, a flock of middle school girls alighted, all in their trim uniforms, chirping like little birds, accompanied by an occasional wave of titters. They were cutting up, making jokes, and generally enjoying each other's company, like young teenagers among their peers are wont to do the world over. Then... they caught sight of my eleven-year-old son, Loren Cedar.

They *saw* my girls and me (we were *together*, after all). They made note of us and factored us into the overall social mix, but it was Loren who had captured their attention. There was something about the equation between these girls, already experiencing puberty, adjusting to the hormonal implications, and pre-pubescent Loren, like a big, cuddly puppy, the more alluring for his *otherness*. Did some of them approach and talk to him? I don't recall. But even if they didn't, it was quite obvious they were fixated on the kid. It was fascinating to watch my daughters' reaction to this highly misplaced display of fawning adoration. They rolled their eyes and occasionally glanced at me as if to say, "Are you seeing this? What are you going to do about it? *You're* the father..."

It was almost as if they were objecting to this gross violation of the Natural Order of Things. It was women who were to be gazed upon and adored (from a safe distance, if you please), *not* young men. This was a deserved consequence of the considerable time and effort young women devote to their wardrobe and makeup, their *presentation*, whereas your average guy will spend more energy/focus on his gamer time than he will on his own hygiene and clothes. So yes, in a sense, this *was* a miscarriage of justice. A travesty. Rock stars are rare exceptions, regrettable aberrations, but under no circumstances should this be happening to little brothers.

I could imagine *O-neichan*, older sister Petra seizing the moment, standing up in front of the chittering school girls, arm raised, snapping her fingers three of four times as she began her declaration: "Hey! Hey, let's back off, do you mind? His name is Loren, and he's our little brother. We love him dearly, but we have to live with him. So, let's don't be giving him a fatter head than he already has, ok? *Wakata*? Understand?"

Ariella would have supported the sentiment, adding her own take if she thought anything important had been left unsaid. On Cedar's behalf, this had never happened to him before and he didn't really know how to react. He did seem to bask in the attention, however, an ominous sign. I'm afraid my response was very little comfort to my daughters. All I could muster was a shrug of my shoulders. It was out of my hands. Fortunately, a train came along

248

and promptly rescued us from the clutches of the incipient Loren Cedar Fan Club.

The whole spontaneous experience took less than five minutes, so I marvel that anyone else could remember this event at all, let alone remotely like I do. Here are Loren's related comments:

I do not recall the train station event specifically, but generally I sure do recall the reaction. It was not so much an awareness of attraction, especially in the first visit. But more of an awareness of being noticed. Coming from a culture and circumstances of being very plain vanilla, entering a culture where that vanilla was a thing rarely seen. Being tow-headed kids drew stares and undue attention. It felt like being a rock star! Many times we would hear "gaijin!" And see folks gawking and pointing. It was a culture shock, for sure. To feel so special at such a young age was wonderful. A true boost to the self-esteem.

On another occasion, we made a one-day excursion to Nikko on probably my kids' last visit. Nikko is a lovely town in the mountains two hours by semi-express train north of Tokyo. This town is primarily famous for *Tosho-gu*, a shrine-and-temple complex unique in all Japan. It is a monument to Tokugawa Ieyasu, Minamoto no Yoritomo, and Toyotomi Hideyoshi, as superior samurai, an elaborate acknowledgement of their deification. At least some of Ieyasu, the dynasty's founder is said to be buried here, while another portion of the cadaver is said to have fetched up for sacred interment in Odawara, or someplace like that. Tosho-gu is unique for being a hybrid expression of Buddhist and Shinto themes, I suppose, a physical representation of Ieyasu's thinking on both religious influences. It was the third Tokugawa, Ieyasu's grandson, Yoshimitsu, who commissioned the final stage of construction of Tosho-gu. Thousands of the country's best craftsmen worked for years on its construction, and it's clear that no cost was spared in the immortalization of Tokugawa Ieyasu, a mortal nevertheless. The place is the antithesis of the normal Japanese aesthetic, at least as I had come to know it. What I learned to love and respect was a subdued presentation, suggestive, understated, and subtle—with effectively no conclusion, or certainly nothing explicitly stated. By contrast, Tosho-gu is over the top and in your face with

249

rococo details of elaborate carving and sculpture, gaudily tarted up in showy colors. However, we delighted in discovering the "Speak, hear, see no evil" display, the three monkeys with their hands covering the appropriate communication organ, looming out at us from a wall cartouche.

All Shinto structures, from Torii gates to enclosed offertories, are covered with a generic red, a bright-rust color; it might as well be called "Shinto red." But this time the Tosho-gu Promotion Committee wanted to go all out. Paint everything in sight, and make it flashy, *O-hade*! I'm telling you, if you've gotten to the point where you actually appreciate the weathered wood of some antiquated architecture on a grand scale as a small antidote to the modern wonders of ferroconcrete, plastic, and glass technology, be prepared for a shock. Given that it's a mid-17th century state-of-the-art temple/shrine construction—and not a late-20th century Disney-inspired testament to razzle-dazzle schlock—it is still a seriously "busy" experience. It is almost jarring to the eyes. The Tosho-gu complex of structures is located in an exquisite location, though; we gotta give 'em that. It was a summer retreat for the Shogun and his entourage, I'm told. Smart folks.

Though she opted to stay behind, this one-day adventure took Kimiko's careful organizing, especially as regards piecing together the train scheduling. We caught the first Odakyu train out of Kugenuma Kaigon shortly past 5 am, transferring in Fujisawa to the JR Tokaido all the way to Tokyo *Eki* (station), changing for another line bound for Ueno Eki where we boarded this special semi-express to Nikko at 7:50 am. I'm sure my troopers would agree that beginning our action-packed day at such an uncivilized hour was brutal. No doubt I'm projecting here, but my recollection is we all more or less kept an open mind on what wonders we might behold, starting on site by 10 am.

Nikko, like many other unique areas, might be said to benefit *and* suffer from its popularity. The number one benefit is the capitalist transfer of wealth; it goes without saying. Visitors bring vacation money—cash for exotic food, lodging, transportation, and features of interest. This infusion of money sets the agenda; the visiting public needs facilities to cater to a range of tastes and financial abilities. As a result, it became inevitable that Nikko get developed. So, it is better that the city and state governments, as necessary evils, took a role in preserving some of the context of this national treasure, thereby preventing the wholesale despoliation of the area's natural and historic beauty through overbuilding greed. *Think, Kyoto.*

So we marveled at all the appropriate phenomena, and walked everywhere, including a short hike away from the Tosho-gu complex, and into a forested area, not unlike the forests we were familiar with back at Small River, Oregon. It was a peaceful respite. We must have eaten somewhere. The food and dining experience was apparently *un*-noteworthy, since I have no memory of it, whatsoever. By about 4 pm, we were back on that limited express returning to Ueno, reversing our train connections. And what I most remember after two and a half decades is how wrung out I felt by the time we got back to our haven in Kugenuma, Fujisawa, Shonan Kaigan, around 8 pm.

* * * * *

Over the years, Howard Levy and I kept in touch. He and his wife, Michiko, were witnesses to our international, official, bureaucratic marriage, sometime in February '88. He and I would schedule a dinner out together once a month or so. The guy was nearly a full generation older than me, plus he'd earned his academic chops in Asian studies. On top of all that, the man was easy-going, relaxed, and just a delight to be around. I think for a while there, neither of us had a fellow gaijin to hang with and share ideas/*shoot the shit.* Once he took my kids and me to a Taiyo Whales baseball game, the Big Leagues in Yokohama, probably the only time any of us had ever attended a major-league game—from any country.

In terms of things Japanese or Asian he was my *Sempai,* and I was his *Kohai,* understudy to the master, though frankly, he never treated me as anything but an equal. Out of those monthly dinners, we agreed to collaborate on a book. Levy-san was an old pro, having self-published several books, many of which were English language aids, e.g., a series of "Two-word Verbs" (30).

We'd stumbled onto the conundrum of all non-native speakers of probably all languages: how to understand and assimilate expressions and idioms that comprise a phrase or a sentence of usually common words, but depending on the unique alignment and *context,* take on a special, culturally driven meaning. As an aid for the Japanese learner, the niche seemed to be

251

under-served. For the next couple of years, every time he or I heard a new idiom, we'd make a note of it and add it to our list. I spent some of the winter holiday of '93 organizing the material—pre- computer—preparing the conceptual layout. We wanted it to be light-hearted, to encourage the student to try out our book. The title I suggested was *Break Bread, or Break Wind* (31). There was supposed to be a sub-title, *Easy words, hard meanings*, to help make sense of the main title, which got dropped in an oversight at the last moment. My daughter Petra helped alphabetize and fine-tune definitions to the collection, as well as compile the list in the run-up to publication. Howard and I ordered 750 copies in the summer of '94, and we dutifully signed each and every damn one of them. According to Levy-Sensei's experience, signing and numbering the copies would make them more valuable, like a numbered Matisse print. Assuming there was a value established in the first place, *Ha!* Our students, bless their hearts, bought our book—out of obligation, in all probability. Its potential utility was made more complicated by its awkwardness of use. It was never the hit we'd hoped for, but it pretty much paid for itself.

My only other experience of being published in Japan was the minor role of English Editor/Rewriter for three books in a series written by Takeuchi Hitoshi (31). Each book contains forty one-page essays about curious phenomena around us, such as, "Why doesn't a spider get caught in its own web?" And "What happens to a salt water fish when thrown into fresh water?" Takeuchi wrote the original pieces, and either he or someone on his staff made a quick and crude translation into English. From these rough scraps I was charged with polishing them up, and rendering them into natural English. And while we're at it, let's make sure the text more-or-less corresponds to a semantic reality I can, at least, recognize. *Acckk!* Much like my All Nippon Airways training manual experience, most of the text required radical reinterpretation. But (*signal the drum roll, the trumpets' fanfare*), I got paid ¥400,000 (exchange rate: ¥126~136 to $1) as side-income for my effort—entailing something more than 80 hours at my pace, over three months.

As a footnote to my connection to Levy-sensei, his son, Hideo (Ian) Levy, received some honorable acclaim in the Japanese literary world for being the first Westerner, first non-native speaker to publish a work of fiction composed exclusively in Nihongo. *A Room Where the Star Spangled Banner*

Cannot Be Heard is a slim (111 pgs.), Holden Caulfield (*Catcher in the Rye*), coming-of-age tale for an American kid thrust into the midst of a very different language and culture, in the gritty aftermath of post-WW II (32). To be charitable toward Hideo-san's writing, I'll refrain from commenting. I have only read his book in translation, but I heartily acknowledge the praise for his mastery of Nihongo, a significant linguistic achievement, to be sure.

Being a barbarian

Have you ever had the experience of suddenly seeing yourself as others see you? On Halloween of 1994, my wife got roped into helping her Japanese associate at an English institute host a party for 60-some children. I was implored to come also, time permitting, as only one other native speaker had been corralled into participating. As some kind of luck would have it, I was free that afternoon, and so followed along out of curiosity.

The associate had gone to no little effort in organizing the "Halloween Experience," at least as she perceived it: in a lesser-used classroom she had placed tables down the center of the room. On the table near the entrance, a series of black vinyl bags were arranged, their openings snugged with rubber bands. The first bag contained peeled grapes suggesting—you guessed it— eyeballs! The second held cold, gelatinous spaghetti noodles, evocative to the fervid imagination of entrails; finely chopped tomatoes, resembling somebody's notion of mashed brains, festered in the third bag.

The other *gaijin* was decked out in a ghoulish mask and I in iridescent fright wig. We were to foster the understanding that the assorted body parts were gleaned from hapless sheep, but we might as well have claimed viscera from human origin since essentially no one believed—let alone *understood*— us anyway. When you ask a kid to stick his hand into a bag to determine its contents, he's likely to haul out a fistful for closer inspection, which happened more often than not.

After weathering the creepy-feely experience the kids, allowed into the room in groups of four, were coaxed down the table for apple bobbing.

Reward? The bobbed apple and a small bag of candy. Occasionally, curious mothers asked to observe the proceedings from positions in the background. Dozens of blown-up balloons littered the floor, though it was difficult to say to what effect.

The sepulchral chamber was, of course, darkened to heighten the aural and tactile effect. I crouched behind a table conjuring up "unearthly" sounds by rubbing a finger across a balloon surface, and uttered grunts and guttural moans as the other gaijin yanked open the door and snatched the next set of kids—much to the shock, dismay, and occasional amusement of many, especially the boys.

Alas, however, among some of the younger girls, the whole phantasmagoria was more than their innocent, fun-loving minds could handle. Let's face it, we gaijin, even in standard trappings, are beyond the ken of some of these folks. So, what do you expect when we get freaked up and try to spook a bunch of seven-year olds? They are apt to wax hysterical and need a little consoling by the likes of my wife and other "normal" hominids in the vicinity.

It was in such a moment, midst the shrieks and gales of tears, that I happened to glance at a couple of housewives along the wall, mouths slightly agape, staring at this scene in utter disbelief. I had this sensation of instant prescience; I felt I could read their minds. They were thinking, *What sort of "cross-cultural experience" could possibly justify terrifying our little kids?* Aghast, they were thinking, *What a strange and unfathomable culture these people come from that they make a holiday "celebrating" ghosts, monsters, witches, and other such fearful specters in order to scare the pee out of little girls...* (33)

Natsukashii mono (nostalgic thing): the curry bun! With variations, this is a simple, fist-sized yeast bun injected with a creamy curry sauce. Sometimes brushed with a batter and sprinkled with "panko" crumbs, it is often deep fried for a few seconds and eaten warm. Virtually every bakery sells its own variation. It's a delightful snack, and I don't know why it hasn't migrated to American shores.

I'd seen these brightly colored prints here and there without paying much attention until, without any inducement, one of my students presented me with two panels of an original three-panel triptych. It was a fairly simple depiction of a young mother holding a suckling baby in her arms, clutching a writing brush in her teeth. On the surface of an unadorned *fusuma*, or sliding papered screen, she is writing a quick note to her husband. It's a full moon, one year since the woodsman, father of her child, found her dazed and lost in the forest, and brought her to his cottage where he nursed her back to health. With the woodsman absent, her true nature is reincarnating. Her hands have become paws; she is reverting to her true *Kitsune* (fox) self. The prints are a skillful evocation of the story, even without having available the final third panel. I was deeply moved by this gift, perhaps even a bit bewitched, and have been an avid *ukiyo-e* collector ever since. I haunt *boro ichi* (flea markets), antique shops, and yes, patronize *ukiyo-e* retail shops in Kamakura and Harajuku—much to the dismay of my wife, who tends not to value her own traditional arts and crafts nearly as highly.

Like Frank Lloyd Wright (34), once I'd paid them any attention at all, I was completely smitten. Ukiyo-e are arguably the best remaining example of the flourishing pictorial arts bought with the "peace dividend" provided by the absolute authority of the Tokugawa Shogunate. Like all the arts during this period, wood-block carving became more detailed and far more colorful than, say, the 17th century. The art of carving eight, ten, even twelve separate slabs of wood, each to illustrate a particular color, texture, or pattern of the overall portrayal, had reached its peak by 1880, by the end of the Tokugawa Dynasty (though Yoshitoshi is a conspicuous exception). The flash and novelty of western technology—*exampli gratia*, photography—superseded, if not overwhelmed, the traditional but suddenly passé styles.

Some of the meticulously carved wood-block sets from the past two and a half centuries have been preserved, so contemporary prints are available, but a piece of information I recently learned has caused me to change some of my evaluation of original, extant prints. Apparently, the well esteemed Ukiyo-e artist Hokusai wrote his publisher that a run of 200 prints from one set of wood blocks was the maximum he would authorize (35). The concern was with repeated use the finely engraved blocks would not hold the ink evenly and begin to show blurred lines. As many as a dozen separate cherrywood blocks to show color and textural distinctions, and 200 prints are the "maximum"?! That should make the surviving copies rarer than I had imagined.

For the most part, the original print you acquire is likely to be the sole remaining copy, or one of very few. They were printed in small runs, and distributed as advertisements often for Kabuki performances, Kabuki itself the creative result of Tokugawa-imposed social stability. If the *ukiyo-e* print you are examining survived the Great Kanto Earthquake of 1923, and the three successive night fire-bombing of Tokyo in March of 1945, then it's rather remarkable that as many survived as have.

About half my collection is a series of dramatic poses struck by Kabuki actors, the other half is of various historical scenes, or imposing landscapes. As an example of the former, just before the dramatic turning point or conclusion of a play, the samurai protagonist, about to win the day or die trying, pauses with sword upraised, full grimace to match the wall-eyed glower. This mid-drama pause is known as *Mi-e*. When it occurs, the die-hard fans shout, *Mate-'mashita!* ("At last!" or "*This* is what I've been waiting for!") The ukiyo-e artists often display famous kabuki actors in one or another of these celebrated poses, which then became advertising for the kabuki play.

In the other category I've got one of Minamoto Yoritomo in a ceremony on the coast of Kamakura, releasing a pair of caged *tsuru*, cranes. Another shows two samurai trying—and failing—to ward off spiders the size of large rats, one of which has attached itself to a samurai's neck, blood around the bite/wound, while the panicked warrior flails around ineffectively with his *katana*, or long sword. Another shows the dramatic conclusion of *Chushingura*, the assembled forty-seven ronin in front of the captured Kira, the courtly despot of proper etiquette, just discovered hiding in the woodshed of his mansion. They are about to decapitate the man and parade his head through the streets of Edo all the way to Sengaku-ji, in Shinagawa, the temple where Lord Asano's restless soul has been waiting this year and nine months for vindication.

Then, there's a somewhat sun-bleached triptych of three Sumo wrestlers of the highest rank, *Yokozuna*, and their entourage, lower ranking *Ozeki* and

256

below, real people from 140 years ago. Another depicts a ghostly apparition of a kimono-clad unmarried woman, the tell-tale sign of her marriage status is the *furi sode*, or the long expanse of material that hangs from the sleeves of her kimono; a married woman's sleeves extend to the wrists, but don't display a lot of material hanging from the underside of the sleeves. Where feet should have been, a fading diaphanous stream trails off, the tell-tale sign of her *other-worldliness*. You get the idea; each print tells a unique story that draws you in all the more.

Among many great *ukiyo-e* artists over the course of the last 250 years, a handful really stand out from a large and productive field. Prominent among them is Hokusai Katsushika (1760~1849), best known for his "Thirty-six Views of Fuji-san." *The* iconic Japanese woodblock print to virtually all foreigners is a scene of fishermen paddling a couple of boats in rough seas. A giant wave is just about to break over a boat, and we have no way of knowing whether these intrepid sea voyagers will survive this tempest, but frozen in time, under the curve of the wave, you can see the snow-capped peak of Fujisan in the distant background. *Wow*, right? If you're not impressed, you are not giving yourself a chance. This is a balanced, tunnel view of serene Fujisan in the distance while in this instant, this never-to-be-repeated flash, this blink-of-the-eye foreground, a handful of men in three boats are braving this sea for the next catch. One message seems to say that brave and skilled men in tight units may successfully cope with daunting natural adversity—in this case, 15 to 25 foot waves—most of the time. But nothing is given.

Utamaru Kitagawa (1753~1806), once you've really looked at one of his *Yoshiwara*, "Floating World," beauties in one of her daily routines—performing her toilette, bathing, brushing her hair, peeling off or putting on her kimono—you'll never forget his distinctive style of languid, erotic indolence. His primary focus, at least what made him famous, was his *bijinga*, pictures of beautiful women in commonplace poses.

Hiroshige Utagawa (1797~1858) and Hokusai display the foregrounding of nature in all her majesty and fury, and the backgrounding of humans in their flimsy, paltry efforts. Hiroshige is most famous for his exquisite landscapes, and rural scenes, and "Fifty-three Stations of the Tokaido," the main road between Kyoto and Edo, the ancient and the new capitals.

The mysterious Sharaku: Where did he come from, and where did he go? Mostly what we know is during the 1794~5 period, this artist produced 150 separate prints, before disappearing. His focus was on the antics of people, often portraits of Kabuki actors. Utamaru inspired a few copycats, whereas Sharaku had a unique, unmistakable style all his own.

Yoshitoshi Tsukioka (1839~1892) is another highly skilled artist at the tail end of the art form. He was perhaps most famous for his depiction of 36 Ghost Stories, each one a graphic if chilling depiction straight out of ancient lore (36).

Another benefit to collecting ukiyo-e prints: they aren't fragile or clunky. They fit in the bottom of your suitcase, weighing nothing and taking up zero room. Since they are such exquisitely made works of art 100 to 200 years old, often retaining their vibrant colors, they make classy gifts. My wife is a pragmatist, eager to point out that they are often in poor condition, have absolutely no utility, and are expensive. My response is, their condition prior to my acquisition was beyond my control. Pure art is rarely utilitarian, and "expensive" compared to what? Fancy clothes? Evenings at this or that cocktail lounge? Among "hobbies," collecting two or three dozen *ukiyo-e*, the top twenty of which cost an average of a couple hundred dollars each, seems fairly reasonable (when you're in the chips), and maybe even an astute investment.

Kotowaza, Proverbs

Hosoku nagaku; "Narrow, but long." *Narrow* gives way to *small, thin, or little. "Small (in numbers, influence, popularity), but in it for the long haul."* Similar to the Spanish, *"Poco a poco," "Little by little."* Or Aesop in "The Tortoise and the Hare:" Slow, but steady wins the race. The expression seems to place a premium on length over breadth/width—the opposite of narrow/ thin. Long soba noodles are served at New Year's to symbolize long life. Long, pleasant friendships, etc., come with narrow, limited conditions included.

Deru kugi wa utareru, "The nail that sticks up gets hammered down." This particular proverb, more than any other in my meager repertoire, is emblematic of Nippon.

Dan son jo hi, "The man leads, the woman follows." Especially in public. This has been traditional since *forever*. It is slowly giving way to gender parity. *Slowly*, I say.

Oni mo ju hachi, "Even a demon is beautiful/desirable at 18 years of age."

Oni no kakuran, Sickbed of the devil. "Even the devil is apt to get sick sometime."

Hogan biki, a preference for the underdog, the disadvantaged party. Students have reported this originated with Minamoto Yoshitsune being hounded to death by his paranoid older brother, Yoritomo, founder of the short-lived Minamoto dynasty (see this story in some detail in "Kamakura," p 182).

Go ju po, hya' po, "Fifty steps one way, or a hundred steps by another"— where the implication of the route, or manner in which you arrive at your destination, is not, and should not be, as important as making the most of your participation and involvement along the way. Since we are all interconnected to everything else, it all matters. A close English approximation is, "Six of one, half a dozen of another," with the same inferences. In the English version, there is a literal equivalence: six equals a half dozen. In the Japanese version, one way is twice as far, but consider the trails that climb in elevation. The trail requiring the most steps might presumably climb more gently, easier, and more comfortably. Also, the meaning and value of the journey should not be exclusively focused on expediency. Rather, *"The road less traveled,"* and all that.

Tsuru sen nen kame man nen, "A crane lives a thousand years, a turtle, ten thousand years." I am stymied as to meaning; what is the metaphoric message? How to casually insert this one into a conversation? Why is this important information to be apprised of? Unless it is to call attention to the

259

extreme longevity of certain creatures, and the all-too-frequent brevity of we foolhardy humans. Since it is blatantly untrue, perhaps it's a test of our gullibility.

Kusa'temo tai, "It's stinky, but it's tai." This fish is past its prime, starting to stink/putrify. But because it is a symbolically special kind of fish (its name, *tai,* an allomorph of *dai,* 大, means "great," as in "magnificent"), we are obliged to use it anyway.

Rai nen no koto yu to oni ga warau, "Conjectures about the future (next year) make the devils laugh." Nobody knows the future, suggesting, the less said about it, the better.

Yu gen fu jiko, "Many words, little or no action."

Fu gen jiko, "(A man of) few words, but consistent, perseverant work ethic."

Minoru hodo kube otareru inaho kana, "As rice matures, it bows its head (in humility)." A hallmark of youth is its vigor, its brash willingness to stand up and defy, having the hormonal effect of superseding or short circuiting the rational function. Only with maturity comes the "weight" of the head—the recognition of interconnectedness, and the sense of responsibility this brings—thus the head is inclined to bow before the many intricacies and complexities of life.

Nana korobi ya oki, "Fall down seven times, get up eight." If at first you don't succeed, try, try again. Perseverence!

Uma no mimi ni nembutsu, "Preaching sutras in a horse's ear." This proverb refers to the futility of trying to engage people who care not a whit about your passions, people with whom you may share a common humanity, but otherwise have no intellectual connections, let alone entwined interests. A situation of live and let live.

Makeru ga kachi, "To lose is to win." (29) This seems counterintuitive on its face, but we learn something with each experience. Many would say, the most important lessons are accompanied by some pain, in one form or another. Many losses make the victory all the sweeter. And if the victory never arrives? Well, you did what you could; there's a kind of nobility in the struggle, regardless of the outcome, though to be sure, any loss smarts in the moment.

Kaeru no ko wa kaeru, "A frog's progeny are frogs." We should expect that the child would turn out like his/her parents—in the spectrum of worldview, temperament, sense of humor, musical interests, etc. And considerable physical resemblance, one would hope. But we shouldn't be surprised by the extent of the divergence, the push-back, one generation to the next—the learned versus the genetic—in behavior, choices, and tastes.

What's!?
(Random sign, noted in passing; the existential dilemma, *sans* context.)

Epilogue

December 29, 2001: I've returned to Japan after 6 ½ years' absence. It is time—arguably long past time—to pay my respects to my Japanese family, to old, dear friends/students who took exceedingly good care of me. They taught me to be an English teacher and, best of all, they taught me their Japan. I've come back to acknowledge my debt to them, and to revisit some of the familiar sites, all in a ten-day visit.

But first, a short digression: What compelled me to leave in the spring of 1995? By any objective measure, I was "successful." I had a full schedule—too full, if the truth be told. Eager students never failing to pay me gobs of money. The learning opportunities from my students grew to be subtler, more nuanced, than the early days, when every revelation was a stunner, but nuance and subtlety lie much closer to the heart of Japanese culture, anyway, there to explore.

The thing is, I felt like I'd reached a surfeit of experience, a satiation of this lifestyle. My Japanese language skills were developing at a painfully slow rate, and everything else had become routinized. To some extent, I was "performing" a role, one I was reasonably good at, but felt trapped in, caught in a snare of my own making. This plateau I'd created for myself wasn't perilous or scary, but neither was it fulfilling—a challenge, well met—in the way it had been in the early years, when teaching was still fairly raw and ragged here and there, and the struggle to get good at it required stretching my normal psychic boundaries. In the beginning, there was a palpable sense of growing, and being conscious/energized by the growth; by this later date, this was not so much the case. Perhaps this phenomenon explains why tenured professors at prestigious universities get sabbaticals, a paid year off to go somewhere and do something else every seven to ten years, and then return to your professorship, refreshed, anew. At this point, though, it felt time to try out a new life while I was still young and malleable enough to rise to the challenge. At 54, however, nothing new was a given. Coming to Japan at 43 I had significantly reinvented myself. Could I do it again?

Kimiko and I had bought a house in Portland back in the fall of '89. It was at the tail end of a summertime vacation to Oregon, including a few days at my cabin in the Coast Range, and visits with friends in Eugene and

Portland. We got wind of this older home on the NE slope of Mt. Tabor for sale, but not yet on the market. It was two days before we were due to fly back to Japan. Our friends heard of the upcoming offering, and facilitated us seeing inside the place. A classic craftsman-style house, it was built in 1918, and had been well cared for. We were charmed in the space of that initial twelve-minute walk through, so we came up with earnest money while a realtor-friend drew up the sales agreement and established an escrow account. All of the transactions thenceforward, took place via the banks and the embassy. We bought the place initially as an investment, a way to grow our money, but it was always there in the back of my mind as a possible future home to move to.

By the spring of 1995 our Mt Tabor house had been completely paid for and was suffering abuse at the hands (and paws) of college students and their prohibited dogs. It was a simple matter to instruct our property managers to evict our tenants, and have the place tidied up by late May. We had a new life to try out in a new city.

* * * * *

This is tricky business connecting with my former students/friends after so many years without contact. I don't know the correct protocol, the polite etiquette. My spouse could tell me but I don't want to rely on her for more than I really need. So out of the blue I would just call a key member of a group of former students, and she would call people and arrange the meeting site, time and date. Assuming I'm able to make that initial contact, the rest gets coordinated by my hosts. I thought I'd lost touch with my original guarantors, Dr. and Tomoko Yoshida. Those first two years of life in Japan when I was skating as a tourist, Yasuo-san was willing to stick his neck out and take formal responsibility for my potentially errant behavior. I believe Tomoko-san had a good look into my character during the first month or two that I was teaching the *futago*, twins, and ultimately realized she could trust me with her children. I taught these twin boys from eight to eighteen years old, their *onei-san* (older sister) in little chunks over the years, and for quite a period, Tomoko-san also. I hosted these three kids plus their cousin for two weeks in Oregon, from Timberline Lodge on Mt. Hood, to my Small River cabin dwelling, complete with an unscripted black bear raid on the front yard garden in broad daylight, horseback riding on the Oregon coast, and canoeing on the Millrace in Eugene. I don't think I ever violated her trust in me. Yasuo-san and I got along well, but as the sole pediatrician of his own clinic, he was a very busy man.

But still, we'd drifted apart; it's hard to make the contact meaningful and current when there has been zero shared experience over the intervening years. It's certainly nobody's fault. Having returned for a few days, and causing social ripples in Fujisawa, Tsujido, and Chigasaki, the three cities along the Shonan beach the housed most of my students, it occurred to me we might not be able to slither through our brief return without it coming to the Yoshidas' attention that we'd come and gone. After all, they'd served as our *Nakoudo-san* (formal go-betweens, or matchmakers) at our wedding. So, I called. Tomoko-san said we "had" to come for a visit. It was arranged for the afternoon of the 31st. She asked us to stay for dinner but the little lady and I anticipated this and agreed to keep it brief; that despite their genuine hospitality, it would lean too heavily on such a special occasion—especially, in such short notice.

When we arrived, they laid out an elegant spread, two large platters of sushi delivered, with drinks all around, if I remember correctly. On hand were Keiichi, one half the twins, and Yamasaki Masako, *onei-san* to Yasuo-san, and my initial introduction to the Yoshida family. It was terrific to see them all. Platitudes ricocheted off the walls; Tomoko-san was effusive with her kind praise. *Honne?* More likely *tatemae*, but very heady stuff to hear, nonetheless.

Upon first alighting from an Odakyu train at Kugenuma Kaigan, on my way to one of three groups I'd arranged to meet on short notice, Hirotaka Nagabuchi happened to be driving by, recognized me and slammed on his brakes, tying up traffic while he proffered his *denwa bango* (telephone number) insisting I call and arrange a meeting. Also on the spur of the moment, we encountered Mon-san near the old house he shares with Chiaki-san; he too insisted we plan to get together. Betty and I needed to visit a few individuals and groups (Nishikori-san, the sponsor of our frequent summertime boarders, was prominent among them) and wanting time to see familiar, dear places, we were hesitant to take on too many visitations, not knowing really how I might be received after 6 ½ years.

Mon and Chiaki laid out a gorgeous spread with sake, beer, *osechi*, and the *coup de grace*, a bottle of the beer I'd made all those years before and left for him to drink, imagining it would be gone in two days, two weeks at the most. He'd kept it in their modest refrigerator all this time. After those first weeks, I suppose it became increasingly harder to drink without a special occasion, which began to require our participation. I was blind-sided! The cap was rusty but still maintained the seal; there was still a decent head on the brew, but truth to tell, it was not one of my better batches. Nothing to shout about and certainly nothing to hoard for nearly seven years. Sometimes, however, it's the simple gestures that are the most heart-wrenching and poignant.

Through this and other examples, I came to see that these people really did value me and our connection, and that their memory of me took on a kind of wholly unrealistic "legendary status." Furthermore, it would have been a grave error for me to come back much sooner, or more often, in order to preserve this exalted image. I think we all know the consequences of *Too much of a good thing*. Also, the case can be made that people need their "heroes," even if such beings don't exist in real life. People will believe what they want to believe; if I am able to nudge/nurture/sustain/perpetuate the "legend" (tongue in cheek, of course), then all the better. Day by day, week in, month out, long live the myth! Mundane existence is dreary enough.

You should know, however, that it has been a phenomenal experience to return to these shores with modest expectations and quite literally be treated, by those who knew me before, as *nobility* returned from an unjust exile.

...as though I'd come back from the dead. A wealth of affection! says Basho (16). Mere gratitude and humility don't adequately serve to capture the feeling.

Some people, like me, discovered our niche at the margins, and we've done alright. We help people navigate the rough waters between the shores of differing social orders, contrasting cultures. We have become adept, even comfortable, in more than one society—and perhaps never fully settled in any. We facilitate the passage from one entity to another. I provide access to the tools of English communication, and a supportive atmosphere where that emergent skill might get exercised.

Personally, I did better than alright. Perhaps, more than at any other time of my life, I thrived. I had very gracious hosts. For a fairly typical, inter-culturally naïve American, I was treated with patient, gentle graciousness beyond anything I'd experienced before. Furthermore, my timing to make a go of English instruction was just about perfect. Leading economic indicators of the late 1980s, early '90s—in considerable hindsight, of course—showed Japan's prosperity to be at an overall high point; I was fortunate to have shared in that prosperity.

There was work involved; it wasn't all magic. It turns out I was not a perpetual fountain of inspired instruction. At the high point, I had over a hundred students. For a somewhat introverted person before coming/going to Japan, it took some getting used to being "on" all the time around my students. Always in character, in the role of *Eigo no sensei,* English teacher: It was all part of making a profound readjustment in lifestyle at the age of 43. It was growing into a new identity.

Channeling the will-o'-the-wisp of Koizumi Yakumo…

finito la musica,
pasada la fiesta

Acknowledgements

Several people deserve praise for help with this book. I wish to thank Sione Aeschliman for her professional editing and organizational advice during an early rewrite phase. I am likewise grateful to Ekubo Sawaura, a Portland Community College student, for being an intrepid researcher, clarifying some fuzzy points for which I needed an insider's interpretation. Also, I commend John "Pollo" Butler for his valuable insights into our shared intercultural experience, and his tenacity in sticking with the editing process. Thanks to Kirsty Munn for her cover-design contribution, and Charlie Magee for his final-stage finesse with format configuring.

Finally, I was delighted to discover that my three children, Petra, Ariel, and Loren—all middle aged now, with children/ families of their own—were willing to contribute to this literary adventure, to dig deep into their childhood/young adulthood recollections, somewhat reliving the experience in the telling.

Sources/Notes

1)   Rexroth, Kenneth. *One Hundred More Poems from the Japanese* (1974). New Directions: New York. No. 50. Many of these are quite delicate and elusive; one was subtly erotic 1100 years after its composition. I guess the basics never change.

2)   Wikipedia.

3)   Levy, Howard S. *Japan's Best Loved Poetry Classic Hyakunin Isshu* (1984). Warm-Soft Publications: Yokohama, Japan. It was Levy-sensei's third and classiest version.

4)   Levy, Howard S. *Chinese Footbinding The History of a Curious Erotic Custom* (1966). Walton Rawls: New York. And *The Tao of Sex*, with Akira Ishida (1989). Integral Publishing: Lower Lake, CA.

5)   Hearn, Lafcadio, *A Japanese Miscellany* (1967). Charles E. Tuttle, Co: Tokyo, Japan.

6)   Hearn, Ladcadio, *Glimpses of Unfamiliar Japan* (1976). Charles E. Tuttle Co: Tokyo.

7)   Hochschild, Adam, *King Leopold's Ghost* (1998). Houghton Mifflin Co: New York. Here's a book depicting latter-day (European) colonialism at its very worst.

8)   Wikipedia: *Greater East Asia Co-Prosperity Sphere*.

9)   Itasaka, Gen. *Gates to Japan Its People and Society* (1986). AOTS Chosaki: Tokyo, Japan.

10) Hearn, Lafcadio. *Japan: an Interpretation* (1984). Charles E. Tuttle, Co: Tokyo, Japan.

11) Reischauer, Edwin O. *Japan Past and Present* (Third Edition) (1985). Alfred A. Knopf: New York. Also, *My Life Between Japan and America* (1986). Harper & Row: New York.

12) Reps, Paul. *Zen Flesh, Zen Bones, A Collection of Zen and Pre-Zen Writings* (1983). Charles E. Tuttle Co: Tokyo, Japan.

13) Perrin, Noel, *Giving Up the Gun: Japan's reversion to the sword, 1543-1879* (1979). David R. Godine: Jaffrey, New Hampshire.

14) Galef, David, *Even Monkeys Fall from Trees, and other Japanese proverbs* (1987). Charles E. Tuttle, Co: Tokyo, Japan.

15) Patric, John, *Yankee Hobo in the Orient* (1945). Self-published. Frying Pan Creek, Florence, Oregon. (This same statistic, percent of arable land in Japan, is supported in Wikipedia.)

16) Chiba, Reiko. *The Japanese Fortune Calendar* (1986). Charles E. Tuttle, Co: Tokyo, Japan.

17) Chiba, Reiko. *The Seven Lucky Gods of Japan* (1986). Charles E. Tuttle, Co: Tokyo, Japan. This and its companion volume are hand-stitched and bound. Printed on a subtle rainbow of colored pages, often illustrated with line drawings.

18) Hearn, Lafcadio. *Kotto, Being Japanese Curios, with Sundry Cobwebs* (1986). Charles E. Tuttle, Co: Tokyo, Japan.

19) *Nihongo: First Lessons in Kanji* (1989). The Japan Foundation: Urawa, Japan. Also, my Portland Community College student researcher Ekubo Sawaura was helpful in uncovering different ways to read that single kanji for *person*, or *people*.

20) Matsuo, Basho. *Narrow Road to the Interior and Other Writings* (1998). Translated by Sam Hamill. Shambhala Publications: Boston, MA.

21) Hearn, Lafcadio. *Kokoro Hints and Echoes of Japanese Inner Life* (1972). Charles E. Tuttle, Co: Tokyo, Japan. I was deeply impressed by this statement and thought this was as good as any to place it.

22) Yoshikawa, Eiji. *The Heike Story* (1956). Trans. by Fuki Wooyenaka Uramatsu. Alfred E. Knopf, Inc: New York.

23) Cooper, Michael. *Exploring Kamakura* (1981). John Weatherhill, Inc. Tokyo, Japan.

24) Of course I'm speculating. But I did consult my doctor, my daughter Ariel, that is, Family Medicine and Geriatrics certified, as to likely pathogens that we are normally resistant to, but can be fatal if allowed to get established, as in an open wound. Her response: Staphylococcus was a likely suspect, though Streptococcus could do the job, as well. *Thanks, Doc.*

25) Wilkinson, Richard, and Kate Pickett. *The Spirit Level, Why Equality Is Better for Everyone* (2009). Penguin Books, Ltd: London, England.

26) Hearn, Lafcadio. *The Romance of the Milky Way and Other Studies and Stories* (1973). Charles E Tuttle: Tokyo, Japan.

27) Akutagawa, Ryunosuke, *Japanese Short Stories* (1961). Trans. By Takashi Kojima. Charles E. Tuttle, Co. Tokyo, Japan. *Rashomon and Other Stories* (1952). Trans. By Takashi Kojima. Charles E. Tuttle, Co: Tokyo, Japan.

28) Stokes, Henry Scott, *The Life and Death of Yukio Mishima* (1975). Charles E. Tuttle Co: Tokyo, Japan. Stokes was a personal friend of Mishima—one of a handful of foreign journalists and writers. This work is well written, well documented.

29) Mishima, Yukio, *Five Modern No Plays* (1957). Trans. by Donald Keene. Charles E. Tuttle Co: Tokyo, Japan.

30) Levy, Howard S. *Fresh American Two-word Verbs* (1988) and *Fresh American Two-word Verbs II* (1987). Sanyo-sha: Tokyo, Japan.

31) Cole, Tony and Howard S. Levy. *Break Bread or Break Wind* (1994). Pine Hill Press: Freeman, South Dakota. 750 copies, each of which we both signed. Heirlooms now, destined for rare book collections. (*Do I hear an offer?*).

32) Takeuchi, Hitoshi and Tony Cole. *How Do They Do That?*, (2) *The Wonderful World of Nature*, and (3) *What a Wonderful World of Human Life* (1992). Dobunshoin: Tokyo, Japan.

33) Levy, Hideo, *A Room Where The Star Spangled Banner Cannot Be Heard* (1992). trans. by Christopher D. Scott. Columbia University Press: New York.

34) The original version of this piece was first published in Cole, Tuna. *Shards A Life in Pieces* (2014). Self-published.

35) Boyle, T. C. *The Women* (2009). Viking Penguin: New York. In this novel Boyle's footnotes document period and source material regarding F L Wright's enchantment with the Japanese aesthetic, *ukiyo-e* in particular.

36) Hiller, J., *Japanese Colour Prints* (1991). Phaidon Press Limited: London, UK.

37) Stevenson, John, *Yoshitoshi's Thirty-six Ghosts* (1983). John Weatherhill, Inc: New York.

Glossary

Adauchi: revenge, vengeance, vendetta—a major theme in Japanese literature.

Aka/akai: red.

Aki: the season of fall.

Arigato: thank you; *Arigato gozaimasu*: A politer form of expressing gratitude.

Asa: morning.

Bakafu: the military (samurai) administration of public affairs; the government.

Bake, but preferably, *Obake*: honorable (or venerable) ghost, apparition, phantom, intangible manifestation of a formerly living person.

Bushi: samurai warrior.

Bushido: the discipline, sacrifice, and training of warriors; the way of the samurai.

Cha, ocha: (honorable) tea.

Chisai: little, small.

Daimyo: the clan leader, or feudal lord, the warrior overlord ruling a particular area.

Dame: It's not acceptable; I don't approve; don't do it.

Dare: who?... Also, *Donata*

Densha: an electrically powered train, by far the most common in Japan. *Den* from *denki*, or electric, and *sha*, or vehicle.

Doko: where?…

Dozo: This comment grants permission by the speaker to the recipient to proceed in the given context. "Go ahead. Carry on. As you like." A statement of assent.

Doyobi: "Earth/soil day," Saturday.

Eigo: the English language.

Eki: a train station.

Fuyu: Winter.

Furo: a Japanese bath. The soaping and scrubbing takes place outside the bath. Following a thorough rinse, the bather may enter the *furo* for what amounts to a soak.

Gaikoku-jin: shortened to *Gaijin*, Outside-country person, foreigner.

Gakko: school. *Sho gakko*, elementary school. *Chu gakko*, middle school. *Dai gakko*, college/ university.

Gak'sei: a school student. *Dai-gak'sei*, a college student.

Genkan: the anteroom, a fully enclosed room at the front of a Japanese house, considered an intermediary space neither inside nor fully outside, where a homecoming family member or a guest has a clean, dry place to remove footwear, hang up raingear, etc. before entering the house proper.

Getsuyobi: "Moon day," Monday.

Gohan: meal, rice.

Hayashi: woods, a mostly tree-covered area, less extensive than a forest.

Haru: spring.

Hito: a person, or people. Nouns in Japanese (and most Asian languages) do not, of themselves, distinguish singular from plural.

Honne: one's truly felt opinion or interpretation. (See *Tatemae* for counterpart.)

Ikura: How much is…?

Itsu: When is…?

Jidai: age, or period. As in the *Meiji jidai*, 1868~1912.

Jieitai: Japan's Self Defense Forces (SDF), deemed justifiable by 1954 (with America's blessing) despite the "No standing military" clause in the MacArthur Constitution.

Jinja: Shinto shrine. *On yomi* pronunciation is *miya* or *omiya*, or *gu*.

Jo, ojo, josei: young woman/women.

Juku: private cram school designed to teach to the entrance exams of many prestigious universities. English language *juku* go through cycles of popularity and presumed utility.

Kabuki: popular theater which flourished in the 18th and 19th centuries owing to the rapid growth of the middle class, particularly the merchants.

Kaisha: a business, corporation, company that produces a good or service to earn money.

Kaisha-in: a businessman, one who works for a corporation.

Kaiyobi: "Fire day," Tuesday.

Kazoku: one's (extended) family.

Kame: turtle. Known for longevity. Compare to *tsuru*.

Kami: god(s)

Kane, or *Okane*: (honorable) money.

Kanji: stylized pictograms, or ideograms, of the real world. Each character can be read in at least two ways. Exampli gratia, 山 is *yama* in *kun yomi*, and *san* in *on yomi*.

Katana: the longer of a Japanese warrior's swords, his principle fighting implement.

Ki: tree, also read as *moku*.

Kinyobi: "Gold day," Friday.

Kohai: the junior understudy to a "wiser," more elderly mentor, *sempai*, in the role of an uncle who takes an interest in the young man's ideas, interests, and choices.

Kozukai, okozukai: spending cash, pocket money; one's allowance.

Kotowaza: proverb; pithy, epigrammatic saying. A statement, usually expressed as a metaphor, that captures a social "truth."

Kuni: country.

Kun yomi: indigenous, native kanji reading.

Kuro/kuroi: dark, or black.

Kuruma: vehicle, car.

Machi: city.

Manga: cartoon figures drawn to represent people in compromising situations. These stories are cranked out by the tens of thousands in pulp magazines, so it should not surprise anyone that they are simplistic and formulaic. The bottom line is they continue to sell in huge volume.

Man-getsu: full moon.

Machi: city, urban center.

Michi: the path, trail.

Mise, O-mise: shop, or store.

Mizu: water.

Mokuyobi: "Wood day," Thursday.

Mori: forest.

Mura: town, village.

Nakoudo-san: a person in the role of matchmaker, or go-between; one who promotes the match to the families, the real seats of power, and they in turn promote the match to their marriageable member, toward the completion of *omiai*, an arranged marriage.

Natsu: summer.

Naze: why?...

Nei-san: though usually preceded by an O: *Onei-san*, Honorable/venerable older sister. It stands to reason, if you had an older sister, she'd be your "honorable" big sis, right?... (*What's that? Dissention in the ranks?*)

Nichi: the sun; also, day.

Nichiyobi: Sunday. Is it just a coincidence that Sunday and *Getsuyobi*, Monday in Japanese, are the literal translation of English (and Latin-based languages)? If not, what's the story? Did Japan operate on seven-day weeks before adopting the Gregorian calendar, or something else, like the six-day Buddhist cycle?

Nii-san: preferably, *Onii-san*, Honorable older brother.

Nihongo: the Japanese language, *aka* "the Devil's language," according to Francis Xavier, *circa* 1551, immediately before abandoning hope of setting up shop in Japan, and returning to Macao.

Nihon-jin: "Japan person/people," Japanese.

Ohki: large, big.

Ok'san: wife.

Okaasan: mother.

Onna: woman/women.

On yomi: the kanji reading (often monosyllabic) that corresponded to 5th or 6th century spoken Chinese.

Otoko: man/men

Otohsan: father

Ototo: younger brother

Samurai: warrior. One from a family of the top rank of Japanese society for some 1500 years.

Sayonara: Goodbye, farewell.

Seito: student(s)

Sempai: an older man in the role of mentor, sage adviser. Co-constructed with *Kohai*.

Sensei: master, or teacher

Shiro/shiroi: white.

Shogun: the supreme military leader of his age.

Suiyobi: "Water day," Wednesday.

Tachi/tatsu: standing, upright.

Taiyo: the sun.

Tatami: a squat straw bale some three inches thick by 30 inches wide by 60 inches long. Packed tightly together, they make up the flooring of traditional Japanese houses; the size of rooms is determined by the number of tatami. A 4½ tatami room is on the small side, while a 10-tatami room would be an average living/dining room.

Tatemae: the art of telling the listener precisely what s/he wants to hear. (Contrast with *Honne*).

Tenki: the weather.

Tenno: Emperor.

Tera, Otera: (honorable) (Buddhist) temple. Often given in *on yomi* form, *ji*, following the name of the temple.

Toshi (*kun yomi*): year. Same kanji, same meaning, is *Nen, on yomi*. E.g., *Ko toshi* means "this year," however, *Kyo nen* means "last year." Go figure…

Tsuyu: the rainy season, occupying five to seven weeks, starting as early as late-June and running as long as mid-August in the Kanto Plain.

Tsuki, otsuki: the moon.

Tsuru: crane. In Japanese lore, the crane is said to live 1000 years, the *kame*, turtle, 10,000 years. *Uh, yeah...* What are we to learn from these astonishing claims?

Uchi: house, home, one's dwelling. Also called *iie*, presumably differentiated by *kun*, then *on yomi*.

Wabi, sabi: the Japanese aesthetic of simple, subtle elegance; the opposite of ostentatious, gauche.

Yama: mountain, in *kun yomi*, or native Japanese reading. The same kanji can also be read as *san*, in *on yomi*. E.g., *Fuji san*, Mount Fuji.

Yoru: evening, night.

Yubin kyoku: post office. Besides postal services, this government office also takes payment for most of one's utilities, and provides a simple saving account service. *What a concept, right, America?*